Praise for Jenn Shapland's

THIN SKIN

"A visceral exploration of the thin membrane between the self, the body, and the systems that control them."
—Katherine May, author of *Wintering*

"*Thin Skin* is a searing and translucent text, personal and collective, showing how porous we are, how vulnerable we are, and how strong, like Earth itself. Our bodies and the body of the land are inextricably linked. And still, we forget the violence that continues to sicken us both. Such an important and visionary book."
—Terry Tempest Williams, author of *The Hour of Land*

"A wrenching, loving, and trenchant examination of feminism, nuclear weapons production, healthcare, queerness, and American life unlike any I can think of. . . . The honesty and art in these essays bring with them a series of welcome awakenings."
—Alexander Chee,
author of *How to Write an Autobiographical Novel*

"With a writing style that recalls the work of Eula Biss. . . . [*Thin Skin*] finds Shapland determined to reckon with the biggest challenges that face us as a society. . . . Books like *Thin Skin* . . . run on hope, which is perhaps the only capital left to those who would like to see the human race survive. Shapland's use of the queer experience is deeply empowering."
—*Los Angeles Times*

"Rigorous. . . . While the future hardly looks bright, Shapland . . . grasps hold of some tentative yet essential hope. 'Each day is a question we ask ourselves—what is life?' she writes, picturing the marvel of growing old beside her partner. 'And answer: *this*.'" —*The New York Times Book Review*

"Shapland's mind is a marvel. . . . A stunning, urgent, and layered consideration of our climate-catastrophe, pandemic-laden day. . . . A brilliant and compassionate guide through loss and the enduring need to find hope."
—Alex Marzano-Lesnevich, author of *The Fact of a Body*

"Shapland finds insight through her nimble and voracious sensibility as a cultural critic. . . . Lucid and rigorous work with an open heart." —*Poets & Writers*

"Shapland probes the capacity of essay as a form to examine and question the lines we draw between ourselves and others, ourselves and the non-human world, and the past we've wrought with the present in which we live." —*The Nation*

"This book is a miracle! . . . Shapland takes on each subject with tenderness and depth. Every essay roams in a wild and thrilling way, holding to the author's own spiritual advice, to yield again and again and to both accept and 'indulge the universe.'" —Darcey Steinke, author of *Flash Count Diary*

"*Thin Skin* confirms that Shapland is one of the most exciting American writers working today. She simultaneously crisscrosses and dissects topics as enormous as personhood, colonization, and climate change with such virtuosic verve and control, I'm still marveling over how she does it."
—Jeannie Vanasco, author of
Things We Didn't Talk About When I Was a Girl

Jenn Shapland

THIN SKIN

Jenn Shapland's first book, *My Autobiography of Carson McCullers*, was a finalist for the National Book Award and won the Lambda Literary Award and the Christian Gauss Award, among other honors, and has been translated into Spanish, French, and Polish. Shapland has a PhD in English from the University of Texas at Austin. She lives in Santa Fe, New Mexico, where she works as an archivist for a visual artist.

jennshapland.com

THIN SKIN

THIN SKIN

Essays

Jenn Shapland

VINTAGE BOOKS
A Division of Penguin Random House LLC
New York

The Library of Congress has cataloged the Pantheon edition as follows:
Name: Shapland, Jenn, [date] author.
Title: Thin Skin : essays / Jenn Shapland.
Description: First edition. | New York : Pantheon Books, 2023.
Identifiers: LCCN 2022049873 (print) | LCCN 2022049874 (ebook)
Subjects: GSAFD: Essays.
Classification: LCC PS3619.H356318 T45 2023 (print) |
LCC PS3619.H356318 (ebook) | DDC 814/.6—dc23
LC record available at https://lccn.loc.gov/2022049873
LC ebook record available at https://lccn.loc.gov/2022049874

**Vintage Books Trade Paperback ISBN: 978-0-593-46953-8
eBook ISBN: 978-0-593-31746-4**

Book design by Michael Collica

vintagebooks.com

Printed in the United States of America
1st Printing

For my mom

She said that the outlines of things and people were delicate, that they broke like cotton thread. She whispered that for her it had always been that way, an object lost its edges and poured into another, into a solution of heterogeneous materials, a merging and mixing. She exclaimed that she had always had to struggle to believe that life had firm boundaries, for she had known since she was a child that it was not like that—*it was absolutely not like that.* . . . And so if she didn't stay alert, if she didn't pay attention to the boundaries, the waters would break through, a flood would rise, carrying everything off in clots of menstrual blood, in cancerous polyps, in bits of yellowish fiber.

—Elena Ferrante, *The Story of the Lost Child*

Contents

Preface

I'm sitting in my office, a converted garage in Santa Fe, New Mexico, in the waning September light, with Lou, the small gray cat, on my lap, while Chelsea is out with a friend. I've just come inside from removing three dead baby mice from our shed. Their mother appears to have abandoned them, and though I tried, naïvely, to revive them—with tortilla chips, with carrot shavings, with oat milk in a syringe—they didn't make it. My editor, Naomi, has asked me to write an author's note for this book, which I've chosen to call a preface, because I like the sound of it better. The preface is meant to tell you what connects these five essays for me, to give you a plan, a sense of direction.

I wanted this book to open with something soft, some easy ground to land on. I wanted to begin with a funny anecdote, relevant to our times but not too taxing. I wanted to ease us all into it, the idea of our utter physical enmeshment with every other being on the planet. I wanted to let the bottom of our bounded individuality fall away beneath us slowly, almost imperceptibly. Instead, this book begins in the free fall of reality: the material fact of our exposure to nuclear and industrial waste, and our political and cultural willingness to wasteland entire human communities and ecosystems. Note that my impulse here is to apologize.

It starts with "Thin Skin," a corporeal account of how thin the membrane is between each of us and one another, between each of us and the world outside. I want it to be clear from the outset that there is no "outside," that the world is a part of our cellular makeup, that we impact it with every tiny choice we make. My thinking for this book began with an essay called "The Toomuchness," which took five years to write. It was inspired by the clothes moths that had infested our closet, which I saw as a metaphor made literal, the ultimate intersection of capitalism's excess and human mortality. I couldn't look away.

I began to see what I now think of as literalized metaphors for my entanglement, my complicity, all over my life: in my dermatological diagnosis of "thin skin," in my friends' having babies as the world burned, in the crystals cropping up everywhere to heal us of something, in my own sense of vulnerability and my desire to feel safe. I began to question the idea of myself as a being in need of protection, indeed as something that could be protected. Nothing can protect us: just look at the mice. It struck me as I wrote that I was utterly vulnerable to every other person, every other creature on Earth, and they were also vulnerable to me. Writing under lockdown during the COVID-19 pandemic only made this more obvious and inescapable. As I wrote, I began to seek other ways of understanding the self that might be more useful than this shivering, weak thing we must shore up against the world.

At times I thought of these essays as a way to document coping mechanisms for capitalism: all the things that I do, that many of us do already, to cope with a broken and violent system. At other times I longed for a way to burn it all down and start again. What would it mean to imagine alternatives to our limited narratives about family, love, labor, longing, pleasure, safety, and legacy? As I thought and read about these intersecting ideas, I grounded the essays in the present conditions of my life, yet each one took me farther back in time—to the makeshift lives of queer women in the 1950s; to the construction of our ideas about work and white femininity during the early days of U.S. colonization and slavery; to the witch hunts in Europe, a point of origin for our dysfunctional healthcare system and the ongoing pressure on women to caretake. I love essays because they can go anywhere, can incorporate any body of knowledge, any question. Nothing is too big or too small.

In writing these pieces, I saw myself as source material—not as a character, not as the story, but as one vehicle among many for probing the ideas that most torment or entice me, that keep me up at night. To be thin-skinned is to feel keenly, to perceive things that might go unseen, unnoticed, that others might prefer not to notice. The essays contain many people's voices other than my own, some of whom express a sensitivity, an ability to feel and sense this profound permeability with others. Writing can be a mode of perception, a sensitivity to the world. This is a book about the joys and perils of our dissolving boundaries: the physical boundary of our skin as it absorbs chemicals, the emotional border where real fear meets cultivated violence, the obscured line from our desires to our material things, the ever-more-fluid overlap between self and work, and the imaginative realm beyond our prescribed expectations for a full life and toward expanded ideas of personhood, meaning, and purpose.

THIN SKIN

Thin Skin

"Do not look to the left or photograph anything on the left," the attendant told us. Chelsea and I had driven an hour north to the Valles Caldera, a wide grassy valley created by a volcano. Usually when we pass through the Los Alamos National Laboratory gates, which block the main road to the Jemez Mountains and the caldera, we're waved through without comment. Sometimes they ask to see a driver's license, sometimes they don't. Sometimes they tell us to have fun. They are always men. As soon as we were past the gate and knowing full well we were on video from all sides, I craned my face to the left. Just beyond the checkpoint, I gaped at a dark Stonehenge of tall cylindrical objects the size of tractors, wrapped in black or white plastic. I kept looking left the whole way up, peering past blue numbered Tech Area signs, into the trees. Whatever it is they started up here—call it the future, call it innovation, call it a war on their own people, call it the end of the world—they're not stopping any time soon.

At the Los Alamos History Museum, a point on the Manhattan Project National Historical Park walking tour, you can buy neon hats with radioactive warning symbols on them, photo postcards of the Trinity test mushroom cloud, pins in the shape of both original nuclear bombs. The museum attendant assured me as I handed over my $5 admission that they used to have missile earrings too. "They were super popular." Now the only earrings I see are in the shapes of paper cranes for Hiroshima.

As I walked the tour route after it opened in 2017, long before I knew the extent of the poisoning around me, unaware of the fault lines below, I became increasingly paranoid. Chelsea admired the plants and trees in Los Alamos's heavily landscaped downtown. Radioactive plants, I said. Radioactive trees.

On our way back down the mountain, I saw a sign for free mulch at the Los Alamos recycling plant. I wanted to suggest we stop and get some for our new raised vegetable beds, but I didn't. I thought back to our apartment search a few months prior, when we had driven out to a hacienda about halfway to Los Alamos. The apartment was enormous, stunning. Cheap. We were ready to say yes and sign a lease when the current tenant walked us around the back of the property to the acequia. "Uranium," she said. "Excuse me?" I said. "We buy our water in plastic jugs down the road at the gas station," she said. "It's fine, just don't open your mouth in the shower." We drove away, silenced, and I dialed the landlord of the more expensive, smaller one-room loft in town. Because the water in town is safe, right? It must be. I still don't know.

MARIAN NARANJO: *I'm really curious about this park. I still stand by what I said years ago when it started. You can talk about the Manhattan Project until the cows come home, as long as you're not doing it anymore. It is shameful that these people would be looking at inviting the public for tourism to come here to this dangerous place at any time.*

Marian and I were seated far across from each other at a table on her friend's patio. I placed a recorder in front of me, hesitant to push it closer to her but concerned about the erratic spring wind interfering with the sound. Her voice comes through soft but certain, scattered with long pauses that I wait through, knowing she always has more to share. On the three-hour recording I can hear birdsong, insects.

Marian's life became entwined with nuclear toxicity in high school. A strong student in science and math, she was chosen for a National Science Foundation summer program at Bowling Green State University. She and other kids from impoverished high schools around the country injected chickens with low-dose radiation, made fish food out of different parts of the chickens, and fed divided swimming pools of fish the radioactive food. The water they were standing in was contaminated, the fish were contaminated, but the fish's fecal matter had zero contamination.

MARIAN NARANJO: *We were the experiments.*

They weren't the only ones. Between 1944 and 1974, several thousand people were involved in what are now known as the Human Radiation Experiments. The Department of Defense, Atomic Energy Commission, and Public Health Service saw fit to feed or inject radioactive material into disabled children, impoverished pregnant women, U.S. soldiers, and the incarcerated. They exposed the dead bodies of children and stillborn infants to radioactive components, cremated them, and then tested them for radiation.

Back in New Mexico, Marian got her first full-time job at Los Alamos National Laboratory, which people here call the Lab, where she worked in dosimetry, testing employees' film badges to determine the extent of their exposure to radioactivity. She left the Lab after deciding she couldn't stay on in good conscience, attended the University of New Mexico, and raised four children while becoming a traditional potter. In 1996, Lab employee Joe Gutierrez blew the whistle on

LANL's lack of compliance with the Clean Air Act. In fact, it was impossible to know how much contamination was entering the air from Los Alamos, as the Lab failed to keep accurate records. As part of the settlement agreement with LANL, Marian was hired as the Native outreach director at Concerned Citizens for Nuclear Safety. When the lawsuit money ran out, she founded Honor Our Pueblo Existence (HOPE), where she works with Native women to help bring their lives closer to the cultural teachings of their people. HOPE holds workshops to increase fluency in the Tewa language; preserves traditional lifeways through the Kwi-tewha, a women's ceremonial house for making sacred bread; and educates people about toxic health risks and contaminated sites in the area. For Marian, there is a deep connection between the Lab's environmental destruction and the preservation of spiritual practices in her community.

MARIAN NARANJO: *We've discovered, me and the geologist, Robert Gilkeson, that when the Lab had applied for the money for the plutonium facility, they put in their folder a map that excluded several faults from the area. The plutonium facility is built on three major faults, right there, feet from where the facility is. They lied and got the money and built it anyway.*

We took a break from talking when Marian got a phone call about a class action lawsuit she and others were pursuing against a brand-new plutonium facility, which had been ordered by the Biden administration. The lawsuit was going forward. In a letter, groups from New Mexico, Georgia, and South Carolina, where the various components of the nuclear weapons are being produced, stated that the order would "saddle the already burdened communities . . . with a significant amount of nuclear waste and pollution," and asked them to perform the legally required environmental impact survey of each site and surrounding area. In August 2022, the U.S. Department of Energy finally began preparations for a survey of the sites for pit production (which was, of course, already well underway).

At the end of our conversation, Marian told me she only wished she were younger, to do it right. Her words stuck with me and turned over and over in my mind for months after we spoke. It amazes me that Marian continues to speak out about this, that she continues to try to make this truth known to the world, when she has been met with such denial and resistance. I wondered how a person could spend their whole life fighting a losing battle. Then I remembered what she told me about "war words." *We have become so accustomed to honoring war. When you start reading articles, or writing your own or whatever, go back and revise. How can I have said this without adding these war words in it? How can I be a more balanced person with my presenting?*

This Downwind Thought

MARIAN NARANJO: *The U.S. government came via anthropologists, Adolph Bandelier and Edgar L. Hewett. They came to the tribes to do the digs at the Pajarito. My mentor, Christina Naranjo, said that was the first divide of our village. We were told that all of our migratory places were covered, and they were to be left covered. This last place of our migration, to our present location. If we uncovered it, we would be opening the mouth of the firing dragon. Nobody knew what it meant, but at that time you always listened to your elders, because there were no such things as lies, she said.*

Bandelier and Hewett excavated the Pajarito Mesa at the turn of the last century, a great uncovering, and what Christina Naranjo refers to as the "first divide" of her village. Today, a national monument named for Bandelier provides hiking access to the cliff dwellings of the ancestral Pueblo people. Fifty years after the excavation began, Robert Oppenheimer, who owned a ranch near Pecos, helped select the mesa for Project Y, a secret military operation run by General Leslie Groves, in part because Oppenheimer believed the beauty of the Sangre de Cristo Mountains would inspire the scientists. Before beginning his freshman year of college, his father sent him to New Mexico with an English teacher, hoping his health would improve with the clean air and some horseback riding, so perhaps he was feeling nostalgic when he suggested it. He and his brother had been camping on the Pajarito Mesa for over a decade when the project began. In a letter to a friend, he wrote that he wished he could marry his love of physics with his love of New Mexico. According to declassified military documents, the site was referred to as a "Demolition Range." New Mexico was a better location than Chicago or Los Angeles or Oak Ridge, Tennessee, or Reno, Nevada, because it's isolated, remote, difficult to reach, good for hiding secrets.

When the United States government used eminent domain to clear the mesa in 1942, it was an act of colonization in line with an ever-unfolding history of colonization: a process of removal, appropriation, destruction, and renaming. Using the Second War Powers Act, they revoked grazing permits and seized or purchased land belonging to San Ildefonso Pueblo and more than one hundred small farms owned by Hispanic families without direct negotiation. Then they dug out cavates, Pueblo dwelling structures dating from 1100 to 1500 C.E., and used them to store plutonium. When these structures weren't of use to the Manhattan Project, they "literally scraped them off the surface of the mesas," according to landscape preservationist Julie McGilvray. They then named the new bomb-testing sites kivas—Kiva 1, Kiva 2—appropriating a Tewa word for a sacred meeting place, until Marian herself demanded that they change the names. Eighty years after the Lab's arrival, a *New York Times* article discussing the disproportionate impact of climate change on Native lands ran under the headline "Dispossessed, Again." But it's not so much "again" as something that never stopped, an ongoing assault.

MARIAN NARANJO: *When the Manhattan Project began, the United States did not have environmental laws. By the time the environmental laws came up, it was already a city, a town. If you go back and look at just the area, the geographical area in itself, it's on the Rio Grande river, Continental Divide, there's movement constantly. It's a very living place. It's very unsafe for the type of nuclear work that's done there. It's extremely unsafe.*

ELIZA NARANJO MORSE: *I started to know the truth from my mom, [Nora Naranjo Morse], from her perspective. She said there was a wagon that came down to the pueblo at some point. And when things were starting to become active in Los Alamos, they began collecting the men from the fields to go up there to work. [The land] was their livelihood. Not just their livelihood, their spirituality, their lifeways, their sense of all the intangible cultural values, relied on the fact that we were growing our own food, and that created this shift. My mom is an artist as well, and she definitely spoke of this with a lot of concern, an awareness that this is a shift that was strange and greatly affected us.*

Perched on a hill overlooking the city of Española, where Eliza grew up, and San Ildefonso and Pojoaque pueblos, Los Alamos is the richest and among the whitest counties in the state of New Mexico. It also had the highest childhood cancer death rate in the state from 1953 to 1987. While scientists at the Lab were regularly exposed to radioactive substances, the people most affected were their children and the residents of Española and the pueblos who worked service jobs at the Lab: custodians, nannies, maids, truck drivers, and construction workers. Between 1943 and 1965, the Lab dumped more than twenty thousand gallons of nuclear waste per day into Los Alamos Canyon and Pueblo Canyon, now known as Acid Canyon. Housing surrounds the southern edge of Acid Canyon, where concentrations of radioactive particles exceed those in the rest of the world by about six hundred times. Hiking trails nearby pass thirty feet from confirmed "hot spots," but the Los Alamos National Laboratory *Daily News Bulletin* claimed this is of no concern to hikers.

ELIZA NARANJO MORSE: *When I started to find out that this place was the cause of a lot of danger for other people, and death, it was frightening for me. I remember for a period of my life not wanting to go up there at all. And then since finding out that at one point, at the beginning, before they knew what the materials really were doing, they were going into radioactive areas, mopping the floors, and then pouring the water out, and having that—it's up high, we're down—all of our canyons lead into our water source. That's something that consistently stays with me, this downwind thought. That regardless of if we go up there or not, we're downwind. These canyons are really precious to us. They're spiritually precious, they're our landscape, they're our water source. That Los Alamos has plopped itself and all it's doing at the top of that, at the beginning of that, certainly it sits with me every time I look in that direction.*

The invisibility of the Lab's effects makes them all the more harmful, yet easier to ignore. Invisibility, of course, for people other than those immediately affected. And among downwinders, the cancers, the ailments, and the disabilities often occur two generations down the line from the contamination itself.

ELIZA NARANJO MORSE: *Just the visual impact of, every morning and every evening, a stream of cars, like a snake going from Black Mesa and beyond, connected car by car by car all the way up the hill and down the hill, that was for me, regardless of what I knew about what they were doing, like a magnet collecting and releasing people every day.*

I'm taking a Tewa class at my auntie's house in the pueblo, and I take it two-thirty to four-thirty, so I'm really aware of this line of cars, because I cannot pull onto the road, because there's hundreds and hundreds of cars all going up there and down there, five days a week, for what, how many years is it now? Fifty years? More than fifty?

And if you're not seeing the cars, you can live your life without thinking about it, you can look at the canyons and not think about the fact that there's probably some amount of material leaking into these water sources that are precious to us. It's all kind of invisible, you know? So that maybe makes it easier for us all to ignore until we start to think about it.

When an independent environmental testing lab discovered plutonium, uranium-235, uranium-234, and strontium-90 in the dust and soil surrounding Los Alamos, scientists from the Lab insisted these residues were due not to the Lab's work but to "worldwide atmospheric nuclear testing in the 1950s or from naturally occurring radiation levels in northern New Mexico." When we had our house inspected before buying it, the inspector found a moderately high level of radon in the air. We tested further and ended up installing a mitigation system identical to the ones on several other houses in the neighborhood. The radon guy explained to me that the noxious gas emitted in our damp crawl space is really the natural decay of elements already present in the soil beneath my house, which occur at a higher rate in the Rocky Mountains.

Am I to believe him, that this is only due to naturally occurring elements? The test of the first atom bomb at Alamogordo sent fallout as far as Vincennes, Indiana, where strawboard produced in a paper mill caused fogging on X-ray film at the Eastman Kodak Company. A Kodak research technician named J. H. Webb wrote in 1949, "All studies point to the conclusion that the radioactive contaminant was an artificially radioactive material which found its way into the mill through the river water. The most likely explanation seems to be that it was a wind-borne fission product derived from the atom-bomb detonation in New Mexico on July 16, 1945." Explosives contamination at levels higher than the EPA's limit has been found as deep as fourteen hundred feet in the groundwater surrounding Los Alamos. Untold quantities of radioactive waste remain buried in undisclosed locations at the Lab, where the mesa/canyon topography and extreme weather events frequently cause flooding and runoff into the region's primary watershed, the Rio Grande. Our house sits near the underground flow of the Santa Fe River, a tributary of the Rio Grande. Yesterday I walked the river trail while the river was flowing. It was filled with white foam collecting in the corners of the rocks like bath bubbles. Once my mind is steeped in this material, the natural world appears threatening in new ways. What is this white foam? Who can I ask?

MARIAN NARANJO: *We were put here to be the caretakers of our territory. In the prayers, our directions of our territory, they have names: the Tsay shun pin to the north, the Tsikomo to the west, Oku Pin to the south, and Ku Shen Pin to the east. The area is from the Colorado–New Mexico border to the Four Corners area, the Jemez down to north Albuquerque, Galisteo Basin, and the Sangres. That is the Tewa world, territory, and it's our church. And the creator planted us here as the caretakers of the gifts of the creator, of the air, of the water, the land, and each of us, and that there were instructions, very simple instructions, on how we do that.*

Our belief was we are part of the earth. We're of the earth. Not that we own it. That's why they couldn't say, "No, you can't be here." They didn't have the right to say that. They still don't have the right to say that.

My mentor said, "And then, as time passed, we became our enemy. Los Alamos came to be. And if that isn't opening the firing dragon, I don't know what else is."

For Marian and her mentor, responsibility for how the land has been used sits not just on the shoulders of Oppenheimer, of the Lab, of the U.S. government. The responsibility, in her view, is also hers.

MARIAN NARANJO: *So now we're in it, we're in it.*

Safer

I was already wearing a mask outside when the mask order for the COVID-19 pandemic came into effect. From February to May, the juniper surrounding Santa Fe throws out clouds of orange pollen. Particles shaped like the metal spiked balls on the end of a medieval flail embed themselves in my sinuses and trigger migraines. Even with the mask, I come in from walking or gardening and immediately rinse my nasal passages with salt water from a neti pot, up to three times in a single day. With migraines, I live at all times in a space of caution, knowing that one false move, one skipped mask or neti, one bite of strawberry or cheddar cheese, can cause days of pain.

It will start with some tightness in my nose or forehead, or a throbbing in my hand. Then one side of my upper body will seize into a rictus that's always there under the surface, lying in wait deep in my neck, my trapezius, along my skull, my forehead, my eye socket, down my upper arm, forearm, and into my thumb. Managing the triggers I know about isn't so hard, after years of practice, but the atmospheric triggers, like pollen or smoke from wildfires, can prompt a migraine almost instantly. I no longer get three or four a week like I used to, but a few days a month I find myself in the full-blown systemic spasm of migraine, which I've learned may be an overreaction to the environment, an immune response out of whack with the level of protection my body needs.

During the pandemic, I watched people become obsessed with the subtle ways their behavior might put them at risk. They fixated on the quality and thickness of their masks, the weave of fabric and number of layers it placed between their respiratory system and others'. They wore gloves long after it was clear the virus wasn't likely to spread by surface contact. They were, like I am, suddenly aware of the thinness of the membrane between us and the world. Between health and illness. Life and death. The fear and ongoing management of worry that I live with, from migraines, from chronic illness, and from my research into environmental toxins, was suddenly everyone's. My systemic sensitivity to the world was mirrored back at me in their frantic rubbing-on of hand sanitizer, in the terror in their eyes when someone nearby coughed.

A few weeks after the mask order was lifted, I wore a mask out in the garden because the mountains had disappeared in a haze of smoke from fires in Arizona and southern New Mexico. Somehow when the fires come from elsewhere it's soothing, gives me someone to blame. It's different when the fires are ours. I was out murdering aphids, wearing gloves to crush them in my fingers while spraying all our beautiful chard and kale and collard greens and tenderest pea sprouts with insecticidal soap. The label on the green plastic bottle reads, "Safer," but I still don't like to get it on my hands. Safer, but still not safe, or safest. Safer than what? It's greasy and hard to get off, and if I wash my hands too many times over the course of a day my skin begins to crack and bleed.

I'm not a compulsive hand washer; I have thin skin. A dermatologist diagnosed it after I endured a summer of fierce rashes up the insides of my arms and down the sides of my chest, red and burning and too painful to sleep. It was the longest stretch of one-hundred-plus-degree days on record and we were living in a loft without air conditioning—lots of buildings in Santa Fe are without AC, a quaint nod to (or desperate homesickness for) decades past, before global warming warmed us. "It didn't used to be this hot," people tell me, over and over, like it's news. We slept upstairs with the windows open, fans blowing, pollen wafting over us, and I lay there sweating and awake, my skin crackling and prickling. "You're allergic to your own sweat," the dermatology PA told me, a little too cheerfully. Peering at me with her giant goggles, seeing some level of detail I've never been privy to in my own epidermis, she informed me that I'm missing a layer. The layer beneath the skin that contains ceramides, which keeps the bad stuff out and holds moisture in, is more like a lazy macramé on me. The fix is easy enough: ceramide cream to replace what's missing. I use CeraVe, the thick kind in the tub, rubbed all over my body every day. My skin feels like it's surrounded by a magic protective bubble. A shield. Manufactured by Big Pharma, the cream makes me suspicious, but it works and I need it. I have to build up my skin each day to face the world.

After reading his book on dreaming, I took Ernest Hartmann's boundary questionnaire, a 146-question survey intended to measure the thickness of your psychological boundaries. It asks you to rank, on a scale of 0 (not at all true of me) to 4 (very true of me) things like, "When I awake in the morning, I am not sure whether I am really awake for a few minutes." "I am unusually sensitive to loud noises and to bright lights." "I believe I am influenced by forces which no

one can understand." "I am afraid I may fall apart completely."
My score was 379, "very thin." In Hartmann's analysis, a person with thin boundaries will struggle to perceive the edges
between things: sleep and waking, others' experiences and her
own, thoughts and feelings. It suggests I am easily overstim-
ulated, have many dreams and nightmares that I remember
clearly (I do), and may have trouble comprehending where I
begin and end. It's similar to being what some psychologists
call a "highly sensitive person," another scale that places me
on the sensitive end of the spectrum. Each diagnosis, each
new sensitivity, makes it clearer that I am living in a place and
time that my body cannot adjust to.

And so, as the world opened back up, sun shining, friends
gathering again, as the disease we had sheltered from for the
last fourteen months was starting to feel distant, less oppres-
sive, I was in my dark garage reading about the seepage, the
leakage of heavy metals and radioactive particles into the
earth, the groundwater. I was on Zoom interviewing experts
on uranium dust's causing lung cancer, the possibility of particles that cannot permeate skin entering through wounds,
through the digestive tract, through stomach ulcers. I was
diagnosed with a stomach ulcer. I was calling the city of Santa
Fe utilities office to ask how much plutonium was in our water,
aware that now it could seep more easily into my body through
my damaged stomach lining. A 2006 water quality report that
went out to every citizen in the county listed plutonium as
one of the water's contaminants, though the report was later
disputed, called a "false positive" by Lab officials, according to
V. B. Price. I simply wanted to know if the plutonium, a man-
made chemical that does not naturally occur in such quantities, was still present. No one returned my calls. Meanwhile I
couldn't step outside without a hazmat suit.

A layer is missing between me and the world. Perhaps this
sense of permeability, of vulnerability, is what got me inter-

ested in exposure. Despite my longing to be strong and able to withstand, the more I learn about contaminants, about the history and trajectory of nuclear research in New Mexico, about the exposures to fertilizer plants and steel manufacture my parents grew up with in Illinois, the more defenseless I feel.

Dissimulation

The early twentieth century marked a great unveiling of unseen forces. X-rays, radio waves, photography, and electricity made it possible to sense energy without seeing it. Marie Curie discovered and named radioactivity, an energy that is emitted from within particular atoms without any molecular interaction, adding to the tide of newly perceived unseen influences. Radioactivity reflected her interest in spiritualism, another obsession with the invisible. Marie and her husband, Pierre, attended séances as though they were scientific experiments. They believed that by connecting with otherworldly sources of energy, they might unlock the source of radioactivity. In radium, they were sure they had discovered something beautiful, something connected to the spirit world. That it was an access point to other planes of existence, to the dead. Along with so many others, they craved and sought proof of something mystical, something sublime.

Working late into the night in her glassed-in ground-floor laboratory to rinse and distill eight tons of pitchblende, the substance she refined to extract radium, Marie wrote, "we then perceived on all sides the feebly luminous silhouettes of the bottles or capsules containing our products. It was really a lovely sight and one always new to us. The glowing tubes looked like faint, fairy lights." "The light," biographer Barbara Goldsmith explains, "was caused by radioactive atoms releasing their energy, but the Curies were unaware that exposure to these substances was affecting their health. A century later the Curies' personal items, clothes, and papers were still radioactive." Even her cookbooks. But imagine believing that something pervasive and unknown could be a power for good, a source of awe, rather than concern or terror.

Curie herself was an invisible force. She attended the Flying University in Warsaw, a secret college for women, who were banned from higher education. Growing up Polish in Russian-occupied Poland, Curie watched as people's names were changed and signs were posted in Russian only. Speaking her native Polish language was forbidden in schools, and no Polish history or literature could be taught. Her third-grade teacher clandestinely taught Polish history during the hour scheduled for botany, Polish literature during German studies. When Russian inspectors showed up at school, a bell would ring to alert the students to swap their books out for the ones they were supposed to be studying. Marie lived in a world of secrets and codes and unspoken but felt realities. As a governess, she taught her pupils how to read and write in Polish. "Even this innocent work presented danger," she writes, "as all initiative of this kind was forbidden by the government and might bring imprisonment or deportation to Siberia."

When she won the Nobel Prize for discovering radioactivity, the prize committee credited her research partner Henri Becquerel three times with her finding. They compared her role in the project to the biblical Eve's, calling her a "help meet for" her husband, and referred to her as Madame, not Professor, as they did Pierre. Marie may have internalized this erasure of her role. Her autobiography can be found tucked away in a short appendix to the biography she wrote about her husband, titled *Pierre Curie*. The couple shared an equal amount of prize money with Becquerel, split between the two of them, as though Marie were not a full person or recipient. The two elements she had discovered, radium and polonium (which she named for her native Poland), were not mentioned. This is likely because the committee wasn't convinced they were real.

And yet soon after its discovery, radium became a multimillion-dollar business. For four decades, you could buy rejuvenating radium skin cream, lipstick, tea, bath salts, hair growth tonic, "a bag containing radium worn near the scrotum" that "was said to restore virility." There was radium toothpaste to boost whitening. Radium therapy, called Curie-therapy in France, began to be used to treat cancer. It was first inserted by fifty needles into breast tissue, or by radon "seeds" that caused serious reactions. There existed a "vaginal radium bomb consisting of a lead sphere supported by a rod for insertion" for cancer treatment. Marie and her daughter Irene took a radiological car to the front in World War I to X-ray soldiers. Later, she supplied radium bulbs to the French health service to treat the military and civilian wounded and sick with radium therapy.

The discovery of radioactivity is a story of willful igno-rance, of knowing but longing not to know, pretending not to know, how powerful and damaging it was. Scientists and sales-people alike believed in its power to cure, to heal. Radium was damaging enough to kill cancer, to burn Pierre's skin through the glass vial in his vest pocket, but somehow not thought to be damaging enough to kill the scientists handling it all day, the people brushing their teeth with it. Marie kept a vial on her nightstand to bask in its glow as she slept. She called it her child.

Curie's mother and sister died when she was young and from then on, Marie suffered from what researchers today equate with major depressive disorder. Of her mother, she writes, "This catastrophe was the first great sorrow of my life and threw me into a profound depression." Research was her coping mechanism. She writes in a letter, "I found out that creatures who feel as keenly as I do and are unable to change this characteristic of their nature have to dissimulate it at least as much as possible." More than depression or grief, what Curie describes is a kind of hypersensitivity, feeling too much.

Soon after reading this, I flee my desk for the garden, where I plant more seedlings than will possibly fit in the beds. I dissimulate it. I try to imagine the excitement of discovering radium while feeling keenly immersed in my own fear and paranoia of the invisible, the unsaid, the unacknowledged, unrecognized, unperceived. Pitchblende mining had been associated with cancer since the 1500s. Scientists in the 1800s and 1900s knew this. Still, people brushed their teeth with radium toothpaste and their jaws dissolved. Pierre's legs disintegrated from within, until he collapsed in the street and was run over by a carriage. Marie was diagnosed with tubercular lesions, gallstones, liver and kidney damage, tinnitus, cataracts. And yet, from the sanatorium in Haute-Savoie Mont-Blanc where she died, she was sure "a dose of fresh air" could cure her. "Perhaps," she once told her sister, "radium has something to do with these troubles, but it cannot be affirmed with certainty." This scientific refusal to believe what is obvious because it cannot be proven, because it is technically uncertain, accompanies our understanding of toxic substances to this day.

Marie didn't live long enough to see what her discovery would be used for, what it would lead to. When physicist Niels Bohr finally understood that nuclear fission could be harnessed as a weapon, he responded, "What idiots we have all been!" A pacifist, Marie writes of her time on the battlefield, "I can never forget the terrible impression of all that destruction of human life and health. To hate the very idea of war, it ought

to be sufficient to see once what I have seen so many times."
All along Marie believed that she was working for beauty, for
a way to access the spirits of the dead, not a way to kill.

Extractivism

In English, the verb "mine" comes from an Old French word,
"*miner*," which started its life meaning "to dig a tunnel under
fortifications to overthrow them." The figurative use, "to
ruin or destroy by slow or secret methods," is from the mid-
fourteenth century, when it combined with "to dig in the
earth" and took on our current usage by the late fourteenth
century, "to extract by mining." In the sixteenth century it
meant "to lay explosives." By 1890 it meant "land-mine, an
explosive device placed on the ground (or just under it) as a
weapon." From its origins, the word "mining" and the practice
of mining were associated with acts of war and destruction,
secretly laying waste to a place from below.

MELANIE LABORWIT: *It's a weird coincidence, but most uranium,
where it is naturally occurring in sufficient quantities for it to be mined,
happens to be on federal lands, most of which are tribal.*

DR. JOHNNYE LEWIS: *The Navajo Nation was extensively mined
for the development of the atomic bomb but most heavily afterward in
the nuclear weapons race from the Cold War. And when that ended, and
the companies left, they left behind over five hundred abandoned mine
sites, many of which are not marked, they're not fenced.*

MELANIE LABORWIT: *Effectively some of the areas in those places
have been made wastelands. The entire area of Jackpile Mine—you*

realize it was a mine if you know what to look for. But it also struck me as I drove away—there were not any animals grazing in these beautiful grasslands. Big vast grasslands, miles and miles. And there were no animals grazing there. Because of—

MALLERY QUETAWKI: *The reason why we fight for a piece of land that looks so barren and ugly—"Oh, we'll build a mine there, there's nothing out there." Well actually, there are shrines, there are sacred placemaking powers that exist within a certain area. And if you don't understand that, yeah, one would be willing to bulldoze a certain area, or pick up a rock and crush it up and test it, where, as us, as people, we're like, "No, that's actually sacred, that's important. As our individual bodies, we're all sacred and we wish to remain whole." So instead of just looking at us as specimens we have to be looked at as more than that.*

During the same years that white colonists mapped, explored, and claimed Indigenous territories across the world, physicians began to map the skin of the body in dermatological atlases. "Skin emerged in early dermatology texts as a mysterious landscape, with flora and fauna to be discovered and mapped," writes Thuy Linh Nguyen Tu in *Experiments in Skin*. Doctors "began to see the body not as open and porous but as closed and demarcated, with skin as its final boundary." From its earliest days, dermatology focused on white skin and its ailments, considering it a fragile protection from the world beyond it. Black skin and brown skin were seen as thicker, as immune to pain and discomfort. This inaccurate prejudice has lasted to the present day. "In a 2016 study published by the National Academy of Sciences, for instance, researchers found that doctors still expressed the belief that black people are less sensitive to pain and that their skin is 'thicker' than white skin." Even now, most dermatology textbooks use photographs of white skin to illustrate conditions, to the extent that physician Neil Singh was unable to diagnose common rashes on his own brown skin.

Because they believed dark skin to be thicker, the U.S. military tested new chemicals on a much higher percentage of soldiers and incarcerated people of color in the mid-twentieth century, as they sought to establish a threshold dosage for chemicals like Agent Orange. They mined the skin of these men to understand what would kill, what would harm, all the while telling themselves that the men felt no pain. "How can we reconcile the fantasy of black invincibility with the reality of black death?" Tu asks. To imagine that a person can feel pain, to imagine them as vulnerable, is to recognize them as human.

The Earth's crust is the Earth's skin. Certain parts of it, desert landscapes in particular, have long been seen by the Western imagination as expendable, as immune to destruction, for they are already wastelands. They are sacrifice zones, inhabited predominantly by people of color, unrecognizable as living landscapes. Chemical residues and contaminants "extend racism in time," writes Michelle Murphy. All the land, water, air, all our bodies, are sacrifice zones on the altar of profit, of might, of power, of nation, but some places and some people have been sacrificed more blatantly, more damagingly. To dig in the earth disturbs and destroys, but it also unearths, aerates. To what extent is my own research a form of extractivism, a digging and unearthing that is painful to me, to the people I interview, to the people I tell about what I learn, to you?

What I find most beautiful, that flaw of early dermatological thought—the undeniable permeability of all things, how substances pass from rain to soil to plant to animal to food to human, how we absorb everything around us through our skin, through the water, through the air—is also the most sinister knowledge I possess.

DR. JOHNNYE LEWIS: *We have some kids, some babies that are born with uranium in their urine. . . . That was really the first indication that the uranium can cross the placental barrier and that the fetus is being exposed.*

MANNY PINO: *Think about that, you know, the metaphor there. These children who are not even, who have nothing to do with this industry, are suffering the consequences by just being born with these radioactive contaminants in their systems. If that isn't a human rights violation, and our government denying responsibility, I don't know what is.*

MELANIE LABORWIT: *One of the uranium mines was out near Paguate, which is one of the six villages on Laguna Pueblo, and at the time that it was running, it was one of the world's largest open pit mines. Of any kind. Uranium, gold, coal, all over the world you have open pit mines, this was among the biggest open pit mines in the world. Which gives you an idea of the scope. I have a really good friend from Laguna, she's from Paguate, and I said, "Did you know about this?" She said, "Yeah, my uncles worked there." I said, "I'd love to talk to them." She said, "They're all gone. They all died of cancer."*

I find I can only read and listen to and transcribe so much of this each day before I feel inundated, overwhelmed, paralyzed. Like I can only take in small sips of this poison. This research, the journey I embarked on when I began to think and read and interview people about toxicity, feels like a sentence, like something I'm forced to do against my will. Because once you start looking at toxic environmental legacies, you can't stop. And once you start looking, you see—I see—it's everywhere. In Santa Fe, nearly half my friends are cancer survivors. I always attributed this to the fact that my friends here are older than I am, they're in their fifties, sixties, seventies, and so the odds that they would have had cancer are much higher than they would be for people my age. But knowing what I know now, I start to have doubts. None of my friends have ever mentioned to me what they think might have caused their cancer, and I haven't asked. Not knowing, not wanting to know, about contamination is a hardening of their shell, a form of protection.

DR. JOHNNYE LEWIS: *I don't think anybody wants to be told that you can have piles and piles and piles of this waste, whether it's nuclear or not—I mean, this is exacerbated because it has a nuclear component— but the waste itself is not good. It's not good psychologically to walk out your door and see somebody else's trash sitting there, in piles that are as big as football fields and taller. We have one community—I have one picture that I should send you, it's the grandson of one of our staff, and he's sitting up on a mesa looking down at the community he grew up in, watching EPA—and he at the time was about four—he's watching EPA scrape away eighteen inches of soil. And this is soil that he and his friends have played in their whole life. He is now close to an age where he will have his own children, and the source of the waste is still in the com- munity. But now so many in the community have moved away, tired of fighting, and it's just not okay. They've moved soil out of that community now four times. And the waste that generated the contamination is still sitting there. Right adjacent to the community. Just right there.*

To dig this up is to poison us, but some part of my psyche believes it's the only way to save us, as though saving were still possible. Drinking in this knowledge and passing it on to you, I know that this is my own coping mechanism. That instead of feeling fear, loss, sadness, anger, I try to understand it. I research it. I seek to learn its roots and causes. But learning and knowing and thinking are not modes of healing, repair. I can't research away the pain of this history, of so many people poisoned without their knowledge, of populations exploited and lied to. The more I learn, the more I want to grab people on the street and tell them what I know. Contaminate them.

MELANIE LABORWIT: *The stories that I started to hear—I can totally imagine it—about people who were driving trucks there, having not been told what any of the dangers of these rocks were that they were blowing to bits. There was detritus all over the place. You blow something to bits, you take the uranium out, and there's all this other rock that was left, and people took it home and built fireplaces with it. The crusher was used to pave roads at Paguate. My friend told me people would come home and they're covered in dust and they'd take off their uniform and throw it in the washer with the baby's diapers. So there are multiple levels of—it was incomprehensible.*

To talk of contamination, of longing for bodily purity and autonomy, longing to be untainted by, among other things, the federal government, bleeds unsettlingly into the broken logic of today's antivaxxers. In the midst of the COVID-19 pandemic, my friend Emily got a call at the spa where she works from someone requesting a massage from an unvaccinated person. "You'll see," they told her. "It's dirty." As though some part of the vaccine could pass through the hands of the masseuse into their skin. But there's no need to invent this, to ascribe to the vaccine a type of contamination that already exists. Vaccines were created to reduce the spread of infection, acknowledging that your body is "both contagious and vulnerable," as Eula Biss writes in *On Immunity.* Often they require that you get closer to the disease to inoculate yourself and others against it. But that doesn't mean the vaccine itself is a poison. Many legal drugs we regularly ingest are; the alarming intentions of the pharmaceutical industry are well-documented, most recently with the opioid crisis.

There's no need to falsely suspect vaccines of waging chemical warfare through the body when legitimate instances of this type of pollution already exist. Consider the water in Flint, Michigan. This type of poisoning affects mostly people on the margins; it's going on in plain sight and has been for more than a century. "Freak out about that!" I want to say to this person on the phone.

The word "toxin" has been popularized in recent years by some massage therapists, health food enthusiasts, and skin care companies that offer "detoxifying" methods of cleansing, eating, and body care. To refer to blanket "toxins" in the environment we might be able to purge from our bodies with a simple fix is to undermine the complex reality of toxins in our air, water, and food that can't be easily removed with a diet or skin scrub. "Toxin" comes from the Greek *"toxikon,"* a word for the poison used on the tip of an arrow. It has always had an association with violence, with the intention to harm another creature using chemicals.

Earlier conceptions of medicine saw the world outside the body as a source of disease, a miasma, a fog of potential harm. However, Steve Kroll-Smith and H. Hugh Floyd write in *Bodies in Protest,* "by the twentieth century, the medical community had abandoned the miasmic theory in favor of the germ theory. The subsequent development of the biomedical paradigm shifted attention away from an exogenous theory of disease"—the idea that disease came from outside of the body—"toward an endogenous theory that located disease inside the body." Because of effective vaccines that prevented the spread of contagious diseases throughout the twentieth century, and with a medical establishment that viewed the body as responsible in some way for its own illness, we lost sight of our fundamental susceptibility to others and our own ability to carry and infect. COVID-19 brought this truth to light again, and a fear of vaccines, like a detox juice blend, suggests to me a longing to control, to rein in the fearsome possibility that we are deeply enmeshed with other bodies and with our environment. To see the external environment as a source of illness is "a blurring of the recognized boundaries between safe and dangerous places." The problem is not that we are newly at risk but that we ever believed we could be "safe."

The Toxic Donut

My mom got cancer when I was eight. She was forty-six. I don't remember her sickness, or her treatment, or understanding what was going on. I remember eating packs and packs of Oreos with my brother in the doctor's waiting room, scraping all the cream out of the cookies and rolling it into a giant ball, which on its own tasted chemical and off. I remember her wig, a dark brown curly mass that matched the perm she'd had since the eighties. And I remember the time we drove go-karts in Wisconsin and the baseball cap she was wearing flew off, a rare exposure of her nearly bald head. She looked small for the first time. I remember that afterward her hair grew back a different color and texture, lighter, softer, unpermed. The radiation treatment she went through was developed from the use of radioactive substances like radium. After chemotherapy, radiation, and ten years of drug treatments, my mom considered herself poisoned for life.

While I was researching this essay, I texted her to ask for her childhood address, taking another stab at confirming my hypothesis that her cancer was related to the place she grew up. I didn't want to speak about it directly. I knew that bringing up the subject was itself toxic. Having been too young during her cancer treatment to experience or understand what it was really like for her, let alone to support her, I always sort of veered around it. I'd grow visibly annoyed or embarrassed when she brought it up to near strangers, like upon meeting my ex's father, a pathologist. Rolled my eyes when she hauled it out in family fights as something she'd been through and survived. Clearly she'd been hoping to be acknowledged, recognized, seen by me and my brother and my dad and the world. Why did I shrug it off for all those years, despite being so interested in toxicity?

But when I pulled up her address, I saw what I knew I would. Mom grew up on the South Side of Chicago, three miles along the Calumet River from a place called Altgeld Gardens. The Environmental Justice Atlas writes,

> Altgeld Gardens had the highest concentration of hazardous waste sites in the nation. The community was surrounded by 50 landfills and 382 industrial facilities. It had 250 leaking underground storage tanks. Several toxicology studies conducted in Altgeld Gardens since the 1980s have revealed dangerous levels of mercury, lead, dichlorodiphenyltrichloroethane (DDT), polychlorinated biphenyls (PCBs), polycyclic aromatic hydrocarbons (PAHs), heavy metals, and xylene.

Altgeld Gardens was and is a largely Black housing community, and the first person to speak out about the cancer plaguing its residents was Hazel Johnson, who is now considered the mother of the environmental justice movement.

HAZEL JOHNSON: *I'm used to calling this area a toxic donut. We're sitting in the center of it, and we're surrounded by all types of pollution. . . . I wanted to know what was going on. My husband had died of lung cancer. Then later I found out that a lot of other people had died of cancer or were in remission. I wanted to know why so many people were dying of cancer. It was up in the hundreds.*

Breast cancer is higher here, even prostate cancer is higher here. But it's the different types of cancer. . . . A lot of people fish in this area. A lot of people are pre-exposed to it, because we had asbestos in our homes. Just living around a bunch of steel mills, refineries, chemical companies, and the emissions that they put into the air, a lot of those particulate matters are carcinogenic.

CHERYL JOHNSON: *The history of contamination in this area goes all the way back to the middle 1800s, when Pullman used to own all of this land and he used it as a sludge dump, so we have multimedia exposure, air, water, and land in this area. . . . There's never been an epidemiological study in this area to determine what's causing this. . . . We still struggle in the environmental justice movement. Because the city of Chicago does not recognize environmental justice. So we always feel like the black sheep in the city of Chicago, because we as Black people should not be talking about environmental inequalities in your neighborhood, we shouldn't be talking about an industry that's polluting your environment, you aren't supposed to know about that.*

HAZEL JOHNSON: *It's like living in hell, because of the odor that makes you sick all the time. And it's sickening to know that the people in our area—it's an isolated area, it's a forgotten area that no one cares about. We have infants that are born with deformities. We have a lot of respiratory problems. We have cancer. We have people that have to live on oxygen tanks in their homes. We have a lot of people that have to be on a machine because of kidney problems. . . . I want to close all the industry down and relocate all the people. Human health comes first. That's the problem with the industry, is the politicians and everybody else, they care about the bucks. But what is happening to people's health? Let's put it where no one lives. I don't think my community should share the burden for the entire city of Chicago, and we've been doing it since 1863.*

Has the connection between cancer and exposure to toxic chemicals always been so obvious? Now I needed to know the history of cancer. When did it start? Can it always be connected to chemical exposures? I went to the library and checked out *The Emperor of All Maladies* and a stack of books on cancer. They each primarily addressed the history of cancer treatment, not its causes. To spare Chelsea yet another dark rabbit hole, I watched the six-hour Ken Burns *Cancer* documentary series on a weekend when she was out of town. I heard Nixon say, "The time has come in America when the same kind of concentrated effort that split the atom and took man to the moon should be turned toward conquering this dread disease." The sponsors listed at the beginning of each episode include David Koch, whose company, Koch Industries, spent most of the twentieth century producing petrochemicals, fertilizers, and paper. Koch, who was treated repeatedly for prostate cancer, paid $395 million for research to cure cancer. How often the cause longs to be the cure.

When eventually I sucked it up and called my mom to ask her questions about her cancer, she wanted to know why I was asking. I could hear the concern in her voice, that she was wondering if I'd had a health scare. I assured her it was research.

CAROL SHAPLAND: *It was February thirteenth. I was making cookies for you to take to school for Valentine's Day, and [the doctor] called me and he told me it was malignant and that I had breast cancer. I was by myself, and I just started crying and walked into the other room; you guys weren't paying any attention. And I said, "My kids are eight and ten years old," and he said, "You are not going to die. You are going to have one horrible year." I still remember it to this day.*

I was forty-five when I was diagnosed. Within how many weeks— I started chemo like April 10, and my last period was May 1995. It put me into menopause. Well, it fried everything.

My hair didn't fall out right away. It started falling out—your First Communion was in May, and Auntie Barbara and I went upstairs and she cut it all off, unbeknownst to all of you. I did nine weeks of chemo and then you get to rest awhile, and then the end of August I started radiation. I would drop you kids off at school and then go over to Lake Forest Hospital to get zapped. You lay on a table and there's this massive machine. First of all you have to go in and—they call it tattoos. They're dots, I can show them to you sometime, they're little black dots that show them where to line up the machine.

When my mom's sister, Barbara, was diagnosed with breast cancer, also in her forties, they both got the BRCA gene test. The mutation of either the BRCA1 or the BRCA2 gene suggests that the cancer is genetic and inherited. They didn't have either, which implies their cancer could be environmental. I started looking into the environment my mom grew up in when I learned this. She didn't.

CAROL SHAPLAND: *Most of the time they never do know, but the doctor said that in my case he thought it was environmental. Not that he knew where I lived or anything. I think it has something to do with the fact that my sister and I got it, there are more cases like that. Maybe our age and the time we grew up, the fifties and sixties. He said that would be his best guess. The fact that the two of us got it and there was no gene.*

We did have neighbors on Carpenter Street, the lady next door died of cancer, the man on the other side died of cancer. Supposedly. Everything was very private then, no one really talked about anything. But it was there.

I'll show you the scar sometime if you want to see it. I'll show you the tattoos.

She was on cancer drugs for ten more years after her chemo and radiation. She recited the names of the drugs for me, spelling each one. Tamoxifen, because of estrogen-positive receptors, for five years. A five-year clinical trial for Femara (letrozole), an aromatase inhibitor. *Ten years of drugs, no wonder I was so nuts.* When I was young, my mom was high-strung; she mellowed significantly in the years after I went to college, the years I now know to coincide with the end of these treatments. Surely they could have affected her level of anxiety. I imagine the act of taking the drugs, knowing what you are taking and why, knowing that they are experimental drugs with undetermined side effects, would aggravate a person's nerves.

My mom didn't buy organic, didn't pay any attention to that. If she'd known what I paid for eggs, she'd have been outraged. When I brought it up, she'd say she'd had enough chemicals pumped into her that nothing could touch her anymore. She was invincible. I always felt maddened by that—of all the things one might take away from cancer, invincibility to chemicals is absolutely the wrong message. But then, I've never had cancer—not yet—so I don't really know what the right message would be.

I talked about my research in therapy, unable to think of anything in my life as important as the things I was learning. My therapist asked if I thought I would get cancer someday, because sometimes when people have illness in their family early on, they have that fear. I paused and replied that of course I did. Of course I assumed I would get cancer. My research is a way to get closer to the cause, to the source, but it's also a way to distance myself. To dissimulate. By knowing everything I can about it, I can somehow prepare myself. I can somehow protect myself and the people I love. Keep it at bay.

Once I told my mom about the mosquitoes in our yard from the nursery next door, how we were spraying this natural garlic concentrate everywhere to try to deter them. In Florida, where she lived then, she said, there weren't any regulations, so *they just have planes and they just fog the snot out of 'em.*

And you know what? It's okay. Her determination to be okay with chemicals, to accept them, to microwave plastic and ignore my questions, her insistence that my dad would use DEET on our yard, recommending Roundup for our weeds: all of this was her own dissimulation, her own attempt to corral her fears to an illness and treatment in the past, to see the boundaries of her body as final and impervious.

There's no way to connect her cancer to the Toxic Donut, not scientifically. *It cannot be affirmed with certainty,* Marie Curie said of her own illness. We are all a product of the stream of toxins flowing into us from the womb. Only what Tu identifies as popular epidemiology—the women skin care workers in Vietnam talking to one another about what they see, exchanging symptoms and questions—diagnosis by word of mouth, can attest to these undeniable connections, these syndemic effects. Hazel Johnson began her efforts by observing the number of cancers in her building, talking to people around her. No certainty can be found, no clear line of fault can be drawn, and yet by talking about it, you begin to draw a map, to connect the contaminants to the vectors of contamination. It is not crazy to begin to notice these connections, to begin to suspect.

Samuel Epstein, a professor at the University of Illinois Chicago School of Public Health, was one of the few experts who spoke loudly and persistently about finding the causes, rather than the cures, for cancer. He insisted on "'run-away petrochemical and radionuclear technologies' as the prime cause of cancer rates rising in the United States some 55% from 1950 to 1995." His 1979 book *The Politics of Cancer* split the field, galvanizing environmentalists and medical professionals while earning accusations of paranoia and conspiracy-mongering from some scientists and the chemical industry. The *New York Times* obituary when he died at age ninety-one of a heart attack—not cancer—called him a "Cassandra of cancer prevention."

Find the Cause

My dad grew up in a landscape opposite my mom's South
Side, a town of six hundred situated between unending fields
of soybeans and corn in Central Illinois. These weren't family
farms but Big Ag, huge monocultures and big business. When
we visited his dad one Christmas, the county road to his house
was covered in six inches of ice. Without power and running
on a generator, the house's brick exterior, gutters, windows,
and roof were encased in ice like the mansion in *Doctor Zhivago*.
My dad doesn't talk much about growing up there. He left
when he was sixteen to study math and then accounting. If he
does talk about it, there's no nostalgia for country life but an
unfiltered disgust. He has memories of beheading chickens, of
chickens eating one another. It's grotesque.

RICK SHAPLAND: *And right on the edge of town there's the railroad
tracks and there's the fertilizer plant. I was probably five or six years
old when we moved to Ashkum. The fertilizer plant was going there full
blast, the grade school was a mile away, and I can still smell the fertilizer. Over time that little plant was bought by Occidental Petroleum, big
outfit, public company, and so they managed it and exploited it. My dad
worked there and sold fertilizer for them for quite a while. And that's
kind of all I remember about it. As far as I know it's still there. I don't
know if it's still operable, it's been a long time ago. It was right there
when you got off I-57.*
    After Carol died, I had some moments—I can still smell it.

When my aunt Carol died in September 2020, my dad
began to talk more about his past, more than he ever had.
Her death was a mystery following a lifetime of unresolved
illnesses. As a teen, bruises began appearing all over her
body, and she was diagnosed with immune thrombocytope-

nia (ITP). She had MS in the early 2000s, walking with a
cane for six months. In 2006, she developed almost total body
bruising, another set of ITP-like symptoms, and a chronic
lesion on her left shin the size of a quarter. I remember her
showing this to me and my mom in our kitchen in Lake Forest when I was home from college. The wound was so close
to the bone doctors thought they might have to amputate
her leg. Later, she was diagnosed with a rare combination
of Graves' disease and Hashimoto's, after which she had her
thyroid removed and went on thyroid replacement therapy.
In 2015, she began to experience the symptoms of myalgic
encephalomyelitis/chronic fatigue syndrome (ME/CFS), for
which she made six trips to the Mayo Clinic. They tested
every major organ group, and all the results came back negative or mild. In the months before she died, she was worried that with her autoimmune disease, she might end up
on a ventilator with COVID-19, so she rarely went out or
saw anyone. In August and September, she was struggling to
walk up the stairs. She was on various medications for high
blood pressure, and the stress of the pandemic could only
have made it worse.

Suffering from increasing fatigue, chest tightness, and
shortness of breath in the last years of her life, Carol never
had a satisfactory diagnosis, let alone a cure. In an email sent
a year before she died, after returning from a visit to Mayo,
she writes, "At least they confirmed that I can't breathe. Keep
seeing notes between drs that say the condition is 'real' &
have to find a cause, not too insulting. Find the cause and quit
being judgmental?" I wrote back to her about POTS (pos-
tural orthostatic tachycardia syndrome), my chronic illness,
because some of the symptoms sounded so similar. They had
recommended that she raise the head of her bed to facilitate
breathing, and I sleep on a tilted bed for POTS. I thought
I could commiserate, because I'm also used to visiting doc-

tors who are unable to find a cause, unwilling to confirm my reality. I'm used to that judgment she called out, that form of ongoing delegitimization.

Despite her progressing illness, in February 2020, she'd thrown a party for my first book publication in Los Angeles with all of her friends and all of my friends in the area. She had worked for decades as an accountant to the stars and helped found Women in Film & Television International. She invited her old clients from the film industry, including Elizabeth Taylor's longtime agent, and everyone from her wine-and-cheese group. It was the last time I saw her, right before the lockdown. When she died in September, ten days after her mom died, we were shocked.

She was sixty-four. She sent chain email jokes. She loved costumes and tchotchkes and had a huge party for the Day of the Dead every year before she got too sick. Her papers indicated that she wanted no autopsy, presumably because she'd spent so much of her life picked apart by doctors. She died, and we don't know how or why. *It was incomprehensible.* When I heard the news from my dad on the phone, my mind went immediately to foul play. I asked too many questions, unable to provide the kind of listening and compassion he probably needed. There wasn't any reason to develop elaborate theories as to who might be responsible for her death. The circumstances are likely things well-known to us.

RICK SHAPLAND: *No one ever knows. And then [my sister] Debbie has rheumatoid arthritis, which is autoimmune. So we grew up in that. It's horrible. I know you're researching Los Alamos, but there's other places in the States, all over the country, where smaller issues happened. In a place like Ashkum, which is all agricultural, you've got fertilizer in the ground—fertilizer, pesticides, you name it—to feed the crops, soaking into the water table, into the wells that people drank. And on top of it, you had fertilizer plants in the air. Some of my dad's friends and contemporaries that passed away had some really weird circumstances, the stuff they died of. Cancers. Parkinson's. Odd stuff that you wouldn't really—I don't mean to get emotional about it, but it was funny, that I could still smell it. Could still smell the fertilizer plant.*

CAROL SHAPLAND: *He always thinks that his sisters, he thinks they all swam in it. He remembers them swimming in those ponds, which he never did.*

RICK SHAPLAND: *I don't know how to describe it. It's sickeningly sweet. There's three chemicals that go into fertilizer, nitrogen, phosphorus, and potassium. But it has a distinctive smell when they're manufacturing it, and that would waft across the town, into the school, you know, we could smell it every day. I just thought about it, and I thought, Geez.*

The thing with Carol was horrible. I don't know. Can't do anything about it. But all in all I think that the Ashkum fertilizer plant had a hell of a lot to do with it. I wasn't aware of the pesticides, but of course they were being used all over the farm country. That was the least of our— every water supply there is on a well, so you get it from two directions.

Occidental Petroleum, the company that bought the Ashkum fertilizer plant, also bought the company responsible for the Love Canal chemical dumping. Finding the most basic information about the plant today is a struggle, as the company has changed hands numerous times, and Occidental is a massive conglomerate with no record on its website of having owned it. But like my dad said, along with Love Canal, along with headline-grabbing disasters like Three Mile Island, there were other, smaller issues. Mine is a chemical inheritance, but so are all of ours. Who has never feared the onset of congenital illness, who hasn't lost a family member or friend to cancer? Somewhere between 5 and 80 percent of cancers are caused by chemicals in the environment, but none of the data is conclusive.

Not Quite Fatal

In the late 1950s, while Rachel Carson was writing *Silent Spring*, her best-known book, on the dangers of chemical pesticides, she was undergoing rounds of radiation treatment, chemotherapy, and surgery for breast cancer. She didn't write about her cancer, apart from her letters to Dorothy Freeman, the love of her life, whom biographers refer to as a friend. She didn't want anyone to know about her illness—or her relationship with Dorothy—because she feared it would undermine her research and its legitimacy, give chemical companies a weapon against her.

The idea for the book arose from a kind of popular epidemiology. Her friend Olga Huckins wrote to her about the prospect of new pesticide spraying in her area and begged Carson to find someone who could help. The request so moved her that she began to research the use of DDT and its effects on wildlife. Answering this question took over her life and reoriented the trajectory of her career, culminating with *Silent Spring*. On the eve of its publication, a friend of Carson's wondered who on earth would want to read a book about chemicals. His wife, Lois, replied, "Anyone who ever held a spray can, and we all have."

Published first in 1962 by *The New Yorker* in three installments, *Silent Spring* gave rise to a new consciousness of chemicals and their possible impacts. Eventually Carson testified before Congress, insisting on "the right of the citizen to be secure in his own home against the intrusion of poisons applied by other persons," stating, "I speak not as a lawyer but as a biologist and as a human being, but I strongly feel that this is or should be one of the basic human rights. I am afraid, however, that it has little or no existence in practice." Her testimony and the conversations that arose from the book led to the banning of a number of chemicals in the United States. In the countless letters she received following its publication, Carson noticed that people no longer "assumed that someone was looking after things." They no longer assumed "that the spraying must be all right or it wouldn't be done." By providing some basic facts about the chemicals being used, coupled with observations of their aftermaths by ordinary people across the country, *Silent Spring* was able to create a shared language and understanding of long-term, difficult-to-trace contamination that led to widespread awareness and legislative action, contradicting the studies by chemical companies and advocates that suggested these effects were nonexistent.

Despite the book's success and its role in mainstreaming ecological consciousness and the environmental movement as we know it, we have failed to learn the most basic lessons of *Silent Spring*. "Who would want to live in a world which is just not quite fatal?" Carson writes, highlighting the compounding effect of chemical pesticides in the environment. When sprayed in "safe" doses, she argues, these chemicals cannot be considered safe because a person is never consuming one single dose, but many different doses through food, water, and air over an extended period of time. Further, the chemicals compound within the bodies of plants and animals, attaining much higher levels of concentration than they had when originally dispersed. It is these long-term, low-level exposures that cause the most damage, in this and subsequent generations, regardless of whether we're talking about pesticides or radiation.

Pesticide manufacturers in Carson's time insisted that their chemicals were never harmful, and yet people reported that birds and fish and wildlife were dying in gruesome, painful ways. The arbitrariness of a "safe" dose of pesticide applies equally to the so-called safe level of uranium or plutonium, the arbitrariness of the length of time needed to make the waters safe, the arbitrariness of the number of years radioactive waste is said to need to become safe—it all starts to seem like a game. The National Agricultural Chemicals Association spent over $250,000 to undermine Carson's work (nearly $2.5 million today, adjusted for inflation).

NIMBY (not in my backyard) is the typical response to the toxic off-spewings of a modern industrial society. We want our cheap energy and gas and food, so whatever has to be done to the land to get it, just do it out of my sight line. We want to believe there is a way to distribute poison in the environment that would keep us safe, that would not harm any particular group unnecessarily, that would not by necessity designate some areas "sacrifice zones."

In *Wastelanding*, her book about uranium mining on the Navajo Nation, Traci Brynne Voyles writes, "To ask for 'just' distribution of industrial pollution, waste sites, mines, unsustainable and toxic labor, and so on, is not to ask for redistribution but rather to ask for modernity to throw up its hands and dismantle itself." Carson asked, what is a safe distribution of poison? Voyles takes the question further, asking, what is a just distribution of poison? The answer is none. But the system we live within has always relied and still relies on poison, producing poison and discarding poison.

The United States banned DDT for most uses after *Silent Spring*, but it is still legal to manufacture. It has been deemed essential to stop the spread of malaria, so it is sent most often to Africa, where it is sprayed on the interior walls of homes. After DDT was banned in the U.S., Monsanto began to manufacture and sell the weedkiller Roundup, which proved to be even more detrimental to humans, animals, and ecosystems. Again, we failed to learn what Carson so painstakingly laid out in all of her writing: "the fundamental truth that nothing lives to itself." *So now we're in it, we're in it.*

She wrote at a time when the fear of radioactive fallout gripped the world. A cartoon in the *Saturday Review* in 1962 reads, "I had just come to terms with fallout, and along comes Rachel Carson." At the time, she thought it would have been easier to write a book about radiation, instead of chemical pesticides, because it was already such a big part of the cultural imagination. Yet, she writes, "whether radiation or chemicals are involved, the basic issue is the contamination of the environment."

Today, considering the ongoing effects of nuclear weapons research and development, I find that people are almost immune to these fears, to understanding that what people are experiencing in New Mexico is the equivalent of fallout, but meted out into the environment slowly over time in insidious, invisible, unreported-on ways. It's as if we're immune to the very idea of nuclear toxicity—like we're not even fazed by it, or we can't look at it, we can't look it in the eye. We don't want to see it, we don't want to talk about it.

If *Silent Spring* were published today, would it make such a splash? Would it change anything? Or would it feel like more of what we already know, more of what we can't bear to know? When I talk to friends in Santa Fe about the plutonium in the water, the response I get is, "Surely not here." Or "Didn't they fix that?" Surely not us. Surely I'm not living in a war zone. Surely the government isn't still poisoning its own people in the pursuit of these weapons. But by many accounts, they are. Like the cartoon, these truths are things we have to adjust to, even as our bodies cannot. Or perhaps, as some bodies cannot.

After wading into the East Fork of the Jemez River at Las Conchas with my friends Brad and Emily, I tracked down water quality data and discovered that the river has contained plutonium-238, plutonium-239, plutonium-240, uranium-234, uranium-235, and uranium-238. Plutonium doesn't occur naturally in this context, so there's only one way it could have gotten there. I debated whether to tell my friends, who swim in the river regularly, about the plutonium. I felt like it would ruin their enjoyment of the place, and yet I also felt a deep imperative to share this information. When I texted to tell them, Brad responded he didn't want to know. "Ignorance is bliss!" He was joking, but I wonder sometimes if maybe he was right. Why do I feel like I have to know all of this and tell people about it? Who actually wants to know?

Carson knew that the treatment she was undergoing to kill her cancer was poisonous to her own body. She wrote to Dorothy,

> I don't question whether it is the right thing. I know that 2-million-volt monster is my only ally in the major battle—but an awesome and terrible ally, for even while it is killing the cancer I know what it is doing to me. That is why it is so hard to subject myself to it each day. That's why I meant I would be happier if I knew less.

If she knew less, she could embrace the treatment, she could feel cured. But knowing what it was doing to her body, she was afraid of it.

In a speech to the New England Wild Flower Preservation Society, she asked,

> Are we being sentimental when we care whether the robin returns to our dooryard and the veery sings in the twilight woods? A world that is no longer fit for wild plants, that is no longer graced by the flight of birds, a world whose streams and forests are empty and lifeless

is not likely to be a fit habitat for man himself, for these things are symptoms of an ailing world.

Is Rachel Carson an example of someone unfit for the world she lives in, unable to adapt? Is the sentimentality she mentions similar to sensitivity, to feeling keenly? Is sensitivity, awareness, a kind of sentimentality? A longing for some other reality, a refusal or inability to live within this one? A dissimulation? To Dorothy, she wrote,

> The main thing I want to say, dear, is that we are not going to get bogged down in unhappiness about all this. We are going to be happy, and go on enjoying all the lovely things that give life meaning—sunrise and sunset, moonlight on the bay, music and good books, the song of thrushes and the wild cries of geese passing over. So—let's think and live happily enjoying whatever time there is.

She was talking about enjoying the summer in Maine, where she and Dorothy spent the most time together each year, and not letting her bone metastases, the tumors in her neck, deter them from finding happiness together in nature. But she could easily have been talking about enjoying a summer, enjoying the world, in the wake of her own research, her own work. She was determined to enjoy the world despite knowing it was poisoned, and yet she also knew she couldn't enjoy it without having written the book. In a letter to a friend, she wrote, "I have felt bound by a solemn obligation to do what I could—if I didn't at least try I could never again be happy in nature." Having dredged up the truth, the only way to enjoyment was to expose these harsh realities. And then to live with them.

—

Critics of *Silent Spring* and of all Carson's writing about the natural world fixated on the fact that she was an unmarried, attractive woman. They called her a spinster, suggested she might be a communist, all common tactics during the McCarthy era for questioning a person's loyalties, their intelligence, their worth. They also harped on the emotionality of her writing, her "mystical attachment to the balance of nature," using a version of the well-trod hysterical woman argument to suggest that her fear of pesticides was a kind of overreaction. This is the same way multiple chemical sensitivity was framed when a group of women in the 1980s insisted their workplaces were toxic and causing chronic illness, what came to be called sick building syndrome. It's the same way all kinds of chronic conditions that afflict women, from migraines to endometriosis, are gaslit and rejected as real cause for concern.

Perhaps living her life as what reads today as a closeted lesbian, as a woman scientist in a field dominated by men, helped Carson to see these chemical realities and give voice to them. It makes sense to me that she'd be used to being gaslit, used to being told that she didn't exist, used to being told that the reality before her eyes—her love for another woman, say—wasn't real, that the facts that she knew to be facts were not real, were not true according to the powers that be and the culture at large. That she'd be used to people's refusing to see her own existence and her own life as valid. And from that ongoing awareness of the disconnection between her reality and others', she'd be able to write something to combat the silence surrounding chemical pesticides, she'd be willing and might find it necessary to scream into that void of people unwilling to talk about it and outright censoring it. Her knowledge of chemical pesticides changed her writing and her understanding of herself as a writer. From the time of her awareness of it, she wrote about little else.

Alterlife

Before I'd looked at the water quality data, Chelsea and I drove back to the Jemez, through the gates and past the caldera, to hike in a place we'd never been. The left side of my head had a low throb that had started the night before, but I was hoping time outdoors would provide a distraction, that blood flow might encourage my system to calm down. With a heavy summer monsoon season under way, the mountains were greener than I'd ever seen them, overgrown with wildflowers and grasses. The vast bowl of the caldera, usually yellowed from the dry heat, was a verdant meadow. As we wound through the mountains, green grew on the hillsides up between the spiny toothpicks of burnt trees and downed wood shining in the sun. The Las Conchas Fire had burned through the area ten years ago, a wildfire massive enough to prompt mandatory evacuation at Los Alamos, to burn sixteen thousand acres of sacred land at Santa Clara Pueblo, and to close the laboratory to nonessential workers. A tree on a power line started the fire, but the landscape needed to burn to recharge. Things periodically have to die, to burn up, in order to carry on. Did they consider the fires when they built the Lab here? Did it occur to them that they would be storing highly explosive radioactive chemicals in a place where fire is a natural part of the climate cycle? Photos of the fire online looked oddly like a mushroom cloud rising up from the distant Pajarito.

It was Sunday morning and the trail offered an idyllic scene. Two men waved fishing poles in the creek. A pregnant woman spread a picnic blanket while two kids in bathing suits splashed around. Climbers made their way up the rock face while a man with a baby in an Osprey backpack belayed, unwilling to let parenthood cramp his extreme sports lifestyle. We moved past the happy gatherings and wound through fields of bright blossoms. Dozens of orange butterflies perched and fluttered in a stand of purple flowers that looked like jester's hats, which I now know to be wild bee balm. Heavy with migraine and too much information, I paused on a rock in the shade while Chelsea photographed the flowers with her Mamiya. I tried to console myself with an upwind thought, imagining that Las Conchas is at a higher altitude than Los Alamos, but in fact the river flows from the direction from which we had come, from the direction of the Lab. Everything sweet about the trail—the robins, the bees, the children caked in mud from bathing their doll in a puddle—was tinged with poison.

Driving back down, we passed a sign for something called the HAZMAT Challenge. A Santa Fe National Forest group campground beckoned to the right of the car, while on the left a barbed wire fence ran all the way to White Rock and beyond. The fence bore three alternating signs that read: "Danger Explosives Keep Out"; "This Area Is Under Surveillance"; and "No Trespassing," with tons of tiny unreadable text beneath. I wanted to ask Chelsea to pull over so I could go read the signs more closely, but I was afraid of what would happen if we stopped, given the surveillance. I was afraid to get too close. The fence was guarding Los Alamos Canyon. The signs didn't mention radioactivity. On AllTrails.com, you can find highly rated hikes in both Acid Canyon and Los Alamos Canyon, the parts that aren't fenced off. As if a fence were all the barrier we needed.

The sky shifted abruptly from blue to dark gray as we merged onto Interstate 25, and lightning crackled across the sky. We passed the exit for the NM 599 Relief Route, which I had always assumed was designed for evacuation purposes or to relieve traffic. Seeing the word "relief" feels relieving somehow; this way lies a reprieve from what ails you. But now I know it was built to transport radioactive waste from the Lab to the Waste Isolation Pilot Plant (WIPP) in southern New Mexico near Carlsbad. It relieves the main Santa Fe artery, U.S. 285, from vehicles transporting waste driving through the center of town. This route seemed necessary because of the likelihood of accidents and how devastating they would be in a heavily populated area. Maybe it also seemed like a good idea to prevent the sight of radioactive waste vehicles in a tourist destination. Regardless, the vehicles traverse 599 and end up on I-25, the interstate that runs to Las Cruces. From Los Alamos to Carlsbad, the trucks skirt around Santa Fe but blow right past a series of pueblos, the fast-growing suburb of Rio Rancho, and the city of Albuquerque, metro population nearly one million.

This is not my holy place. But the mesas and canyons of northern New Mexico are one of the most beautiful, most moving landscapes I've ever experienced. They are the reason the state nickname is the Land of Enchantment. The government has poisoned so much of it, and they are just getting started.

In 2021, the Lab announced that they would be opening an office in downtown Santa Fe to facilitate the production of hundreds of new plutonium pits, along with the Savannah River site in South Carolina. The Trump and Biden administrations deemed it necessary to ramp up the supply of nuclear warheads to keep the U.S. in top form for potential nuclear war. In response, the Democratic legislators I helped elect issued a joint statement.

> Los Alamos National Laboratory employs the best and brightest minds in the nation and plays an essential role in America's national security—including keeping the nation's nuclear stockpile safe and secure and supporting nonproliferation efforts around the

world. It is paramount that the Department of Energy and its contractors carry out this mission with the highest standards of security and safety in operating its laboratories. LANL's clean-up program must have sufficient resources to ensure all planned restoration and protection efforts remain on schedule and critical milestones are met. We will continue to support LANL's workers and mission and advocate for waste clean up to remain a top funding priority for DOE during the appropriations process.

U.S. Senator Martin Heinrich (D)
U.S. Senator Ben Ray Luján (D)
U.S. Representative Teresa Leger Fernandez (D)

It's all well and good to advocate for waste cleanup, but they do so in the same breath that they champion the activities of waste production as "essential." What is a just distribution of poison? None. Biden's infrastructure proposal, the American Jobs Plan, calls for the manufacture of advanced nuclear reactors to aid the transition to green energy. Nuclear power plants, touted by many on the left as the only way to carbon neutrality, require highly refined uranium, and where do you suppose they're going to get it?

MELANIE LABORWIT: *I think a lot of New Mexicans have no idea that tiny little Eunice, down near Hobbs, has the country's newest uranium enrichment plant. And we are not enriching New Mexico uranium. The uranium mines in New Mexico closed down a long time ago. They're actually bringing in raw uranium all the way down to Eunice from Canada, from Saskatchewan. I asked the hazardous waste committee at the legislature, "What are the regulations on these trucks? Where are they driving?" They're driving anywhere they want, from Canada, and nobody has any clue that raw uranium is coming through New Mexico, probably on a daily basis.*

—

Saskatchewan is home to seventy-five First Nations communities. It's one thing to realize we are all downwinders, that heavy industry and chemicals have polluted our soil, water, and air to the point that we are born altered. It's another thing to know the contamination was ordered, and continues to be ordered, by the U.S. government, an attack on its own people, overwhelmingly an attack on the people who originally inhabited this land, that carries on today. We are still at war. New Mexico isn't the only state with this kind of radioactive waste, but we have the most, store the most, and are currently ramping up to produce more.

The Manhattan Project the park seeks to historicize is very much alive, is probably in my cells, mutating them as I write. Along with the Ashkum fertilizer runoff and the Toxic Donut slurry, my legacy is resting poisons and symptoms with undetermined causes. The Stockholm Convention on Persistent Organic Pollutants in 2009 found that "all people alive today contain PCBs within them," writes Michelle Murphy. PCBs, or polychlorinated biphenyls, are man-made toxic chemicals found in paint, electrical equipment, copy paper, and plastics that do not break down in the environment, accumulating in plants, food crops, small organisms, and fish. Here in the alterlife, Murphy writes, you are called to "an unflinchingly pessimistic acknowledgment that these chemical relations are racist, harmful, even deadly, and that it is up to you to take on the ways that you are caught up in this killing (even if they are killing you, too, just more softly)."

I made an appointment with an HVAC specialist to install an air purifier, hoping to cut down on the smoke particles that circulate in my home. This summer my migraines have been especially bad, rising up to meet me almost every day. I feel a heightened sensitivity to my surroundings, an inability to manage triggers that are vague, multifactorial, atmospheric. Still, I find myself wondering: At what point am I covering my windows with aluminum foil or doing the equivalent? While I wait for an estimate, I borrow an air purifier from my friend Merry and carry it with me from room to room like a precious pet, like a lifeline.

Culturally we ridicule the very idea of multiple chemical sensitivity, environmental sensitivity, sensitivity in general. Toughen up. Don't be a snowflake. But to be sensitive is to be aware. Being and becoming more aware of these toxins, these omnipresent chemicals, makes me have to face something most people adamantly refuse to look at. Do not want to know. It's easier to deride such idle, small worries, these traces, in the face of whatever bigger, more obvious threat we encounter. To be sensitive is sometimes to err, to overreact, to be too finely calibrated or tightly strung, to be overly cautious. But to be thick-skinned is to be what? Obtuse. To see the hurt and gloss over it, dismiss it, laugh it off.

Humans are way more allergic, more sensitive now, and no one seems to know why. My biggest migraine triggers are foods high in histamine, a random-seeming assortment including strawberries, eggplant, soy sauce, red wine, aged cheese. If I decided my sensitivity was a form of weakness and wanted to toughen up, I could eat all these foods. I'd go back to how I used to be, living in a constant migraine, a state of ongoing hurt. I could grit my teeth and bear it, as I imagine people with more physically demanding jobs, living in more highly polluted areas, must do to get by. Migraineurs make up a significantly higher proportion of annual suicide rates. Why should I toughen when I know we are all tender, we are all sponges? Chronic illnesses are ignored, maligned, derided, denied. But my aunt died of something.

Perhaps it is a question of adjustment. If humans are a species like any other, it is not inherently bad to alter the planet with our industry, weapons, chemicals, extraction, construction, projects. All animals do this. Beavers build dams, too. Those who survive are the so-called fittest, and not all species, not all humans, will make it. Maybe the least sensitive of us, the thickest-skinned, will survive, a chilling thought. Maybe none of us will. And that's also fine. A bumper sticker on a car at the end of our street reads, "Nature Bats Last," and it always makes me smile. Our demise can be a sort of comfort.

Some forms of chronic illness are starting to receive more attention lately due to the persistence of long COVID. Many of the symptoms overlap with long-understudied syndromes like chronic fatigue and POTS. As with the invisible syndemic effects of chemical exposures, chronic illnesses are often unseen, undiagnosed, and misunderstood. It is more common for doctors to wave them aside, to ignore them, or even to consider them psychosomatic than to treat them. In my own life, I've found that the only way to repair chronic illness is to live with it and forgive myself, be kind to myself, be gentle. These actions require an awareness of what I'm feeling, an acknowledgment of what my body is going through. When I don't acknowledge the onset of a migraine, I go about my day and everything I do makes it worse, until I collapse in a dark space unable to move, waiting for the pain to let go. Toxic histories and legacies are in this way like illnesses, and in many ways, they are literal illnesses we must all live with and acknowledge if they are not to take us unawares, to be compounded by our every action. The only way to acknowledge them is to call them out, to name them, to talk about them when no one else wants to hear. We cannot care for something without first acknowledging its existence.

And yet naming the problem is not enough—to solve it

would mean for "modernity to throw up its hands and dis-mantle itself." Moving forward now will be a process of coping with what is and resisting further damage, a set of practices that require an awareness of what has happened, what is still happening.

MARIAN NARANJO: *Whoever's here in this Tewa world just can do that daily, acknowledge that you're here in this sacred place and that there are ancestral spirits that knew and know how to live in peace and harmony, and just ask for their guidance to do so. Come today and tomorrow, if everyone would just do that in the morning, we would see what doesn't belong. We would know how to be caretakers. We're not there. But that's the next circle, that circle of balance. Where we do put back our heaven and earth, our heaven back on earth. Get it back. How do we do that? It's this, it's talking face-to-face. It's doing more of this.*

Biographical Notes

Between January and July 2021, I interviewed a number of people, some engaged in the ongoing fight against nuclear weapons production in New Mexico, others attempting to understand its impacts on the Navajo and Pueblo peoples through art, activism, and museum education. Starred interviews appear at greater length in *Exposure: Native Art and Political Ecology* (Radius Books, 2022).

Marian Naranjo (Santa Clara Pueblo) is the founder of HOPE (Honor Our Pueblo Existence). She was the Native Communities outreach director for Concerned Citizens for Nuclear Safety and has been an antinuclear activist for many years.

Eliza Naranjo Morse (Santa Clara Pueblo) was raised, lives, and works on, around, and beyond Kha'p'o Owinge land. She has participated in creative activity individually, communally, nationally, and internationally for more than twenty years.

Melanie LaBorwit* is the Native arts and culture coordinator at American Indian Alaska Native Tourism Association Inc. and formerly the museum educator at the New Mexico History Museum, where she curated the exhibition *Atomic Histories*.

Dr. Johnnye Lewis* is the director of the METALS Superfund Research Center and co-director of the Community Environmental Health Program, the Center for Native Environmental Health Equity Research, and the Navajo Birth Cohort Study, the first study of the impacts of uranium mine waste on pregnant women and children. She is professor emerita at the University of New Mexico College of Pharmacy.

Manny Pino* (Acoma Pueblo) is the president of Laguna-Acoma Coalition for a Safe Environment.

Mallery Quetawki* (Zuni Pueblo) is the artist-in-residence and training specialist at the University of New Mexico College of Pharmacy Community Environmental Health Program.

Hazel Johnson was the founder of People for Community Recovery in Chicago. Interview source: Daniel Hautzinger, "The Chicago Woman Who Fought to Clean Up the Southeast Side," WTTW Chicago Public Media, February 4, 2020.

Cheryl Johnson, Hazel's daughter, is the director of People for Community Recovery in Chicago. Interview source: Jennifer T. Lacey, *Altgeld Gardens: Life in a Toxic Environment*, Vimeo, September 21, 2009, https://vimeo.com/6688840.

Carol Shapland is my mom.

Rick Shapland is my dad.

Strangers on a Train

We have been paddling for days. Or maybe just one day, a few hours, but it feels like days of skimming my paddle an inch underwater, trailing it, my arms jelly, eyes scorched by the reflection in the lake water, mind, as ever, elsewhere. It's the third or fourth hundred-plus-degree day in northern Wisconsin. Up north, my family calls it, emphasis on *up*. These are not normal temperatures, and this is the 1990s, so we aren't accustomed to seeing abnormal weather as part of a larger conspiracy. It is hot, and it is god-awful, and I am mentally vowing it will be my last-ever summer at camp of any kind.

When the two counselors and ten or so campers arrive on the shore where we will spend the night and start pitching tents and swatting mosquitoes, I sit with my legs in the water, scrubbing them with sand. That morning, in the dark van on the way to our canoe launch, I put on this new waterproof spray sunscreen, which caused all the sweat and dirt and lake sludge to adhere to my skin, and I'm thinking maybe the sand will serve as some kind of exfoliant, to remove the layers of filth. I am an adolescent who much prefers a summer day spent inside, experimenting with skin products. After twenty minutes of scrubbing, my skin reddens, the scum stays. The sky overhead is yellow-green and menacing. Or is that my mood?

For dinner, we eat couscous, which I've certainly never heard of, and hang our bear packs high in the trees (does Wisconsin even have bears?), and I keep hearing the counselors' radio walkie-talkies go off with some kind of weather alert. They appear bored, and no one else seems to notice. As we're about to get into our tents—still hazy light out, still five thousand degrees—the counselors return from an impromptu meeting they've been having at the edge of the woods with their radios and say that some storms are coming in. The safest way to spend the night, they've determined, is under our canoes. So we crawl in groups of two and three under the overturned aluminum shells, and I hear myself saying out loud more times than anyone needs to hear that aluminum doesn't seem like the *safest* option for riding out a thunderstorm, but soon enough the cracks of lightning and thunder drown out my shrill know-it-all voice, which masks only terror.

The storm comes fast, rain pummeling the canoes like rocks thrown from a second-story window, like the rock my brother once threw from the top of a hill while our house was being built that split my head right open. My dad showed up on the doorstep of the neighbors we'd never met covered in my blood, and they slammed the door on him.

Just as I get used to the rhythm of the rain and tune my heartbeat to it, someone rips the canoe off us and we're being pulled from the ground by the counselors and told to run. Run into the woods, all together, leave your stuff. So we run. Unlike my weak efforts at paddling, I am a born sprinter—my dad calls me the cheetah—and I keep having to stop to let everyone catch up to me. Where are we running? Where are we? The woods stretch endlessly in every direction, dark, messy, and we are soaked and pelted with sideways rain, occasionally illumined by lightning. The wind scatters us. My unwashed blond hair blows out of its low ponytail and sticks to my face, my mouth. We keep running.

Eventually, somehow still all together, we come to a road. A road! Salvation. We begin running along the road, on the splashing pavement to avoid the rushing drainage ditch beside it. Lights come up behind us and we stop. A van! For my whole short life I have been taught to fear vans of this sort: windowless, unmarked, pulling over for us, a group of girls. Suddenly it becomes obvious that we are all girls. I was likewise taught to fear this kind of road: backwoods, empty, dark. But we pile into the strangers' van, relieved to be taken out of the rain and back to camp, where there are cabins, though instead of walls they have screens that let in bugs and cold and rain and every night sound. The rain keeps on and the van passes nothing at all, except a dreary bar called the Rustic Inn, all lit up and surrounded by cars. Those suckers are stranded, I smirk.

We ride along, my head bumping against the window as I try to fall asleep, a fear nap, until we come to a stop. Why are we stopping? A massive pine tree lies across the road. No way around it. The jig is up. Panic floods my abdomen again. The van turns around and drives us back to the Rustic Inn, where we are instructed to sleep on the floor, which is covered in Astroturf carpet, like so many restaurants and bars in northern Wisconsin. It is dark enough when I lie down that I blissfully do not see the maraschino cherries crushed into the carpet until I wake the next morning. My legs are still covered in gray streaks from the sunscreen-dirt-rain combination, but I can't see these either.

Three tornadoes plowed through our campsite that night. Our bear packs were never found. I don't remember much about the couple who picked us up in their van, but I remember how terrified I was of the Rustic Inn. I was certain we had crossed into horror-movie territory the moment the van turned around and headed back there. After camp was over, I made my parents drive to the Rustic Inn so they could see what I'd been through. The only time during my childhood, during my twelve years of life, when I was genuinely threatened, and I was more afraid of the other people, the people who rescued us, than the storm.

This is the story I trot out when anyone brings up tornadoes, or rural dive bars, or summer camp. I usually lean into my own stereotype when I tell it to new people, my sheltered upbringing in an affluent suburb north of Chicago, my youth, my naïveté, my frailty. It's good to ham that part up, to heighten the terror of the storm, the strangers, the bar. Terror was a major part of my daily life growing up, not because I actually experienced frightening things, but because of the contrast between my immediate surroundings and the news. In Lake Forest, our local news was Chicago news, and each night I sat with my parents and watched a scroll of drive-by shootings, gang violence, and armed robberies march across the screen. Someone had always been murdered by the time the ten o'clock news came on, usually a kid caught in the crossfire. The mom was onscreen, shrieking, "My baby," and the stoic news anchor was telling us what number murder this was this week, month, year. They never mentioned what number had been killed by the cops.

These news stories taught me to fear what I referred to as the Big City, to fear the small, close-together houses in the background, to fear the people in mugshots, most of them men of color. I have to imagine that this was the intent: to make us afraid. And to make white children afraid enough that they never explored beyond the safety of the suburbs. Chicago, then and now, is among the most segregated cities in the country, and this was by design. Its long history of redlining confined immigrants and people of color to the south and west of the city, white people to the north. The gun violence was itself a product of redlining, a symptom of the systematic disenfranchisement of communities on the South and West sides. The news focused on these instances of violence to reinforce the segregation. When a twenty-one-year-old shot thirty people, killing seven, at a Fourth of July parade in a North Shore suburb in 2022, one citizen told *The New York Times,* "We said it could happen anywhere. But we didn't realize 'anywhere' could include here." This was the belief that governed my childhood. The world was a dangerous, scary place out there, but not the North Shore, not our community. Danger and violence only happened elsewhere.

My childhood was the era of so-called superpredators, the fictional idea that people raised in certain urban settings were actual monsters that needed to be found and locked away. The racist term, coined by political scientist John Dilulio and picked up by Hillary Clinton, was part of the messaging that rendered Black male children liable in the criminal system, a way to try thirteen- or fourteen-year-old boys as adults and then sentence them for life. As the framework of fear and vulnerability existed to shelter and infantilize me, it was used to make legal adults of Black children. Claudia Rankine writes, "The inability of white people to see children other than white children as children is a reality that frankly leaves one hopeless about a change in attitudes regarding the perceived humanity of Black people." To see only white children as children, to see only white children as vulnerable, is to dehumanize every other person. It also ascribes an undue preciousness to white children.

In the eighties and nineties and aughts, a slew of students from my high school committed suicide by walking in front of trains. No one talked about it, and most of the deaths were not reported as suicides. The causes are unknowable, but it's hard for me not to attribute the copycat suicides to the extreme pressure placed on children to be perfect—to excel in everything, to be popular, to attend an Ivy League college.

Maintaining the shimmering surface of the bubble was all of our responsibility. The father of the family living next door to us walked in front of a train and killed himself after I'd left home. He had lost his job and suffered from depression. Any kind of failure could be the catalyst for self-harm in the community where I grew up. My peers had eating disorders (like I did), addictions, and nervous breakdowns. These were only discussed in murmurs among the moms, among the kids, nothing ever spoken of outright or treated as a real problem.

If we had anything to fear as privileged white kids in the suburbs, it was our own psyches and their ability to stand up to the pressures of living in a place defined by flawlessness. But instead of learning how to feel mentally and psychologically okay, I was taught to be afraid for my safety constantly. Why was my safety, my vulnerability, such a priority? What exactly was I supposed to be afraid of? Over time, the blanket fear of strangers that was purportedly intended to protect me as a child morphed into a different fear as I became a young woman. I had something else to protect, but no one would say what it was.

I was an extremely sheltered kid. It wasn't easy to see from within how strange Lake Forest was, but on some level we all recognized that we were growing up in a fantasy. Turn on the news if you want to learn what the rest of the world is like. When Chelsea visited Lake Forest for the first time, she said it was like being inside a train set. Like the outwardly perfect vision of suburbia depicted in John Hughes's movies, a vision she'd always found hard to believe, come to life. Those movies were filmed in towns like mine along the North Shore. They filmed *Ordinary People*, a movie about teen suicide, in Lake Forest, and photos from the set decorated a room in my public high school, an ivy-covered mansion on the tony east side. To be sheltered is to live in a world where certain things are never said, where language itself is limited and therefore limits the reality you are able to perceive. It creates a constant state of cognitive dissonance. The information I gleaned from the world around me, from the news, from rumors or gossip at school, from eavesdropping on my mom's phone calls, sharply diverged from the world we all pretended to live in.

I began to apprehend the bubble that surrounded me only by prodding its edges. As a kid, I didn't have a lot of freedom, apart from roaming the neighborhood on my bike, and it wasn't until I had a car and a license that I started to explore beyond the limits of my few residential streets. I drove first to the mall, then to a further-away mall down the highway, then to Evanston, where I spent long afternoons walking around, drinking coffee, trying to imagine what it would be like to live in a city and be a whole person. Eventually I followed Sheridan Road along the lake until I was actually in the city. Only Rogers Park, Lincoln Park, and only to shop or wander or find pastries, but still, it felt like a victory. A boundary transgressed.

The boundary was my own sense of safety, the edge of where I was allowed to go alone as a white teenage girl. Sometimes I felt afraid, usually if I found myself alone on the street or passing through an alley. I didn't know where these fears came from, exactly, but I sensed that on my own I wasn't okay. I came back from these jaunts to a mom infuriated, demanding to know where I'd been for so many hours. Often I lied, knowing that to say I had gone into the city was to invite more reminders of my own vulnerability. Of my smallness and weakness and perceived inability to protect myself outside the prescribed limits of suburbia, of white geographies.

But the fear I felt, despite my attraction to it, despite my inching ever closer to it, was real, even if its cause was a fiction. Right when I entered high school, which I had also been made to fear—kids from the town over went there, kids we didn't know—9/11 happened. I watched it on a big screen in one of the school auditoriums, transfixed, terrified. I had never been to New York, I didn't know what the World Trade Center was, but now all the buildings in downtown Chicago—the one where my dad worked, and the Sears Tower, and the ones we peered up at through sleet on the river architecture tour that seemed to be every teacher's favorite spring field trip— all of these were flimsy, vulnerable structures, biding their time until impact and collapse. On the news, people began to fear immigrants, expanding the post-9/11 rhetoric against Muslims and Middle Easterners to any person with an accent. When I graduated college I feared the recession. I lived with a sense of scarcity, threat, anxiety. Fear has its own logic. It thrives in the absence of clarity and reason, in euphemisms and unfinished sentences, in any atmosphere that breeds it.

After the Rustic Inn, I swore off camping and all wilderness activities until I signed up for a doomed college orientation camping trip, wanting to try out a new, less cautious version of myself after leaving home. I registered for the least-experienced-level hiking trip, but it turned out everyone else in my group had wanted to be in the expert tier, so after a vote we hiked the hardest route up the mountain, me out of breath for three days and holding up my new so-called friends at every turn.

For the rest of my time in Vermont, I did not hike, or camp, or ski like all the other kids at my school, which had boasted diversity among the student body, listing all the languages spoken on campus, but failed to note that 95 percent of the class came from the same small set of prep schools outside of Boston and New York. I'd thought I could escape the suburbs by moving across the country, but wherever I went, there they were.

I sheltered myself from these familiarly self-tanned faces

and spent most of my time holed up with my secret girlfriend, reading books that weren't on the syllabus and judging everyone. I didn't go home for Thanksgiving or allow my parents to visit for parents' weekend. I hardly called home, because it was too hard to talk about my life when so much of it was dictated by a relationship I couldn't acknowledge.

Then in my sophomore year I decided to leave school for a semester and go to New York for a program at NYU—my girlfriend had gone to Greece, so this was the best I could come up with. I wandered the streets of Manhattan on foot, alone, afraid only when returning to my apartment in the Financial District after dark, not because of the people I met there, but because all the people had vacated the office buildings and the streets were perfectly empty. I was afraid of no one.

I spent the following year abroad in Italy, flexing my newfound independence in a new language but still insulated by the other students in my program. We made some Italian friends, but for the most part we all hung out together, drinking two-euro bottles of wine and riding our bikes along the medieval cobblestones. I had flashes of the autonomy I'd been craving—eating a rectangular slice of pizza while walking down the street at twilight, finding the words to explain what was wrong with the washing machine to a handyman (*La lavatrice ha inondato la cucina!*), holding my own when every old lady tried to cut in front of me in the grocery line—and flashes of fear, when men I didn't know walked close behind or beside me, whispering obscenities so that only I could hear them. These were interspersed with devastating homesickness, which was confusing because I couldn't stand my hometown.

Instead of hopping trains and exploring cities on my own, as some part of me longed to, I took fifty-euro flights to Bordeaux to visit my girlfriend, our lives still bound by each other despite our having lived in different countries for a year and a half, despite her multiplying entanglements with others. On the phone with her late at night, or trying to answer her texts before she had a chance to ask why it had taken me so long to respond, the restrictions on my sense of my own independence had never been stronger, and part of me longed to escape even my escape.

Despite whatever reservations I had about the relationship, I moved with her to Austin after graduating college and we lived together for several more years. In retrospect I can see how a codependent relationship might follow from a sheltered childhood, a form of rushing from one safe zone to another to avoid the storm of the world beyond myself. The closet as a kind of shelter. When I realized that neither place was safe for me to be fully myself, I messily fled the relationship and landed squarely in my twenties, living alone for the first time and finally out, at least to my friends and peers. No longer defined by a secret, I felt I could at last do whatever I wanted. I was reading feminist theory for the first time and beginning to see the structures that had kept me confined all my life by fear for my safety. Armed with my new visibility, some part of me still believed that traveling alone would be a way to reclaim my independence and freedom.

After a week at a writing workshop in Portland, Oregon, the first time I called myself a writer, called myself queer among strangers, at age twenty-seven, I booked a treehouse near Mount Rainier, the closest I'd come to camping since college. I still had gauze taped to my knee from falling during a drunken footrace with a fiction writer—when it happened, I didn't notice I was hurt until an older poet offered me a large maxi pad to staunch the bleeding—and the memory of J, a shy and brilliant girl I'd met at the workshop, pushing me on a swing. Coming out is a kind of second adolescence. The treehouse was magical enough when I arrived but tilted into a horror movie when I returned to it after dark.

I treated myself to dinner at a lodge facing the mountain and had my photo taken by kind strangers with the peak lit up in the setting sun behind me. I, a born flatlander, knew little about mountains, but I wanted to get to know this one better. Longing to explore, but due in Seattle early the next morning, I drove after dinner up the mountain road by myself, and my GPS stopped working and I turned the wrong way, struggled to find my way back to the treehouse village. I peered at every driveway, every turnoff, trying to recognize it as the way I'd come. Was I lost? What if I was lost, where would I go in the night alone with no service? I finally saw a turn that seemed familiar and found my way back to the treehouses.

When I got to mine, I had to climb up in the pitch dark, suddenly cold, suddenly equally afraid of large insects and other people waiting for me in the tiny house. I found the single lamp and looked under the bed. No one. I needed to shower and knew there was no chance I would wake early enough to do it in the morning, so I climbed down the tree in the dark and took off my clothes in the shower stall, afraid for my privacy even in the dark, in the woods. I took the fastest shower of all time, shampoo still dripping, certain someone—who?—was going to come for me.

The next day I caught the Amtrak Cascades in Seattle, back in cell service, high on thoughts of J and all the ideas I'd had at the last week of talks and writing workshops in Portland. The romance and the creative energy were one and the same, a rush of pheromones in the air around me. I was still drinking it all in through my skin. The train made a "fresh air stop" in Eugene, right after taking a thirty-minute "smoking stop" in Portland; this time I left my bags and got off the train, unaware of the difference between the length of the two stops. I was basking in the sun beside my train, taking its pic-

ture, texting J, along with two of my still-circling exes, telling
everyone that I was quitting smoking. This was at least the
seventh time I'd quit smoking and it would be years before I
really did. I was daydreaming about J, our unending kiss on
the bridge the night before, and then the train was moving.
The train was leaving. I was not on it. The conductor looked
me straight in the face, unable to stop the train but able to
recognize, feel responsible, emote with his expression from
the small window above.

Instantly I was sobbing, raving, panicked. An old Amtrak
woman, gray hair and fluorescent yellow vest, understanding the situation immediately, offered to help me, told me I
couldn't delay. My crying was delaying. She called me a cab
to chase the train, while I tried to understand what she was
even talking about. You can't *catch* a train. Can you? What did
I know about honestly anything. I grabbed a cigarette from
my pack to calm me down. A man with a thick tongue, drunk-
seeming, called me over to ask how many of my cigarettes a
dollar would buy. I gave him the rest of the pack, quitting for
the eighth time. On one of my trips outside the train station to
check for the cab he asked why I was crying, and I told him,
and he said he'd thought they were tears of joy, of adulation,
A-D-U-L-A-T-I-O-N. Sometimes you need it spelled out to
appreciate the person conjuring it.

Up until I got in the cab, I felt relieved, grateful for the
real adults around helping me along. The Amtrak woman
had been with me, my fairy godmother. But once I was on
the road, I became afraid. Zee, the cab driver, wanted to talk.
After we pulled out of the station he offered a flat fee of two
hundred dollars to get me to Chemult (where?), the next stop,
two hours away. Who was this guy? Where were the cab signs,
the official stuff? He turned the meter off—why?—and then
he told me, since it was a long ride, that we could smoke a
cigarette on the way. He'd seen me smoking on the curb. I

said okay, then later when he lit up I told him that I'd given my pack away. So after I quit smoking and missed my train I bummed a Camel Crush in solidarity, though I did not crush it, and smoked in the blue dusty velour backseat with the window cracked at sixty miles per hour, unable to ash without the ash flying back in at me. A chunk of hot ash flew straight into my ear. Zee was ashing into a blue Mountain Dew bottle. The car smelled of menthols and blue Mountain Dew, which somehow smells blue. We got off the highway and I worried more. Why was my phone getting no signal? Where was he taking me? All the old lessons about strangers flashed before my eyes, along with the clear message, "This is how I'm going to die: blond twentysomething murdered, side of the road, Oregon woods."

But soon enough, half-listening to Zee tell me about his poetry and ask for my email so he could send me some of the poems he'd written for his girlfriend, I began to trust. What makes us trust strangers? I mused as the trees blurred by. What makes us doubt? The fact that Zee was a poet, this loose tie to the writing world I'd found entry into in the past week, calmed my fears instantly. The fact of his girlfriend, too, made me relax—serial killers never have girlfriends, do they? And then: How is it so easy to fall for something? Someone, that is. With the other half of my mind I was thinking only about J, even though I knew little about her. We'd just met. I knew so little and remembered so much. Her hair, shaved at the sides; the way she rifled her hands through it, messing it up, her smile. The lingering electricity running through our bodies.

At Chemult, Zee pulled away and I was momentarily a white woman alone again, I was Cheryl Strayed, until I was joined on the platform by a man who was actually hiking the Pacific Crest Trail. We waited for the train. White man, beard, dirt, backpack. Fear. But then, conversation. He'd encountered snow and had to get to a different part of the trail, but he also wasn't sure if the train had already come. We waited together, uncertain how long we'd be standing there, whether we were characters in an existentialist play. Somehow, miraculously, the train appeared and then I was back on it, winding through the Sierras. I walked the aisles to my car like I was back from the war, awake from some apocalyptic nightmare I had thought would never end. I found my seat, assuming that my backpack with my computer in it, my suitcase, all my things were probably long gone. But everything was exactly where I had left it. My big headphones crumpled in my sweatshirt, nothing touched.

"Where'd you go, man?" asked Tyler, my seatmate. I filled him in, along with the other passengers looking on with interest, even the loud guy across the aisle. I was the object of great curiosity in this car; everyone had been wondering where I'd gone. Starving, embarrassed, I made my way toward the dining car. It had been three when I got off the train and now it was eight.

"Don't get lost this time!" they heckled. Dinner was over, and the staff was eating in the dining car. Fuck. I was peering through the window, hoping someone might take pity on me, when the conductor who saw me miss the train caught my eye and lit up. "Let her in, oh my God, she made it." I ate with the staff, lasagna and sad green beans and the saddest salad of all. While I ate, after narrating my cab ride, I learned about an accident they'd come upon last night en route to Eugene, two people by the side of the tracks; they thought it was a double suicide. I was researching suicide by train then for an essay about Lake Forest and I'd unwittingly landed myself in a pool of experts. Every person I met seemed to have something in common with me—Zee's poetry, the hiker waiting for the train, the railroad staff—like I was a little girl in a fable, a lesson waiting for me at the end of every encounter. But what was I meant to learn from all this? That I was safe?

That night I barely slept, all the adrenaline still pumping

through me, the awkward train seat, the smell of Tyler. And of course, thoughts of J. We arrived at Sacramento at four in the morning, where I was to change trains and start heading east. But the next train wouldn't be there until nine. The train station was under intense construction, nothing open anywhere, and I was completely exhausted and couldn't imagine schlepping my bags even a block. Even a few more feet. I collapsed bodily onto one of the wooden benches in the outdoor station and fell so soundly asleep, backpack under my head, purse by my side, suitcase in front of me. When I woke up around eight, I realized how stupid I was to sleep like that in public, with all my stuff. I panicked for a second, then gathered my belongings and began to look around for the bathroom. The loud guy from across the car waved from his spot a few benches over. "I've been watching you, gotta make sure you don't miss your train again."

While in most situations the idea of a stranger or semi-stranger watching me while I slept would have been terrifying, in the train station tears flooded my eyes. Who were these people, watching out for me? Just people. I headed to the bathroom of a Starbucks and took a navy shower in the sink, tried to make myself look less like a disaster. I felt, for the only time in my life, what it might be like to be homeless, without a place to go. Would I have watched out for myself in this situation, if I'd come across me sleeping on a bench with dirty hair? Why did these men take it upon themselves to watch out for me? Is it because I am female, white, young, blond? The same things that are supposed to make me vulnerable, the same things that are supposed to make me afraid. They are protecting me every second as I move through the world. The fear I feel is real, but the threat never is.

Four years later, Chelsea and I drove from Birmingham, Alabama, her hometown, to Montgomery to visit the Memorial for Peace and Justice. It's the first memorial to lynching in American history; it's also a chronicle of white womanhood. As we descended into the labyrinth of the memorial, concrete walls rose up out of nowhere on either side of us. Rusting body-sized metal weights with the names of counties and people who were killed etched into them hung in front of us. The floor continued to sink beneath our feet as we walked down a ramp, craning our necks until we couldn't read the text anymore, the heavy metal boxes by then overhead. White women littered the walls to our left and right, which were covered with plaques listing the cause given for killing the people named on the weights above.

Parks Banks was lynched near Yazoo City, Mississippi, in 1922 for carrying a photograph of a white woman in his hat.

A black man recently discharged from the army and a black woman were lynched near Pickens, Mississippi, in 1919 for writing a note to a white woman.

In 1889, in Aberdeen, Mississippi, Keith Bowen allegedly tried to enter a room where three white women were sitting.

In 1934, after being accused of "associating with a white woman" in Newton, Texas, John Griggs was hanged and shot seventeen times and his body was dragged behind a car through the town for hours.

While lynching was an act of domestic terrorism perpetrated by white supremacists against Black people in the South, and against Spanish American, Mexican American, and Indigenous people in the Southwest, its defenders claimed it was an important means of protecting vulnerable white women. This national narrative was faster and stronger and more compelling to white audiences than any reality. And it came from the top. "The greatest existing cause of lynching," said President Theodore Roosevelt in 1906, "is the perpetration, especially by Black men, of the hideous crime of rape." The threat against white women's bodies was far more palatable to the white masses than systemic racism; it mobilized puritanical communities hungry for a sex scandal and reliably silenced those who were supposed to be enforcing the laws. "[If] it requires lynching to protect woman's dearest possession from ravening, drunken human beasts," white women's rights activist Rebecca Felton (and Georgia's only female senator prior to 2020) told the Agricultural Society in 1898, "then I say lynch a thousand a week if necessary."

We had just stepped inside the Legacy Museum, down the road from the Memorial for Peace and Justice, when we were informed that we were standing in a former slave warehouse. I overheard a child asking her mother a question about some of the wall text. The wall listed the recorded sale prices for various slaves. "They sold us for *how* much?" the girl wanted to know. She and her mother were both Black. "Twenty dollars," the mother sighed after a long pause. My eyes blurred and I turned to the next part of the exhibit, shelves and shelves of soil and sand in glass jars. All of it collected from lynching sites, an attempt to make physical and local and visible centuries of unhindered violent white crime. The museum had holograms of former slaves and phone carrels where you could listen to the stories of currently incarcerated people, but it was those jars that stuck with me. Even in places where blood seeped into the soil, it all looked like ordinary dirt.

On I-65 back to Birmingham we stopped at Peach Park and bought a basket of peaches and two cones of peach ice cream, which was perfect, though I later learned, trying to re-create the recipe at home, that theirs was made mostly of peach-flavored gelatin. But it was numbing for a moment, licking my cone, patrolling the drips at its rim, until a little later, the largest Confederate flag I've ever seen waved down at us from the east side of the interstate, unhindered. "We put the flag up so people could see it," said Leonard Wilson, commander of the Alabama Sons of Confederate Veterans, after the organization purchased the land to raise the flag in 2005. Flying alongside the main artery that runs to Montgomery from anywhere north, the vast majority of visitors to the National Memorial for Peace and Justice will see the flag on their way. Will be reminded.

In Alabama, a Black pastor named Michael Jennings was arrested for watering his neighbors' hydrangeas while they were out of town. One of his other neighbors, Amanda, called the police on him for "suspicious activity," despite having invited him to her son's graduation party weeks earlier. When the police were putting him into the back of the car, she realized her mistake and told them "it was normal for him to be watering flowers at that time." She told them, "This is probably my fault." Reverend Jennings asked if she would speak to the news about what had happened, but her husband replied to his text, "My wife is not going to have anything to do with this." All of this occurred in August 2022.

In the post-Trump era, it's easy to hate white women, those Karens who vote consistently for white supremacy. In its report on lynching, the Equal Justice Initiative, which built the Memorial for Peace and Justice and the Legacy Museum, reminds us that white women's fear comes from the racist cultural system in which they are raised. EJI writes, "Socializing girls in such an amoral framework communicated a devaluation of Black life and inflicted psychological damage on them." Votes for white supremacy are votes bought by fear, votes for self-preservation. All their lives, the Karens have heard the same cultural narratives: that they are constantly in danger and must protect their "dearest possession," i.e., their white pussy, and that only armed white men, misogynists or not, will act as their guardians. Lynching provided a framework, a scapegoat, a nexus for their fear.

My friend Emily is often reminding us, "Kill the cop inside your head!" But here I think it might be valuable to kill the white voice of Rebecca Felton, of anyone who ever held you captive by telling you to be afraid. "I realized this is what white people do to each other—they cultivate each other's fear. It's very violent," Eula Biss's cousin tells her in "No Man's Land," her essay about living in Rogers Park as a white woman, constantly reminded by others that her neighborhood is unsafe. She continues,

> We are afraid, my husband suggests, because we have guilty consciences. We secretly suspect that we might have more than we deserve. We know that white folks have reaped some ill-gotten gains in this country. And so, privately, quietly, as a result of our own complicated guilt, we believe that we deserve to be hated, to be hurt, and to be killed.

He's missing part of it, though. If it's white women whose safety we will do anything to protect, white women who we falsely believe are most threatened, most at risk, that suggests that we also believe deep down that white women are the ones who most deserve to be hurt and killed. Our fears are caught up in our desires, and our desires are shaped by what we are taught to hate. We believe this is likely, we expect it to happen, perhaps think it should happen, relish its happening, though statistically it is rare. I've watched it happen over and over on TV all my life.

In fact, white women are the least at risk of murder, but their murders most captivate the dominant cultural imagination. Picture blond Laura Palmer's dead body wrapped in plastic, which opens the series *Twin Peaks*. By the end of the show, the lesson is clear: *Young women who display independence and/or sexual curiosity will probably be murdered by a deep-woods demon.*

And then there are all of the British mystery TV shows that Chelsea and I watch. Why do we love these shows so much? What is it about women's being killed that appeals to us? I tell myself we're hooked on the satisfaction of crimes solved, justice served, often by a powerful female detective like Helen Mirren as DCI Jane Tennison or Olivia Colman as DS Ellie Miller. It's a relief to imagine a world in which the justice system functions, in which criminals are evil people who get what they deserve, a world so utterly different from the one we live in.

These stories of capture and murder date back to the earliest days of imperialism and conquest, a time when it was helpful to the interests of the colonizers, who sought to occupy as much land as they could, for women to be encouraged to protect themselves—i.e., stay home and reproduce. The "first distinctly American best-seller," writes scholar Christopher Castiglia, was a captivity narrative published in 1682. It tells the story of Mary White Rowlandson, the wife of a Puritan minister, who was dragged from a burning house and held captive for eleven weeks by Narragansett Indians. In Castiglia's view, this story and others like it, stories of white women captured by Native people, were "circulated to justify imperialistic expansion." They were a way to assuage whatever guilt white people might feel when learning about the genocide of Indigenous peoples and the stealing of their land: cast the Native people as violent, cunning murderers—deep-woods demons—out to capture, to steal, and to destroy white America's most precious resource, white women's bodies. Never mind the fact that most "set-tlers adopted into indigenous societies almost never wanted to go back," as David Graeber and David Wengrow write in *The Dawn of Everything*.

What were the news narratives of violence I grew up with in Chicago but a reiteration of this, a means of justifying seg-regation, redlining, and mass incarceration? "These are the murders we find most compelling," Biss writes, "because these are the murders that allow us to be afraid of the people we want to be afraid of." "We," of course, being white people.

When I got on the train I wanted to be free, to be auton-omous, to be independent, but all the cultural narratives I inherited remind me that as a white woman I am not an agent, I am biding my time until victimhood. Castiglia writes that the victim and the perpetrator are denied agency by these narratives, the aggressor a figure without reason or control, the woman a preyed-upon "passive item of exchange in battles fought by and for men." By coming out as a lesbian I thought I could free myself from the narrative that had kept me hostage my entire life. But I was still a white woman and I still could not be independent, autonomous, free—or I could, but in the back of my mind I was always in danger. The safest place for me is a house with a fence in the suburbs where no one can get me, and the best thing I can do with my life is hurry myself from one fenced suburban home to the next, from father to husband. Without those things, without a man by my side, even with a partner I would always be seen as—would always see myself as—a woman traveling alone.

Because I fear capture, I am a hostage to my own safety and my perceived and culturally reinforced need for protec-tion. "In reading captivity narratives . . . women and people of color are interpellated within an ideological system that grants agency only to white, male subjects." I am trapped in this narrative that traps others. But by being afraid, I become an agent of the larger mission of the state. "Captive white women, by generating fear and hatred of the Indians and their allies, helped to further the colonization of the shifting western frontiers." During his reelection campaign, in the midst of a massive uprising for the rights of Black people to exist without being murdered, Trump kept talking about the suburbs, claiming it was this particular geographic and sociological construct that was truly under attack in this country, and only he could protect them. White women, perhaps stoked by the same man to fear Black Lives Matter activists relabeled "Antifa" or refugees fleeing the utterly American drug wars in Central America relabeled rapists, white women, reminded constantly of the white futurity lodged in their bodies, voted for him, their professed protector, 53 percent the first time, 55 percent the second time, according to exit polls.

The narrative of violent Native Americans waiting to capture white women undergirds the myth of the threatened white woman to this day, whether or not we're aware of it. But the women who suffered the most at the hands of colonization, and who continue to be at the highest risk of violence and death today, are Native women. Today, there are "thousands of human trafficking victims targeted and exploited in the U.S. every year, of whom only 10% are ever identified. And while Native Americans make up about 11% of New Mexico's population, they account for nearly a quarter of its trafficking victims." I read about all this in my local papers, the *Santa Fe New Mexican* and more often the harder-hitting *Albuquerque Journal*. "It is a growing crime that's estimated to generate $99 billion a year globally, and in the U.S., people of color are victimized at the highest rates." Native women are most likely to be taken because the laws do not protect them or fail to recognize them. They fall into a no-man's-land, a no-woman's-land, between the laws of their tribal nations and the laws of the occupying nation, and the U.S. tribal courts do not possess jurisdictional power over non-Native people, their kidnappers. While this has in recent years become newsworthy, so much so that a multiseason Canadian podcast called *Missing & Murdered* was made about the ongoing kidnapping of Native women, the practice has clear historical precedents. Sarah Deer, a Muscogee (Creek) law professor, writes that contemporary sex trafficking of Indigenous women is "almost indistinguishable from the colonial tactics of enslavement, exploitation, exportation, and relocation."

The commissions and task forces recently formed in the U.S. and Canada raise awareness of violence against Indigenous women, but they do so in a manner that deploys what Leanne Betasamosake Simpson (Michi Saagiig Nishnaabeg) calls "the politics of grief." Rather than focusing on structural changes or connecting current problems to historical injustices, she explains, the politics of grief avoids "substantive changes . . . in favor of superficial status quo ones," and blames the victims and their lifestyles, while positioning "the state as benevolent and caring." A father figure, stepping up to watch out for these poor vulnerable women whose trauma is always figured as individual, personal, a freak incident, rather than a "collective, community, or nation-based" loss. This narrative renders Indigenous women and Indigenous communities helpless victims of an unnamed violent force. They are the grammatical subjects that are elided in calling people "missing" or "murdered." We are missing the kidnapper, the murderer who should be held accountable, who should be stopped. Perhaps the media narrative should focus on the perpetrators and the systems that support their ongoing existence. While vital for drawing attention to the reality of Indigenous women's lives, victim narratives reinscribe fear and threat as conditions of their existence.

While I'm reading in the local paper about the ongoing capture of Indigenous women and children, QAnon conspiracy theorists insist that white children are being sold on the popular furniture website Wayfair. Some of them are angry enough about this fictional narrative to scale the Capitol walls and mount an insurrection. Have they not heard about the Indigenous women? Or do they find their narrative preferable to reality, somehow? They have grown used to worrying about white children, white women. They don't want to worry about Black women and Indigenous women and Latinx women and trans women, the real targets for violence. Why do they need to invent another narrative when reality is terrifying enough? Because their narrative allows them to control and to fear the people they want to control and fear? Because choosing the threat, rendering it as a population outside or separate from their own community, gives them a sense of control over the ongoing threats we all face?

I like to believe that what I know distances me from these whites, from QAnon truthers, from Karens. I am not like them, because they are—what? Ignorant? Undereducated? Confused? Duped? Straight? Misogynists? White supremacists? What is the distancing mechanism I employ to separate my whiteness from theirs? It makes no difference. "Guilt and defensiveness are bricks in a wall against which we will all perish, for they serve none of our futures," said Audre Lorde.

In her essay "Know Your Whites," Tressie McMillan Cottom writes, "What *is* necessary for the paradox of whiteness to maintain the internal tension that defines it is for superiority to coexist with fragility." Is my superiority the way I distance myself from other whites, and my fragility the fear I felt in the cab? Is my fragility what I perform when I tell my camping story, when I cry in a train station and people rush to my aid? My perceived fragility, my deeply felt fear, is a performance, whether or not I'm aware of it as such, and it's a performance—like all those white women's bodies in British whodunits—that erases and devalues the real victims of violent crime and recenters the white woman.

A year and a half after the treehouse, two months after we started dating, Chelsea convinced me to go camping with her. We drove from Austin to the *Spiral Jetty,* a land artwork by Robert Smithson north of the Great Salt Lake in Utah, where we curled up in the nest of Chelsea's 4Runner, which was facing the rock spiral out the back, so we could wake up to it. This was the first big road trip we took together, fifty hours in total, and all our friends told us we were insane. Who would take such a trip so early in a relationship? Why would you drive halfway across the country to look at some delicately stacked rocks? But our time together had been spent dreaming of other places to be, spaces we might inhabit that would feel less confining, less cloistered, than Austin, than Texas. With Chelsea, camping seemed suddenly wonderful, a way not just to see the jetty but to sleep beside it. The car air felt cool from under the warm, heavy blankets. Chelsea slept in her red and navy sweater, and we used her big ivory cardigan as our pillow. I had toe warmers in my socks and wool tights on. It was so quiet. No stars, a few satellites. Beyond the car was sand, soft sand, and dark rocks and white rocks, and some salt crusted in rings. And out at the horizon, past the rim of white salt, a pink expanse of water that I pictured as I fell asleep.

I'd gotten nervous driving out there, on the long dirt road past a fully militarized zone. I'd locked the doors of the car. When we'd arrived there'd been two other cars of people. All women. Not scary. One dog. One baby. But they left and then it was just us, and I kept hearing what I thought were tires on the road. We'd spent the night before in a Taos Earthship after winding our way through snowy creeks and mountains covered in tall pine trees and eating green chile for the first time. We fell asleep in a big bed, where I'd had bad dreams of someone—these two guys—who kept leaving my front door open and threatening to sell my rental house or take it over. I never had time to call for help because they kept coming back. At the *Spiral Jetty,* I kept waking to sounds of scratching around the cooler, and other rumbles, thunder maybe, and I'd imagine that a tide—a lake tide—had come in, that when we opened our eyes we'd be surrounded by water.

Instead by morning the car's windows were covered in what appeared to be frost; we couldn't see anything. Chelsea braved the cold and took one arm out of her sleeping bag to wipe the fog from the window, and there was the jetty, in dark grayscale, the sky to the left all pink. We warmed our pants under the covers and put on our layers, me in thermal Southwest Airlines coveralls, and stepped out into air that was hardly cold at all. The mountains were reflected in the water way out, and there was a white horizon line beneath. Salt. We'd walk there later. First I sat in a camp chair and wrote while Chelsea walked up the hill behind me. For a moment I couldn't find her, scanning the hills and hilltops frantically. I thought of *L'avventura* and Monica Vitti's blond hair against rocks. Disappearance. And then there she was, tiny earth-tone Waldo, halfway up. She shouted to me and I shouted back and it was clear as day.

We were falling in love in this landscape, and we were listening to Patti Smith read *Just Kids,* thinking about her relationship with Robert Mapplethorpe, how they created a whole world unto themselves. Perhaps here, beyond the confines of the university and the city and all the bougie condos that were sprouting up near our homes in Austin, perhaps in one of these states with a tiny population in a huge area, we could find our own lives.

In northwest Utah, almost Nevada, trying to find Nancy Holt's *Sun Tunnels*, we missed the last handwritten sign, which looked nothing like the previous copper ones that wobbled in the wind. We drove and drove and the GPS started flashing because there was no signal, and suddenly we saw a group of buildings, the first in many miles, and felt relieved to find a town. As we got closer, the town morphed into a compound of buildings and trailers and outbuildings and dead cars, a place where surely many murders had taken place. We turned the car around, gas tank low, and careened back to the highway and safety. We stopped at an old gas station and paid inside. It was full of dolls. No bathroom. I was dying to pee. The gas station doll collector told me to go to the café two blocks down, a bar we'd passed called Coyote Club. It was windy, cold. I started walking and Chelsea said she'd pick me up after she'd finished with the gas. A man in a red truck leaned through his window and practically leered at me, seeing where I was headed, and turned sharply into the bar's parking lot. To apprehend me, presumably. I turned around, terrified, and ran to the car.

None of this would matter by the time we got to Santa Fe, where we forewent the yurt we'd rented on a llama farm after discovering it had no hot water and only bean bags for beds, and found ourselves snowed in at a hotel with fireplaces in every room, no choice but to stay an extra night. We soaked in the women's communal tub at the Ten Thousand Waves spa, naked bodies of all shapes, colors, sizes sharing the water beneath the pine trees, snow softly falling all around us. I'd never felt so free, but I also saw how each woman carried and displayed and hid her nakedness differently, as though her body were her personal thing, her fault, when it was suddenly so clear to me that bodies are just iterations, permutations of a form. Crystals, grown from imperfections.

Six months later we upended our lives and moved there, all because of this trip. I remembered not the compound or the dolls or the fear of cars' approaching on the gravel road but the way no one was around to look at us or bother us, how the jetty and the salt and the pines and the whole landscape let us be.

The massive earthworks of the West, like Smithson's *Spiral Jetty*, Nancy Holt's *Sun Tunnels*, Walter De Maria's *The Lightning Field*, and Michael Heizer's *City*, can be seen as their own form of colonization. They imply an attempt by white artists to take over the vastness of the American West with enormous installations that require the movement of huge quantities of earth, the disruption of the land. What has been viewed in art history as a movement out of the studio and the gallery and the museum, a gesture away from the commodification of the artwork as a product, an attempt by artists to free themselves from the market, is in effect a laying claim to a place that is not theirs to take. Any attempt to be free diminishes another's freedom, encroaches on their space and safety. How can a person take up space without claiming something that isn't theirs? It depends on who is doing the claiming and how they are doing it. Georgia O'Keeffe came to New Mexico and decided that Pedernal was her mountain. She told people about this all the time, *that's my mountain*. In the same way explorers came West in the early days of colonization and renamed the rivers, the mountains, and the lakes after themselves.

Space seems like safety to those whom society polices. Women, queers, gender-nonconforming people. All it took was one camping trip out west for me to love camping and hiking again, to want to move to New Mexico to have more access to the outside, to the freedom I might find in nature. But the very fact that I view nature as available for my enjoyment separates me from those who feel more unsafe in the wilderness, burdened by cultural narratives of escape and pursuit. In her essay "Black Women and the Wilderness," Evelyn White writes, "My genetic memory of ancestors hunted down and preyed upon in rural settings counters my fervent hopes of finding peace in the wilderness. Instead of the solace and comfort I seek, I imagine myself in the country as my forebears were—exposed, vulnerable, and unprotected—a target of cruelty and hate." Nature isn't free and open if it is a site of intergenerational trauma. White's fear is as justified as it is limiting.

In their essay "How I Became Free in the Mountains and Never Left," Shea Martin writes after coming to Vermont: "I do not know when I decided I would stay. Perhaps it was when I decided I deserved to stay, which I guess came after I decided I deserved to breathe, which came after I decided I deserved to dream." For Martin, who describes themself as a Black fat queer, inhabiting the natural world is a way to claim and take up space. In recent years, a whole movement has arisen, most visibly in the group Outdoor Afro, to reclaim the outdoors for Black people. To claim the outdoors is to take up space in a world that asks Black and brown and Native women to make themselves small and inconspicuous, that asks some not to exist at all.

I keep coming back to the image of a woman tied to the train tracks in the cartoon West. She needed to be saved. But there is also this mythology of the West as a place of freedom and independence for women. There are the many women who found ways to be independent and to be queer, to reject certain gender norms for at least some of the time, out west. White women, Black women, Native women, Mexican women. I wrote a monthly column for a while profiling these women; I know they existed and exist. Isabel de Olvera, Maria Varela, Paula Angel, Maria Gertrudis Barceló, Laura Gilpin, Agueda Salazar Martinez, Esther Martinez, Dorothy Stewart; those are some of their names.

Because coming out as a lesbian is such a touchstone in this narrative I've created for myself, I have to wonder if my queerness is what I felt needed protecting, what made me feel most free in New Mexico. Where I live now, the population is less dense than in most other places in the country, meaning I am less likely to be perceived by others. There are simply fewer people around to do the perceiving. Like when Carol and Therese leave New York and take a road trip in Patricia Highsmith's *The Price of Salt*, adapted by Todd Haynes into the movie *Carol*. Driving west all the way to Salt Lake City offers a chance for two white queer women finally to find freedom, to have sex. But of course, this is the 1940s, so the surveillance state reinscribes their captivity. The man Carol's husband hired to listen to them through the hotel wall poses as a women's magazine salesman. And what are women's magazines but tiny prisons, glossy surveillance states for our psyches?

Captivity still exists all over the world for queer people. Zanele Muholi, a queer South African photographer and activist, says,

> Just existing daily is political in itself and visibility also has its own politics especially for those in a space where some people are regarded as deviants. You are told you can exist, but at the same time there is this violence which also exists as a constant threat that denies you the right to be who you are, or who you want to be.

I've never been threatened with violence for being who I am, and being queer isn't illegal in the United States, as it is in so many countries. I don't know what it's like to hide or flee violence; I don't know the threat of being outed as a threat on my life. As a white queer woman in the United States, my encounters with the forces that restrict freedom are subtler, the kinds of policing that act on the psyche rather than the body. I remember going with J to get barbecue in Lockhart, Texas, how the woman behind the counter took one look at J's undercut and put down her spoon, refusing to serve us. Someone else came up to help us, while she stood back with her arms crossed, staring. Later I told J what had happened, knowing she hadn't noticed. "In the future," she said, "please don't tell me when things like that happen." I was doing it again, acting as an agent for the fear, the threat that sought to put us in our place. The fear wouldn't exist without people like me, reporting on it and reminding people when they've crossed a line.

The usual suspects in American literature about the outdoors and the wilderness are not Black women but three-named white men like Ralph Waldo Emerson and Henry David Thoreau (whose mother did his laundry so he could bond with a pond and create a mythology to underpin Manifest Destiny so that other white men could take all the land and choose to exploit it or preserve it). White cis male nature writers, as earnest and poetic and radical as they might be on the page, laid the groundwork for the men in fluorescent gear climbing Everest, with their undying desperation to *summit* and underpaid Sherpas schlepping their belongings, dying en route. They are the forebears of the artists who came to the West to make earthworks and claim huge swaths of land for their art. They are not Evelyn White, who wants to go kayaking, or Shea Martin, who wants to be with lakes and trees and mountains that ask for nothing.

The leaders of Outdoor Afro tell stories about Black naturalists on their hikes and excursions, referring to

> protesters who marched in Selma as "hikers." Harriet Tubman, abolitionist and hero of the Underground Railroad, is remembered as a naturalist who understood waterways, astronomy, herbal medicine and geography. That understanding helped her move enslaved Africans from the South to freedom in the North. George Washington Carver is honored as a scientist who employed sustainable agricultural practices more than a century ago.

These suggest other ways of knowing and drawing power from the outdoors, directly from the ground, rather than the aerial view you might take from a nature documentary. For Tubman, finding freedom in nature means something quite different from what it meant for Thoreau. The Black Lives Matter movement formed around the idea that Black people should be free to move about in public spaces, outdoors, without their lives being threatened by violence or incarceration. The Memorial for Peace and Justice commemorates centuries of patrolling the ability of Black people to walk down the street, to exist in public without being hunted down and killed by white mobs. For Black people to enjoy nature, for anyone to enjoy nature without a colonialist mindset of exploration and conquest, or precarity and fear, we need to reimagine the history of the wilderness and its narratives.

The project of colonization required the outdoors to be framed as white, masculine space. In order to justify claiming vast swaths of already occupied land, any body other than that of the colonizer—Black bodies, Native bodies, women's bodies—had to be rendered and reinforced by the dominant culture as not belonging to that space. Women and wilderness are both constructs, categories that have been defined in service of some other project. Women were domesticated and defined by the interior of the home so they would reproduce a workforce efficiently, and wilderness was separated from the human so it could be either exploited or preserved, conquered or claimed. Neither entity, woman nor wilderness, existed on its own terms, and both were and are feminized, fetishized. These two processes, both of which Silvia Federici, an Italian Marxist historian, considers forms of "primitive accumulation" like the enclosure of common lands as private property, are the ways that capitalist governments gather up resources. And both of these processes occurred on a massive scale in Europe and the Americas simultaneously in human history: the witch hunts, during which hundreds of thousands of women were terrorized in a state-sponsored attempt to corral them into keeping house for the new waged workforce, coincided precisely with the conquest of the Americas and genocide of the Indigenous populations. Both enterprises demanded narrative rationales, reasons for the subjugation of others. Federici writes, "The demonization of the American Indigenous people served to justify their enslavement and the plunder of their resources. In Europe, the attack waged on women justified the appropriation of their labor by men and the criminalization of their control over reproduction. Always, the price of resistance was extermination."

The narrative of the wilderness eventually became a way to justify exterminating the Indigenous people who had lived on the land for centuries, who occupied spaces that the transcendentalists and conservationists wanted to view as pristine and untouched, so that they could chart them, rename them, own them, and make it possible for future generations to hunt on them, mine them, drill them, frack them, profit from them. And as the "wilderness" of the western United States was being parceled out, so too were our bodies, the newly enclosed territory of Western medicine taking the place of healing practices rooted in knowledge of herbs and natural processes best known by women who were burned or drowned for such so-called witchery. Men in power needed to show how a woman's natural resources, like the land's, might be exploited. They certainly needed to take away the contraceptive knowledge that women healers had been cultivating for centuries. When they started calling women witches, it was a way to chase them inside, to keep them away from the healing arts, from nature, from independence, freedom, and community, to house them in prisons for procreation and reproduction of a male labor force.

The two things most often "raped" in the English language are women and the land. Virgin soil, Mother Nature's bounty. Meanwhile, I've read that in the twentieth and twenty-first centuries, landscape designers have been planting only male trees, to decrease the alleged mess of seeds and fruit from female trees, but the male trees are the pollinators and have caused exorbitant increases in pollen counts and our allergies. I don't know if this is true where I live, I would have to ask an arborist and he would probably deny the whole thing, gaslight me, but it feels true, these New Mexico junipers spraying their pollen all over my face, into my orifices.

The logic of primitive accumulation continues to play out as the United States seeks access for ever deeper and scarcer quantities of oil under its surface. When I try to find a map of fracking locations in the United States, the first link I click takes me to one covered in skulls and crossbones, marking all the places where fracking accidents have occurred. Finding basic information about fracking locations is difficult, and at times seems to be intentionally hidden or paywalled. In the frenzy for oil, nowhere is safe.

We first saw them on the way to Marfa, an eight-hour drive from Santa Fe, our eyes blurring out by the time we hit Carlsbad, where the air is brown with methane and smells like farts from all the fracking in the Permian Basin, the country's largest oil producer, though we didn't know it then. We passed so many temporary structures, metal buildings and prefab homes, and the road was suddenly crowded with trucks carrying massive unfathomable equipment, and pipes shooting fire into the sky, and as we looked back at the fire we saw a tank marked HALLIBURTON, and a little ways farther a woman standing on the side of the road alone. Trucks everywhere. "The heart of darkness," Chelsea said. "There should be a Google Maps filter for hellscapes."

These, we learned later, are man camps, the massive temporary communities of oil and gas workers hired from all over to frack southern New Mexico and West Texas and Pennsylvania and the Dakotas and California and countless other places to hell in search of oil. Criminals at the man camps also benefit from the "loophole" that protects non-Native people from being prosecuted by tribal governments for crimes against Native people. The presence of man camps "correspond[s] to increased rates of violence against women" but not increased rates of enforcement. It's the drug war, it's the oil, it's the land that needs to be protected. These are the excuses they give. At a rally for missing and murdered Indigenous women, activist Delee Nikal (Wet'suwet'en) said, "The femicide is directly linked to the ecocide . . . there needs to be more awareness that these extractive industries, all that is affecting our climate and destroying our territories, is intertwined with violence against our women and girls."

—

While Indigenous women are being murdered and kidnapped with very little awareness from the public, I have been told all my life that I am under threat, that I am powerless, that I have something to protect, that my only recourse is vigilance: not drawing too much attention to myself, not ever being alone in public, not putting myself into bad situations. How else might I access feelings of agency or security without giving in to that formulated fear? There is no such thing as safety, only the sense of entitlement to it.

That summer of the tornadoes and the missing bear packs, when the campers were all girls and we did nighttime candle-light ceremonies at the campground for which we all had to dress in white—why?—one of the campers in my age group was a witch. This was my only personal encounter growing up with the existence of witchery, apart from *Sabrina*. She was outside in the night making circles on the ground, chant-ing. She had objects. Spells. Books. We were afraid of her, the witch, and other campers definitely told the counselors about her practices, and she may have been sent home. But now reflecting back I can understand what she was after and what we were all afraid of. Power.

In Frances Denny's *Major Arcana,* a photo book of people who identify as witches today, one writes that she became a witch after moving to New Orleans, where "there is a pretty strong occult community."

I was maybe too young to feel like I was in danger until a particularly violent summer when the crime started closing in on me. I was hearing gunshots at night. A delivery boy was stabbed on my front stoop and then my apartment was broken into. I couldn't sleep there anymore, so a friend of mine came over and did a *veve*, a Haitian Voudou ritual where you create a drawing on the ground with corn flour to draw in the presence of a certain spirit. The desperate fear that I was feeling allowed me to be open to the healing that took place that day. It showed me how empowering ritual could be—that if you were feeling lost and out of control, you could perform a symbolic action that would summon your personal power and get you through whatever was happening.

The witch camper was trying to reclaim her power, which felt threatened, perhaps by the tornadoes or the mean bitches who surrounded us, the other campers, policing any behavior that seemed out of line, perhaps by the demand that we wear white and carry candles and sing in unison, but more likely by her own girlhood. Another contemporary witch, Ébun Zoule, writes,

> "Witch" is totally political for me. It is a political practice in that it allows folks to manifest things for themselves and their communities rather than relying on a capitalist system. Solutions are found through community and self-spiritual guidance instead of capitalism and all the ways it drains people of their power. I think capitalism is afraid of the word "witch" because it implies self-sufficiency. How could capitalism work if everyone was self-sufficient?

In other words, one way to resist a system that tells women that they must be afraid, that they are potential victims, that they must protect themselves, is to claim independence and self-sufficiency, to find ways, even symbolic ways—sleeping outside, driving downtown, reclaiming the streets—not to be afraid, to kill the cop in all our heads telling us what to fear. Rather than avoid situations that might make us afraid, we can examine our fear, sit with it, ask what it is trying to tell us about the world and whether or not we believe it.

I was sitting on a rock in the shade of a juniper, which thankfully wasn't pollinating at that moment, meditating. *I am a lake.* I breathed in. *I am cool and still and held by the earth.* I breathed out. *I reflect things as they are.*

"Hi there," a man said from the trail with a laugh, and I was no longer a lake. I was a woman alone in the shade and my stomach had dropped through my legs into the rock below me. My heart raced and I closed my eyes again—when did I open them?—and heard the footsteps of the man passing. I tried to become a lake again, but I could not. I was still a woman alone.

The Toomuchness

The Moths

We were surrounded by sweaters. In the air, I caught a whiff of grandparents, the elderly, conjured by damp wool and moth-balls we'd never use. They'd poison the cats. The scent must have stowed away in the thrift store sweaters. Regardless, the lingering chemicals failed. The moths got everywhere and ate the high-ends and personal faves, holes on holes. They loved cashmere most. Upstairs in our loft, which had previously been our landlady Fran's tapestry studio, the turquoise floor-boards had disappeared under all the clothes. The toomuch-ness was up to our knees.

The late October sun at seven thousand feet is strong enough to make the afternoon sweaty as high summer, but the mornings and evenings plunge into jacket weather, and anyway, I'd gotten tired of short sleeves. I love that moment in the year, switching my clothes over, and the opportunity to sort, to discard, to pare down, to reconsider. For months I look forward to pulling the bins of winter clothes from the back of the closet, opening them, and seeing all the sweaters and corduroys and scarves I've forgotten about. A breath of fresh air, a chance to reclaim dormant, wintry aspects of my personality, as the spring switch ushers in airy, lighter, sunnier selves.

Stacking the sweaters on newly cleared closet shelves, at first we didn't notice the moths. Their residues left clues: unremembered holes in a sleeve, a conspicuous amount of dust at the bottom of the bins. Then one flew up from Chelsea's Mexico City cardigan, a big cream and red and orange patterned shawl collar with a tie at the waist, good for clutching to your chest while making coffee on cold mornings. We didn't see where it went, the beige flutter, but it headed toward the closet.

After reading online that their eggs nestle in the very fibers of our knitted winter skins, my first thought was *Burn it all*, the clothes, the bins, and start over. Instead, I kept reading and learned that freezing the sweaters for forty-eight hours would kill the pernicious moth eggs, so then I cleaned out the freezer, too. Old hamburger buns, stale Christmas cookies, frozen fruit no longer recognizable. In my house growing up in Illinois we had three freezers. My mom froze everything, and dinner often involved a thawing stage. This is a comment not on her cooking but on her extreme resourcefulness, which I attribute to Catholicism and hardscrabble Midwesternism, and which I know lives deeply and unalterably in me. My freezer is packed with things we'll never eat, because when I'm not sure what to do with something, I freeze it. I keep it, whatever it is, imagining some future time when a use for it might emerge. It's never felt clear to me what to keep, what is useful, if usefulness is enough. When I'm out of town, Chelsea goes through the freezer or the cabinets without telling me, to save me from witnessing the process of throwing things out. No matter how necessary, throwing things out, even thinning the sprouts in our vegetable garden, registers in my psyche as violence, a separation, a loss.

The moths, however, felt unfair. They were eating holes in

all our clothes, making us look shabbier than we were, and to begin with, in the era of the moths, we were underemployed freelancers in secondhand sweaters. We had just moved to Santa Fe from Austin, hoping to shed our connection to the corporate university and careerism and find a life that was simpler, pared down. Obamacare and the Medicaid expansion in New Mexico made this fantasy seem more feasible, though then I had to spend inordinate amounts of time on hold with the automated state human services system YES New Mexico—so long that I memorized its hold music, which I sometimes found myself singing throughout the day, a soundtrack invading my dreams. During what we referred to as the Lean Years (broke, but not broke enough to lose a sense of irony, of humor about it), I still managed to acquire more and more things: too many funny secondhand shirts from the men's or boys' sections at Savers; piles of clothes from new friends trying to Marie Kondo their homes; clothes that I made myself, an attempt to corral some of my desire for new looks into a time-consuming project, to slow down the time between a want and its fulfillment. Inside the clothes lurk a tangle of desires, fears, and guilt.

Lake Forest, the town on Chicago's North Shore where I grew up, is a place obsessed with its own wealth. The town square was built around a Marshall Field's and is a paean to consumerism, a bastion of shopping. A junior high friend lived in Marshall Field's palatial mansion, replete with crumbling tennis courts, a pool, an entire additional house behind the pool, maids, drivers. The Walgreens lived nearby, and one of my classmates was a Swift, of Chicago meatpacking fame. In the miasma of old and new money, we discussed relative class among ourselves even as children—the Wrigleys gave out gum in bulk at Halloween. I was able to recognize, to some extent, the community's privilege, but it was confusing to know where my family stood in relation to it. As children, we interpret the world that surrounds us as the world itself. I knew I never wanted for anything, and yet I wanted so many things.

Clothes have always been a source of class dysphoria for me. When I was about to start kindergarten, right after we moved to Lake Forest, my mom and I went to the upscale clothing store the Children's Place with my new best friend Molly and her mom. The moms bought us each identical periwinkle collared dresses, which we wore on the first day of school. All of my other clothes came from Kohl's, so this dress was a big deal. I remember being excited to wear it that first day and wearing it much more often than Molly for the rest of the warm days of the year—once a week, at least. My mom had made it clear to me somehow that this dress was expensive, a one-time thing. So I knew, at age five, how class could be expressed through fashion. Living in a hyper-affluent community, surely my parents could afford to buy these clothes, but it was "the principle of the thing," as they told me frequently. Why spend so much on things I would inevitably outgrow within a year? Instead of absorbing their principles, I became aware of other people's clothes, recognizing that they were more expensive than mine.

I started shopping in earnest in high school. I'd shop during lunch period, leaving school in my red Civic and driving a town or two over, perusing sale racks whose contents were already familiar to me, spending all my dance-teaching money, and when that was gone, using the credit card my parents had given me for "emergencies." A sale felt like an emergency to me. It still does. I needed to look different, to be someone else, and shopping was the way to achieve that. The catalogs of the late 1990s and early 2000s—dELiA*s, J.Crew, Anthropologie—made that clear. As a teen I felt out of place wherever I went, and my social life became increasingly competitive as my friends and I sought to perfect a life on paper in pursuit of prestigious college admission. This was the goal we'd all been working toward and one-upping each other for since kindergarten. You could blame all this millennial striving on neoliberal precarity and inevitable downward mobility, like Malcolm Harris does in *Kids These Days,* but I didn't have words for it then. I thought—I still think—that if I had the right outfit, everything else would fall into place.

In the stores, I would scrutinize each piece of clothing, each object I found, and picture a version of my life it fit into. A person who might have such a thing. And what her life would look like, feel like. Anthropologie was especially generative for these fantasies, for construing alternatives to the self and the life I longed to escape. One of the early lifestyle brands, Anthropologie sold not just clothes but dishes, bedding, candles, stationery. Muted rainbow latte bowls that I somehow still own three of. The objects were arranged into charming environments, whole worlds that I could see myself inhabiting, each corner of the store a place I can vividly remember. A long table set with napkins and dishes outside a Tuscan farmhouse. A vaguely Eastern room full of multicolored print pillows. A rolltop desk with hidden drawers half open to expose a collection of pastel pencils, watercolors, a wax seal kit, where some other me might sit and make something of her important thoughts. The objects created a fantasy in my mind of a woman in a floral silk robe on her white, ruffled, four-poster canopy bed, sipping from her latte bowl while writing a letter with seven candles burning in the middle of a dappled forest clearing.

It wasn't my imagination. For their fall 2003 line, which came out during my junior year, Anthropologie's head of home furnishings, Polly Dickens, great-granddaughter of Charles Dickens, and her team envisioned three distinct women as inspiration for the collections. "Estella" is based on the character in *Great Expectations* and is "a very grown-up and feminine" line of bedding in smoky pastel colors and cobwebby fabrics. "Licia" is a blend of wares from Turkey and Morocco. And "Sonia" is a very clean, Swedish-inspired line of furnishings.

The women were themselves objects, acquirable lines of products. How often products are named after women! Meandering from staged room to staged room, I could be any of these women-made-of-objects; I didn't have to be me. Expanding on the marketing concept of "self-construal," whereby an individual uses brands and objects to bolster a sense of identity, the stores were designed to be "transformational," tasking the customer with inventing entirely new selves, new lives, to accommodate its products. Not fitting into any current version of femininity I saw, I gravitated toward these manufactured ones. It felt easier than being myself: Here are the pieces, collect them all and you'll be normal, you'll fit in, you'll stand out.

Like its parent company Urban Outfitters, Anthropologie was designed as a place not only to shop but to spend time and immerse yourself in the narratives. The average customer spent seventy-five minutes in the store. My fifty-minute lunch period never felt long enough. It was seductive on purpose, and I was seduced. The rooms suggested travel to far-off places, independent women's lives fueled by creativity and friendship and ease. Estella, Licia, and Sonia had a lot of things, but they definitely didn't seem to have jobs. No one asked Licia what her major would be, or where she was going on a Saturday, or when she'd be home, or what she'd bought. In fact, she never actually had to buy anything—her life was magically appointed and kept for her by fairies, birds, some forest-dwelling labor class. The store's white paper bags and tissue paper had an earthy, fresh scent that can still bring this whole era back to mind, if I pass by one of their stores. Employees lit incense before opening hours to create precisely this scent memory. The clothes were outrageously expensive, but the discount room was tucked away, a world of its own, and made it seem reasonable to buy doilylike blouses and vanilla fig candles, fully believing as the salesperson wrapped my dinky items in tissue that my life would surely change, that with this precise purchase I would become enough. Buying things on sale was a way to have more, and in the moment, it always felt like that discounted thing I was buying was not a random leftover but the final piece. And then, back home, hanging the new thing in my closet, it never was. None of the new things I bought went with what I had, because to truly be what I wanted I'd need to have all of it. And a new life, body, family, home, personality. I longed for the transformation these stores promised.

My closet had big, wide double doors that opened out. At some point in adolescence I became obsessed with organizing all of my clothes by color. I spaced the hangers out with my fingers so they were perfectly even. In my closet was a tiny TV on which I'd watch *What Not to Wear* and *Trading Spaces,* shows that reaffirmed my belief in self-transformation through material things. I kept the closet doors open while I was in there, watching TV in my papasan chair and basking in the glory of my perfectly ordered universe of objects, while my family fought downstairs and I turned up the volume. I watched Martha Stewart wrap her plastic hangers in white fabric, and I hung a sign on my bedroom door from Anthropologie that read "Baking a Cake," with an image of a 1950s housewife on it. Somehow these cues became a sort of drag, a performance of femininity and domesticity and perfection that took over my life for a while. My favorite thing to wear was a pale green cotton sundress from Anthropologie that tied around the waist with four faded pastel ribbons. It had lace at the neck and the hem, embroidery, darts, a perfect storm of nostalgic ladylikeness. I wore it with a coordinating ribbon in my hair, half up. I still have it. I wonder now if I was performing these past versions of femininity because I couldn't understand or find my place in the present version, which looked like $150 7-brand jeans and belly button rings and three-inch skirts and platform sandals and tiny tank tops my mom wouldn't let me wear. But regardless, from an early age I was using clothes, outfits, as a language, a way to speak some truth or lie about who I was underneath.

All of these on-sale clothes, in their garish early-2000s hues, most of them hardly worn, followed me to college in Vermont, to Texas, through graduate school. And all the while, I kept shopping. I never had quite enough money to support myself, but I did have a credit card of my own, and in graduate school I won a few writing prizes that made me feel flush. I bought beers for all my friends, bought an aspirational professor costume of satchels and Oxford shoes and blazers, bought ill-fitting bathing suits on sale year after year, until the prizes evaporated and my credit card debt bloated. I ignored it. The clothes took up more and more space, over-flowing from the closet into bins under my bed and sofa in my duplex in Austin, and eventually into garbage bags I planned to donate, but the bags hibernated in my car for months. Having been closeted in my first relationship with a woman for six years prior, I could see there was some irony here, in my jamming the closet door shut, shoving everything into the trunk or under the bed. I wanted to get rid of it all, but I couldn't. I was holding on to the fantasy of a past self, past selves, past lives, some way to return to the person I pretended to be as a teen, cracking through icy sidewalks in heels and a size zero

A-line skirt from the J.Crew sale rack, another honest-to-god ribbon tied in my long blond hair.

We talk about the closet as a place to come out of, or to be outed from, but how many theorists have talked about what it's really like inside? Maybe it's a two-way street. Maybe sometimes the closet is a refuge, a warm, quiet place to nestle back into, like Edmund before the wardrobe leads him to Narnia, like any kid playing hide-and-seek. The wool and canvas and leather closing around you, the dark, the stable smells of old things, the past. All of my previous selves and their outfits, and all the things I've never worn but could still someday become, surrounding me and keeping me company at my loneliest, my most lost.

Perhaps then—perhaps now—I'm afraid to get rid of things because I don't want to lose these former selves, these other versions of womanhood, as cringey as they feel to me as I outgrow them. "I think we are well advised to keep on nodding terms with the people we used to be, whether we find them attractive company or not," Joan Didion says. "Otherwise they turn up unannounced and surprise us, come hammering on the mind's door at 4 a.m. of a bad night and demand to know who deserted them, who betrayed them, who is going to make amends." The closeted years are so fuzzy, my memory falters, has little to grab on to. The clothes hang around to remind me of what I don't have access to otherwise.

In our loft, none of the closets had doors, an unusually common feature of homes in Santa Fe. Instead, in their place, curtains hung precariously across the two downstairs and two upstairs closets. When I washed the curtains to try to rid another surface of potential moth activity, suddenly there was nowhere to hide any of it anymore—the high school dresses, the high-waisted skirts and scarves I wore in grad school. The same was true of my relationship. Chelsea was there and willing to see and be with all of me, but I wasn't ready to see or reckon with these contradictory styles yet. With the curtains off I was fully uncloseted, exposed in all my excess.

During the worst of the moths, we were sharing sets of microscopic wasp eggs with our Zen friend, Susan. She ordered them from the same place the Smithsonian does, and we hung the little gray egg-speckled cards in the closets, hoping the specks would hatch and eat the invisible moth eggs, which was their job. The moths kept appearing, right as we were trying to go to sleep, so eventually I panic-ordered cedar pieces off Amazon and put them all—seventy-one of them—everywhere, and routinely sprayed every garment with cedar oil spray, but we continued to find and kill moths. The moths leave an iridescent gold paint on your skin when you kill them. I really don't want to kill them, I've been a vegetarian since I was twelve, but it happens instinctively. I'm so mad at them. They made me buy stuff for my stuff, and I already have too much.

The moths are a sign of the dark side of excess: deterioration, decay. All my stuff food for bugs, like my body will be someday. They may well have originated with Fran and her tapestries, but they came for us, and we must contend with them and their significance. Why do I have so much and buy more? Am I greedy and materialistic, am I wasteful, or am I just swimming through so-called late capitalism? Maybe I should get rid of my copy of *Postmodernism, or The Cultural Logic of Late Capitalism*, while I'm thinking about it.

If you ask the Buddhists, attachment to material things is a sign of ego and self-attachment, which basically amounts to a curse. For Hindus, restraining from greed is one of the core *yamas*. Jewish tradition underscores satisfaction with what one has, Islam has a charity requirement that is meant to deter acquisitiveness and wealth hoarding, and the Bible warns about the moths: "Do not store up for yourselves treasure on earth, where moths and vermin destroy, and where thieves break in and steal" (Matthew 6:19). But, raised Catholic, I shed the skin of religion a long time ago, and a popular current iteration of the Christian church is the "prosperity gospel." Religious leaders take on celebrity status, wealth. Not to mention that capitalism's been entangled with the Catholic Church from its origins, quashing the lower classes to maintain its own power. There are moneylenders in the temple, etc.

I still have to get dressed every day, and even though I feel more comfortable, more myself in what I wear now—a combination of androgynous, long-lasting Muji basics, Everlane jeans, and thrift store gems—it's always a kind of costume, a performed self I select and buy and keep. And what if my idea of myself changes again? If there's no easy moral way out of this, out of consumption, if it's not as easy as rejecting it wholesale, what can we do? Why do we shop? What do we want? Do we want against death? Or toward it?

The Hedonic Treadmill

A few weeks into the COVID-19 lockdown in New Mexico, I drove to my acupuncturist's house to pick up the herbs she'd mixed for me, set out on a bench in a little wax-paper bag with sharks all over it, a bag I saved for months, trying to discern a way to reuse it. The alert sign at the side of the overpass that had been issuing mask warnings flashed out our national anthem at the empty highway all day long: "SHOP ALONE_SHOP ALONE."

Wanting to be more than a consumer, I started to make my own clothes. I'd learned to sew in what was termed Home Arts at my junior high school, a class in which I made a pair of flannel boxer shorts and learned the proper part of scissors for cutting (the tips). In my twenties in Austin I started to hate all of my clothes. I couldn't get rid of them, but I didn't want to wear them. Since college I'd been wearing skinny jeans that clung to every inch of my skin in the humid 105-degree Austin summer. I shopped exclusively at Urban Outfitters. I'd transitioned to this uniform when I met my college girlfriend and suddenly all my femme outfits felt obsolete. I erased that version of myself and replaced her with a style identical to my girlfriend's, who wasn't calling herself my girlfriend or telling any of our friends we were together. Maybe I thought that if I looked like her, people would just know. I erased myself to fit her. Now free of that relationship, I needed to kick the jeans, too, along with the blazers and skirts of academia. None of these made sense anymore. All I wanted to wear was clothes that didn't touch my body at all, but I couldn't find these in stores. Women's styles had swung back to the ruffles and lace of my teen years and I couldn't stand it. First I made a navy linen button-down dress with a Mandarin collar. I followed a pattern, but the pattern offended me instantly. The pattern was designed for my former self, for a woman in the 1950s. It had a woman's name, like Sally or Susie. I modified everything about it: I rejected the bust darts, straightened the A-line skirt, took out the curve for the waist, added pockets (except I forgot the second one, so it has only one pocket).

My mom sewed, my grandmothers both sewed; when I started making clothes I knew I was part of a tradition. In her history of waste in America, Susan Strasser writes,

> At one time, it fell upon American women—virtually all American women—to do the miles of stitching required to keep their families and, collectively, the nation in clothing. . . . Because they sewed, they intimately understood the fabric and cut of old clothing—

mending, patching, accumulating pieces that could be used again, and composing new garments from old ones.... They knew just what pieces would do for what purpose, and how to make what they had into precisely what they needed.

What a pleasant idea, this sense of purposefulness, of using what one has. It reminds me of my mom's approach to dinner, of Lévi-Strauss's theory of bricolage, an idea I dwelled on in my dissertation. Bricolage emphasizes the element of contingency: it's not about "the availability of raw materials and tools conceived and procured for the purpose of the project"; rather, the bricoleur will "make do with 'whatever is at hand.'" These materials are "heterogeneous" and include "the remains of previous constructions or destructions." Their imaginary landscape is not the market of new things but castoffs and remains, the detritus, the leftovers.

Over the years, as I sewed clothes and baby blankets and quilts, I amassed a collection of fabric, some partially used, some untouched, brimming from a bin in my closet. No matter how small the scrap, I found myself unable to get rid of it. Surely I could use it for something—a bookmark, a headband, a cat scarf, a fraying bow on makeshift giftwrap. Looking through the bin for moths, I realized that when the fabrics are not used I forget they exist. I can't keep all the patterns in my head. But if I have used it for something I can look at the scrap and recall what I made—it reminds me of the making, of extended use. The unused things have no meaning. The spare cords and screws and parts in our junk drawer with unknown functions. An unread book with no memory attached to it. Unworn clothing at the bottom of the drawer. Wittgenstein in Italian, how I first read him, sits on my shelf, calling out, *Il significato è dato dal uso.* Significance is given by use, to translate it literally. Certain texts I keep reusing, and these are the ones I recall most frequently and still find generative. Each time I revisit, revise, rephrase, reconsider, new depths and possibilities emerge.

Learning to make my own clothes, I marveled at the slowness of the process. Sewing patterns all seemed too complicated, too rigid, so I studied my own clothes and tried to re-create them. I eyeballed every seam and stitch to comprehend how the piece was put together. Soon I couldn't unsee it, the labor that went into my own clothing and everyone else's. Someone sewed every seam of what you are wearing right now! A machine helped, but a person was involved. Cutting and sewing and turning it right side out, pressing and trimming threads. In recent months I've learned to knit, and I can't get over the fact that every time I make a mistake the only way to fix it is to tear the entire thing out and start over. I am not adept enough at reading my work to undo it without messing it up further. I've restarted this single first hat twenty times and will probably restart it again, and it has taken many hours already. This teaches me the value of a hat.

"As one western woman wrote in 1867 of her new gray dress, 'I finished my sacque and entered it to live therein till its last days arrive.'" When I first read this sentence in Strasser's book, I saw it as "until *my* last days arrive," which seems likely, too. For most of human history, most people had only one or two outfits at a time. They washed and mended and altered those items for as long as possible, then shredded the fabric into rags to use for household cleaning, insulation, or rag rug making. Mending was a part of life, and care was something people expected to show for things, a set of practices and habits around which to build a life. "Domestic writers counseled readers to keep on top of their mending tasks, both by working on thinning areas before they developed holes and by establishing regular times for inspecting garments and linens to see if they needed mending." I picture my mom in the green armchair with her glasses on, sucking a needle and peering at a hole in my brother's pant knee, at the inside of my pointe shoe whose ribbon had snapped.

Wealth creation has followed the production of fabric for centuries, from the status of silk in China to the woolen sails of the Vikings to the textiles that funded the Italian Renaissance. The Medici started out as producers of wool before they became bankers. Cotton was already a major global industry when America was colonized, and it was one of the first plants Christopher Columbus encountered in the Caribbean. Up until the eighteenth century, farmers had grown cotton on a small scale alongside other crops, but the demand was increasing in England's factories, and the colonists had an abundance of free land—after they had killed and dispersed the Native populations that inhabited it. To work this land they stole and enslaved people from Africa, using the cotton gin invented in 1793 to speed up production. In her history of textiles, Kassia St. Clair writes, "By the late 1850s nearly 80 percent of the cotton consumed in Britain came from America." The free land and labor made clothes manufactured outside of the home much cheaper.

As the price and availability of cloth decreased, the practices of care, of keeping up with the thinning places, disappeared. Adam Minter writes in *Secondhand,* his book about the thrift industry, "The idea that a garment or other object was a resource that should be renewed at home was eroding. In the process, the sentimental value associated with clothing declined as quickly as the material value. After all, it's easier to discard a store-bought shirt than one made at home by a mother, a wife, or a sister." A capitalist society values money above all, money as a means of buying things, having new things, having all the things we need, but within it we don't value the things themselves. We discard them and replace them as quickly as possible.

By making it easier—to get things, to do things, to survive, to get places—consumer capitalism seems to have made it harder to be happy, at ease, satisfied. Maybe not in equal measure. Surely it was much harder when there was sewage everywhere and you had only one set of clothes and bathed once a month. But we lost things. Mending. Dirtying. I consider my until-now-inexplicable love of washing my feet at the end of a messy day outside. We lost our proximity to filth, to aging things. To animals, plants, nature, seasons, weather. Sensuality. Embodiment. Instead, we have proximity to plastic. I feel plastic running down the seams of the pajamas I ordered online, a clear marker of a fast-fashion garment. The feeling this inspires in me: I need to get some new pajamas. And now I have proximity to moths. To the lives that will feed off of me when I'm gone. I've become obsessed with getting rid of them, needing to keep all the things I'm not wearing pristine.

My clothes making grew from a hobby in grad school into a small business after we left Austin, an effort to supplement my income as an adjunct and part-time grader. Soon I was making caftans and bag dresses and kimonos for friends and friends of friends and strangers who saw my clothes on Instagram. Apparently I wasn't the only person who wanted clothes without gender or size or shape. I spent afternoons up in the eighty-degree unair-conditioned loft, ironing yards and yards of woven cotton ordered on Etsy from India. I was cranking out garments as quickly as I could, wrapping them and mailing them, adding new pieces to my website. I thought making clothes was a way out of buying and discarding, a way to control the means of production. Instead it was a way into buying and branding and making and selling. It didn't feel any better.

When did people decide that our desires could be fulfilled by things? In medieval and early modern Europe, the popular version of paradise was not a collection of objects or big houses or tons of great outfits but "bodily indulgence and enormity, pleasures sexual as well as gastronomic and every other kind," with a notable "emphasis on food." People imagined heaven as a place where you ate and drank and fucked as much as you wanted. But for the upper classes, anthropologist and economist David Graeber writes, paradise was about not excess but rarity, the

> elite consumables, the exotic commodities of the day that were primarily essences: spices above all but also incense, perfumes, and similar scents and flavors. . . . Rather than a land of complete fatty indulgence in every sort of food, these were often conceived as lands whose ethereal inhabitants did not have to eat at all but simply subsisted on beautiful smells . . . the familiar elite consumption worlds of fashion, style, and the pursuit of ungraspable novelty.

The elite version of paradise sounds like a place Gwyneth Paltrow might enjoy, or any of the other thin blond white women who proffer "clean eating"—eating less, making yourself smaller—as a solution to whatever bad feelings you might have about capitalism. These concepts of heaven marked a shift from the erotic-love model of desire, in which longing was fundamentally not meant to be fulfilled and the object of desire always out of reach. The virtue of unfulfilled longing—refraining from acting on one's desires—came to the West via Saint Augustine and medieval Christian doctrine, with "the idea of human beings as creatures tainted by original sin and therefore cursed with infinite wants, as beings living in a finite universe who were inevitably in a state of generalized competition." Sounds familiar! But instead of love and longing, the new ideas of heaven took the shape of material goods. At this moment, with the advent of global trade routes for tea, coffee, spices, and silk, and the enclosure of common lands into private property, desire shifted from the longing for collective excess and leisure to the aspiration for personal gain. But people did resist this for some time, lolling on hillsides sharing bottles of wine.

What changed was their sense of security. As Europe shifted from a feudal society to a capitalist one, human beings lost the sense of position or place that being born into a particular class, occupation, and religion bestowed, writes Erich Fromm, a humanist and refugee from Nazi Germany. To overcome one's underlying insecurity,

> his self was backed up by the possession of property. "He" as a person and the property he owned could not be separated. A man's clothes or his house were parts of his self just as much as his body. The less he felt he was being somebody the more he needed to have possessions. If the individual had no property or lost it, he was lacking an important part of his "self" and to a certain extent was not considered to be a full-fledged person, either by others or by himself.

Fromm uses the typical midcentury "he/him/his" pronouns here, but it's technically accurate: women could not legally own property at this time and were treated as objects a man could acquire to shore up his sense of self and standing. In this way, stuff began to bolster identity, and the longing for more stuff offered a possibility to change one's fate. This is how we ended up with a word like "homeless," a term first used in English right around this time, in the 1600s. If you could demonstrate that you were a whole person only by having property, being without a home indicated you were without a self, and thus you were treated as less than human. In Europe, your name and family signaled your status and wealth. For those colonizing a "new" country, the markers were reset and new ones had to be found. From the earliest days of settler colonialism, people bought clothes, land, and horses to show that they were worthy of respect, dignity, and credit. A society in which one's genealogy did not determine one's class offered endless possibilities for reinvention in pursuit of status.

For years I've loved the Emmylou Harris song "White Shoes," from her album by the same name. She wants 'em, she needs 'em, and she's gonna go out and get 'em. She sings, "I know I'll feel better / When I slide down into the leather." It's a song about class aspirations, about getting out, about young womanhood, about independence. But it's also about shoes. And what her new shoes, her new outfit, give her: a new sense of self.

I bought the record used at Waterloo Records. The store is one of the few remaining independent businesses on a corner in downtown Austin that, in the twenty aughts and twenty teens, was overhauled by an organization called Schlosser Development. They replaced one indie shop after another with chain stores: an Anthropologie, an REI, a Chico's. I worked across the street from Waterloo at BookPeople, another holdout. Rumors at the store pinned the changes on the then-CEO of the neighboring flagship Whole Foods, who owned our building and a majority share in BookPeople. At work in retail for an hourly wage, I loved to daydream myself out of my day-to-day, but, perhaps due to the immediate surroundings on the block, the only out I saw was through. I went shopping on my lunch break, assailed by lifestyle brands new and old, buying on-sale pillowcases; picnic blankets; records; organic cotton Whole Foods yoga clothes, again on sale. I wandered the aisles of these big consumer spaces as a way to calm my mind, to be not employee but customer, to be anonymous and alone, to be someone. At the front desk of the bookstore I scrolled endlessly through home décor blogs, paint colors, furniture. I tried to imagine a home, a life, that felt like what I wanted, to distance myself from the immediate reality: asking for and never getting a raise from my $7.25 an hour, watching mostly men be promoted to manager, while I was being asked to dust the shelves. I thought it was punishment for my scrolling on the clock, but now I see it as a sick, coerced performance— why else was I told to use the feather duster when the dust cloths worked much better? If we asked Marx, he'd say I was feeling alienated from my labor.

I had retreated back into a self I'd last occupied in high school, when the shopping was at its peak. As I'd waited until my parents were asleep to bring the shopping bags from my car to my closet, I was smuggling bags back into work, ashamed at my purchases and my credit card debt. Perhaps I needed a secret, something to protect and keep from other people, to feel whole. After six years without telling any of my friends or coworkers about my relationship, I was finally out, and outed by our dramatic breakup. Throughout our relationship, which controlled every aspect of my life, I had been quiet, wordless, on the subject of myself. The secret made it impossible for me to share anything deep with my friends, so I never got close to anyone. To tell them anything about myself without revealing the relationship would have been a lie. I barely wrote in my notebook, but when I did, I wrote of the sliver of space I took up. In our apartment, my room was half the size of hers.

Now that I was on my own, I approached the new task of filling in and filling out my life, becoming a whole person the only way I knew how. I started buying myself things. I couldn't really articulate my identity in words; keeping a secret for so long had cut me off from language. Instead I communicated in stuff, even when I was talking to myself. Coming out of the closeted relationship was a process of repossessing myself, my things, my body. I was also aware that I was more secure and could be more frivolous with money—or rather with debt—than most of my coworkers who didn't have the elite bubble of funded grad school to keep them insured and afloat, or the safety net of higher-earning parents, or a decent credit limit. I wanted—I still want—to buy my way out of capitalism, out of work.

After a six-month post-breakup interlude in a tiny, roach-infested studio apartment, my friends helped me move to the duplex my coworker Laura was moving out of. The rent was a stretch, but I was starting to feel like I could take up space. You can picture me then, in the 1920s duplex, peeling laminate and popcorn ceiling suddenly replaced by original wood floors, crown molding, a clawfoot tub, and two wide porches made for reading or having drinks with friends. I was twenty-five and in the process of exercising autonomy for what felt like the first time, disentangling myself from the secret of my first relationship, which had hung over my life before this point so that I was barely there. It's hard for me to remember the years before the duplex, before I had my own space and my own self, before I stopped being a secret. For years I'd imagined what it would be like to live alone, never having done so apart from my dorm room senior year of college, which was next door to my girlfriend's and decorated almost identically (we'd each cut up copies of the art magazine *Esopus* and pasted them in a pattern all over one wall). Until this point, until this duplex, really, I hadn't totally owned my identity, had merely borrowed the shadow of hers. Yet throughout those years of being sort-of-together I had in the back of my mind a vision of the life I'd have someday: a quiet place, a vegetable garden, endless hours to mill about in and read and think.

In the duplex I could start to bring some of that fantasy to life. I did it with paint colors: mint green for the kitchen, deep aquamarine for the living room. And strings of lights in the backyard, and a picnic table that my ex bought me, during one of the moments we found ourselves back togetherish. I had my own space, my own closets. I chose how to arrange everything, chose the paint colors. I did everything as I wanted. And I had friends, finally, real friends I could talk to, who slowly grew to know me, who I was out of the relationship. I had a tiny closet for clothes, a big closet for the cats' litter boxes, and a closet that used to house a washer and dryer that I turned into my office. The first designated writing space I ever had was a closet. The duplex wasn't perfect, with North Loop's neighborhood plague of cat fleas, an agoraphobic neighbor whose snoring I could hear through the wall, a shotgun layout in which my bedroom was situated at the very front of the house, next to the entrance and barely hidden by a bookshelf. But it was a start.

These years, 2009–2015 or so, were the heyday of food and lifestyle blogs like *Orangette, Smitten Kitchen, 101 Cookbooks, Apartment Therapy, Design Sponge.* I was a sponge for this content, desperate to learn what kind of life I might have, unsure that any of the paths I found myself on—minimum-wage misogyny at the bookstore, elite but likewise misogynistic power dynamics in academia—were right for me. I started writing at this time, I was slowly coming out as a lesbian and starting to date women, and the blogs and the house were a canvas for me to try out all these possible lives and selves, to consider where I was headed. I was shopping again for a self, after not having had one during such formative years.

What I really wanted, what I'd been picturing all along, it turned out, was to be a writer, to have that quiet space and endless time, but this wasn't as easy as buying the furnishings of an artist's life I saw on some blog. I wrote about this longing in 2010 and 2011, when I was starting graduate school, but I couldn't figure out how to make that a life. When Chelsea and I started dating in 2015, we spent a weekend at a yellow-walled Airbnb in Houston. Under the skylights we talked about the lives we longed to have. In the letters we exchanged furiously during these early months, we contemplate starting some kind of art space, building our lives around creative work, structuring our own time. Imagining our lives together offers an opportunity for Chelsea to rearrange her priorities, which would look like, she writes, "privileging my mental life and my creativity instead of the things I hold in my hands, my pristine apartment, everything in its right place." We considered living in a remote place and how that might give us more of the quiet time and empty space for reading, talking, scheming, and thinking we were both craving. I shared my longing to escape academia and my dream of being a writer with her, and she took it seriously. We both took it so seriously that we moved to Santa Fe six months later to try to make a new life happen in a small city surrounded by mountains. The Craigslist ad for Fran's loft read, "MAGICAL / ART / LIVING."

Capitalism is fueled in part by desire, longing. It's our fantasies and daydreams that advertisements prey on. While we think that what we desire looks like a perfect home or body or wardrobe, in truth our longings are always for something human, not material. The object of our desire is a sense of completion for a broken self, a longing to be loved, to be recognized by another human. Our whole social order, Graeber writes, is "a vast apparatus for the fashioning of daydreams," and we enjoy the dream far more than the objects themselves.

Chelsea and I got our space, our remote place, but we also each had multiple freelance jobs, impossible deadlines, barely enough money for rent and food. It was a happy time, the Lean Years. It was also cramped. The daydream of Santa Fe was real, but the loft meant we were surrounded by our stuff all the time, could see everything we owned from everywhere in the house. The brackets beneath the shelves in the closet began to pull out from the wall. The moths destroyed everything. We tried to get rid of things—an old rug, a broken Craigslist rowing machine—by placing them out on the curb, only to find them repurposed by Tenzin, one of Fran's tenants who lived in an egg trailer on the driveway. The rowing machine was stationed upright as a fence post on his makeshift patio fortress. Fran's hoarding was becoming more extreme the longer we lived there. She'd even held on to her bad ex-boyfriend, Joe, who lived in an attached wing of her house that had been partitioned into an apartment. He was a hoarder, too. I put my mom's old bike—a yellow Schwinn Collegiate too heavy to ride—in the shed behind our studio, and he removed it. The shed was filled with old clothes and boxes of discarded objects. Fran had three huge trash cans on her porch filled with the things she didn't have room for, but she wasn't getting rid of them, she was keeping them. Surrounded by the evidence of excess's material burden, I longed to go to her house and clear out everything, as though what she needed was simply a helping hand. I wanted a physical solution to a psychological problem. Fran, we learned later, had early-onset dementia, and perhaps her belongings were a way of holding on to something while her memories slipped from her.

Maybe the disruption, the disturbance, the disconnection, arises when the life-sized worlds we buy ourselves don't match up to or connote anything alive, anything that could possibly live. We long for a social relation, for connection, and we end up with a material one. We end up having to relate to, to deal with, stuff. We make a purchase, trying to acquire the fantasy, only for our own longings to have shifted by the time the purchase reaches our house. No object, no matter how carefully selected, can make us feel seen or loved or known. We long for time and space and end up filling our coveted free time with cleaning, organizing, discarding. We grow out of life-sized dreams, we discard entire parts of our personalities. I acquired a closet full of identities, but building these exteriors feeds on a person's interior. It's not just that these catalogs of perfectible possibilities provide no sustenance; the things we consume are eating us alive.

Instead of heaven, we find ourselves in unending purgatory, an in-between, never-complete state. The state of constant flux with goods coming in and going out, the unfinished quality of a life spent waiting on new things and getting rid of old, the boxes, the trash. Thirty percent of American solid waste is from packaging from home deliveries, I learn from the umpteenth *Guardian* article about the perils of consumerism. It's never still, never fixed, always cycling en route to a perfectly framed scene on Instagram.

Chelsea keeps saying that we are entering a new dark age, and I think she's right. When desire shifted from erotic love to food to stuff, we forgot the part where you can never actually be satisfied, that desire is meant to remain unfulfilled. Graeber writes,

> Anyone who got the idea that one could resolve the matter by "embracing" the object of his or her fantasy was missing the point. The very idea was considered a symptom of a profound mental disorder, a species of "melancholia." . . . This leads to the interesting suggestion that from the perspective of this particular form of medieval psychological theory, our entire civilization . . . is really a form of clinical depression.

A note goes on to say that clinical depression rises sharply in consumer-oriented societies. We are supposed to contemplate that which we desire but not try to consume it, not try to possess it or keep it. We are supposed to preserve our longing. Instead, we try over and over to embrace it, to consume it, to fulfill it, and we always just miss. We shop. A scholar responds to Graeber, "In hell, your appetites are turned against you. The separation of appetite or desires and consumption, we might conclude, is tantamount to hell. In short, capitalism, for most people for most of the time, is a lot like hell. And it is capitalism that produces this separation (or 'scarcity' in the language of economics) just as it consumes we who labor within it."

I thought the moths came from greed, but perhaps they come from desire. Greed is singular and about quantity—wanting *more*. Desires are complicated, are plural. They provide no easy moralistic tale, no real way to corral them. When basic needs are covered, other desires can flourish. Can flower, like the weeds in the yard outside our last rental house that Chelsea valiantly slayed with a Weedwacker, only to find them regrown the next day. The weeds were high and everywhere, all types. The yard was supposed to be xeriscaped, but nature disagreed. Still, our lease stipulated that we were to maintain the absence of weeds. Some weeds crept on the rocks laterally like grass or vines, some encroached on the plants and bulbs, choking out their light. Some had purple flowers that I felt bad pulling out. Some were prickly and ugly and mean looking, reddish tinged, with milk that gushed from the stem when it broke and roots that held fast like tiny fists underground. After Chelsea's weed-whacking frenzy, the dead weeds lay there, turning to straw, and then I composted them. Weeds, like waste, like excess, are defined by one's perspective.

It's comforting to me to remember that we aren't the only ones who gather up belongings and keep them. In her book *The Second Body,* Daisy Hildyard writes, "The desire to have some room of your own and a nice cup and bowl comes for us all in the end. The human buying himself an emerald green velvet sofa from Habitat is not so very far from the badger who drags the dirty leaf mould out of her sett every night or the pigeon building a nest out of elder twigs and cable ties." At our loft, I longed to get rid of Fran's outdoor cushions, whose stuffing poked through the threadbare, sun-worn fabric, until I saw birds perched on the chairs plucking the fluff out and carrying it off, to renovate their nests. With synthetics, that is.

When I was little, up until age four or so, I sucked my thumb, and when I did so I liked to hold in my hand a piece of cloth. The cloths I gravitated toward were these tiny undershirts I wore when I was younger, a version of me embedded in the fibers of the white cotton or the faded pastel bunny print. Sucking my thumb and smelling the cloth, which my mom referred to as "diapers," maybe to deter the behavior, was the most deliriously comforting thing I knew. I couldn't get rid of the shirts. Long after I stopped sucking my thumb, I squirreled them away—again, my mom's word for it, which she also applied to my tendency to hide candy in my room, and later, secret clothing purchases—and would take them out now and again to smell, the scent surely tied to some memory no longer consciously accessible but there. An early hoard. Maybe I was lonely all along and taught myself in infancy that clothes could comfort me. Knowing how to care for ourselves under capitalism means soothing ourselves with material things in the face of the terror of the world beyond us and the precarity of our own immediate lives. We are all wired to soothe ourselves.

Maybe I'm looking for excuses.

The Unfathomable

A very obvious recurring dream that I've been having for years now, a few times each month: I'm already late and I have too many bags and the bags are heavy and full and things are falling out of them and I'm trying to shove everything back into the too-small bags, trying to carry everything and get from place to place. Sometimes people along the way offer to help me, and I wave them off—ashamed of my excess, my inability to contain it.

To be alive right now and to try to be aware of the broader impacts of my own actions feels like drowning. But also like a deprivation, like casting about for sustenance and finding only dust. The whole world is marked increasingly by excess and lack, too much rain or none, fire and blizzard and flood and tsunami and ebbing glacial ice, drowning coastlands. Billions of birds, entire species extinguished—two-thirds of global wildlife since 1970, according to the World Wildlife Fund!—while humans keep multiplying and running out of food, water, space to live. Too many people, too many lives, too much activity. Too many refugees fleeing too much violence to be confined in too-small spaces. Can you feel claustrophobic vicariously?

A memory surfaces. I could be ten or eleven, so it's the midnineties. We are at a stadium for a concert or a basketball game, probably the Bulls. Whatever it is, I have no interest in it. Stacked up around me are thousands of people in stands, more than I've ever seen at once, and tons of bright lights and loud music and voices yelling over loudspeakers. I start thinking about all the things that are plugged in, all the electricity and the pipes filled with water, all the floors and all the seats and the weight of the people above me, and I feel vertigo, the floor collapsing beneath me, the people all tumbling down, none of it able to withstand the weight of so many bodies, so many cords, my psyche ticking into overload, unable to monitor so many external stimuli. Sweat pricks at my skin and I can't keep my mind in my body and everything is whirling around me at a high speed, and I start pulling on someone's arm saying I have to go, I have to get out of here, and soon I'm walking at full tilt on tiny legs for the exit, back the way we came, down a giant ramp, I have to go, I need to be outside. These panic attacks followed me through college, recurring in any big indoor crowd, in snaking airport or amusement park lines, huge hotels, theaters, city blocks. It will still flare up in a crowded movie theater or concert: the feeling of impossibility, that it can't possibly stand up, the building, and I'll close my eyes and focus on my exhales, tightrope-walking along the edge of passing out. Being alive right now feels like this, like I'm waiting for it all to explode, implode, go under, go up in flames. This is what so many books and movies and shows promise us, a cataclysmic offscreen ending that makes way for some postapocalyptic world. But instead, none of it seems to go anywhere; the space—physical, mental, psychological— keeps filling. We are in it.

In April 2013, the eight-story Rana Plaza building in Dhaka, Bangladesh, collapsed. The building housed five garment factories, and its collapse killed at least 1,132 people at work making clothes, injuring more than 2,500. They were making clothes for Prada, Gucci, Versace, and Walmart, among other retailers. One hundred and twelve workers had died in the Tazreen Fashions factory on the outskirts of Dhaka five months prior, when the building caught fire and the workers were unable to escape.

It's not only people and electricity and new products and clothes that are piling up around us, always collapsing or on the verge of collapse. Pope Francis said in 2015, "The earth, our home, is beginning to look more and more like an immense pile of filth." We are drowning in our own filth, or, more accurately, people in less wealthy countries, and in marginalized parts of our own, are drowning from the waste produced by people with disposable income, disposing left and right. Waste from cars and factories and production, in the form of carbon gases that heat the oceans and the air. Waste from the farts of cows. Waste from our trash cans. The more a society consumes, the more it discards and the more waste it produces. This is obvious but became more tangible to me when we started feeding our cats more each day, realizing when they kept trying to eat the food off our plates that we had been depriving them of calories. Suddenly, of course, the litter boxes were twice as full. The bags weighed more. We had to buy bigger bags.

On a pilgrimage to the Walmart in Portales, New Mexico, three hours from Santa Fe, where vaccines were being handed out like candy, we tracked a two-story line of train cars running parallel to Highway 60 that seemed like it wasn't ever going to end. We drove beside it for over an hour, until finally a break, a view of land and sky beyond, and then within seconds another identical train charged through going the opposite direction. The multicolored cars said Amazon or FedEx or Maersk or Hamburg Süd or Cosco or Evergreen or Yang Ming or China Shipping or Walmart or MSC or DAL.

The cars going east were filled with objects made in China purchased by Americans online. Until 2017, cars going west would have been filled with cardboard, the most cost-efficient backhaul. The boxes that our purchases arrive in were sent back to China, where the cardboard was recycled and made into new boxes, new garbage objects for us to order, unpack, and eventually recycle or throw away. Eventually, China passed legislation sharply restricting the amount of recyclables they would take on. Minter described the other end of the backhaul in Shenzhen, China, in 2005 as "a checkerboard landscape built from tens of thousands—maybe hundreds of thousands—of twenty- and forty-foot-long metal shipping containers painted red, yellow, blue, and gray. The containers cover hundreds of acres, starting from the long piers and running right to the base of the tropical mountainside in stacks that rise as high as sixty feet." On Highway 60 it was easy to imagine dual channels of stuff coming in and trash going out extending along the entire continent from east to west, a conveyer belt. What were all these cars filled with now? Were they empty, car after car of blank space, returning to the port to be filled again?

Loitering in the Walmart after a pandemic year of avoiding stores, high on our shots, we were gobsmacked by the array of consumer goods on the shelves, the sheer enormity of items in one place. We bought the unlikeliest things: a basketball, yoga blocks, extension cords for the garden. I'd been avoiding buying some of these things on Amazon, which was the most obvious way to acquire household goods during the pandemic. I try to avoid Amazon because I read the articles and listen to the podcasts about the workers giving birth and dying on the job, all because people want things immediately, two-day, one-day, one-hour shipping. Because if the thing does not arrive immediately, the need/want/urge might naturally subside. As I veer away from shopping online, try to wait out the random call of the shopping cart, I wonder if desires are not bottomless. Perhaps they can be interrupted. Perhaps their nemesis is patience.

But they're after our patience, too. In 24/7 Jonathan Crary writes, "Billions of dollars are spent every year researching how to reduce decision-making time, how to eliminate the useless time of reflection and contemplation. This is the form of contemporary progress—the relentless capture and control of time and experience." This is why we have fast internet, one-click shopping, two-day shipping, saved credit card numbers and passwords in our phones. This is why we have phones, actually. To remove the time needed to leave the house to acquire something. In the 24/7 marketplace you can acquire from bed. As Crary notes, "one of the forms of disempowerment within 24/7 environments is the incapacitation of daydream or of any mode of absent-minded introspection that would otherwise occur in intervals of slow or vacant time. Now one of the attractions of current systems and products is their operating speed." When you're unable to sleep from all the blue light in your eyes throughout the day, the blue light will summon you again to the slot machine of app checking that advertises to you in your most private moments. And the first thing many of us do upon waking is open an app engineered to ping us with new desires: Instagram, Twitter, Facebook, your email. You can buy things without being fully awake, without remembering you've done so.

In this light capitalism can start to take shape as a force, a violence that forecloses other options, bends us to its will. Considering the use of force in epic poetry, Simone Weil writes, "Where there is no room for reflection, there is none either for justice or prudence. Hence we see men in arms behaving harshly or madly." From the vantage point of 1939 France, on the eve of German occupation, Weil's response to her own cultural moment seeps into her reading of Greek texts. Rereading it now, I begin to see excess itself as a force, a kind of violence, a wave under which we crumble, to which we surrender.

In this shallow yet consuming present, where we're all trying to stay afloat, not to drown, it's hard to connect your individual actions to larger impacts at a great distance in time and space. And yet, I find, it's also hard not to. Hard not to see my every action as having much bigger and unintended and unstoppable consequences. On some level we, the consumers, feel bad about this—about ordering things, about throwing things away, about using energy, considering all that we now have no choice but to know. We must feel it, because they've monetized our guilt, too. Now you can buy from conscious companies, you can pay extra on your shipping for carbon offsets. The guilt that the producers of all of these desires and products and indelible plastic garbage should feel has been pawned off on us, and we're happy to pay for it, a modern form of Catholic indulgence.

There's a Japanese word for the feeling that waste inspires: *mottainai*, the shame or the despair or the feeling of failure that wasting provokes in a person. Japanese historian of waste Eiko Maruko Siniawer writes, "'*Mottainai*' was said to capture not only the act of wasting, but the principles and feelings associated with the consciousness of wastefulness, such as "regret and shame for the loss of things, appreciation and respect for things as well as those who made them, and empathy and compassion." We don't have a word for this in English.

For a few weeks this winter, I had two glass canisters of water sitting by the back door. Each night I would pour the water into the electric kettle to heat and then pour it back into the canisters to place in our covered vegetable beds to keep the plants warm. After we got the extension cords from Walmart, we put in lightbulbs under flowerpots, makeshift heaters, so the plants didn't need their hot water bottles, but the jars were still full of water, and I couldn't bring myself to pour it down the drain. Instead I placed them by the door and waited for a day when one of my other plants needed water. Chelsea told me about a water main that burst downtown where she works, the streets flooded and the water gushing out, and how it made her think of my two little jars. My pointless little jars, I said. And yet the feeling of watching the clean, clear water flow down the drain, knowing that our rivers are dry and the drought is encroaching and the plants are desperate and the water is expensive—I can't bear it. *Mottainai*, my heart cries.

Though my actions are minuscule, are, like the average American's, .0000000003 of global carbon emissions, I know they have effects. I know that, as Hildyard writes, I have more than one body acting in this world. Your first body is "the place you live in, made out of your own personal skin." Your second body is "a body which is not so solid as the other one, but much larger." Hildyard continues,

> This second body is your own literal and physical bio-logical existence—it is a version of you. It is not a concept, it is your own body.... It is understandably difficult to remember that you have anything to do with this second body—your first body is the body you inhabit in your daily life. However, you are alive in both. You have two bodies.

To see this second body, to see these minuscule but extant material impacts, we have to retool our sense of scale. Our approach to the unfathomable. It's confusing to learn about the immensity of my global existence from the smallness of my most private spaces, like on my phone in my bed or on the sofa or on a podcast in my car as I drive around town contributing to my meaningless carbon footprint. "Your first body could be sitting alone in a church in the centre of Marseille," writes Hildyard, "but your second body is floating above a pharmaceutical plant on the outskirts of the city, it is inside a freight container in the docks, and it is also thousands of miles away, on a flood plain in Bangladesh, in another man's lungs." This derangement of scale makes the tiniest decision seem fraught with meaning, with impact. Yet the ease of making that decision to buy something, to gas up the car—coupled with incessant advertising that deprives us of the time and capacity in which to make a decision—implies that we are autonomous free agents with no responsibility to anything but our desires.

If the United States is built on ideas like individualism and some mythical rugged independence, it makes sense that climate change—but more completely the coterminous quality of any body on a planet—disrupts and confuses the citizens of that society, causing some to reject it wholesale, many to live in denial or maintain ignorance, and others to feel a deep psychological shattering. We are not individuals, we are not autonomous, we are not independent, because we are also enmeshed, coextensive with all others.

This is unfathomable to us. The root of the word "unfathomable" is the Old English "*fæðm*," the length of an outstretched arm, from "*fæðmian*," "to embrace, surround, envelop." It is the measure used to take the depth of the ocean, to sound it. How we long to get our arms around it all, how I want to embrace all our waste and excess, all our desires. To sound them. Grasp them, hold on to them. But my arms are only so long. Often when I come in the house from running errands I try to carry everything from the car at once, and I'm so laden with bags and stacks of library books that I barely make it to the door.

Our boundaries are overrun, yet we want to fathom our own place in it all, we want to remain autonomous, we want to know where we begin and end. Capitalism, the drive for profit, also dissolves all our boundaries, but not in the pleasant way that love or sex or mind-altering chemicals or immersing yourself in the natural world does. It dissolves boundaries between work and pleasure, between private and public, between sharing and publicity, connecting with others and selling ourselves to others. Many of our current social issues can be seen in this light as a fight over boundaries, a longing for some kind of clear separation.

I overheard a person recently describe her new home as a place for her son and niece to "gun up" and ride out some future apocalypse. There is a longing, whether it's for revolution or collapse, for some final and definitive moment when this system will break down and people can return to their bounded individualism, even if it's a bunker at the end of the world in their imagination. It would be much more difficult to accept that the end is no climax but a deterioration happening slowly in our midst, and that it's always been happening, and that it will never end. That the bunkers so many are building will need to somehow sustain themselves into the future, that someone will need to make fabric and clothing, grind grain into flour, cut wood for warmth. That, inevitably, we will again be relying on one another. That we are vulnerable, violable, and dependent on the system that poisons us.

The label "late capitalism" is a container unto itself, the concept overflowing, bursting its borders, unfathomable. "Late capitalism" suggests longing for an end, for it to be almost over, for it to have passed. Fredric Jameson himself, author of *Postmodernism, or The Cultural Logic of Late Capitalism,* commented recently on the ubiquity of the phrase "late capitalism": "It's very interesting! It's kind of—how should I say it—symptomatic of people's feelings about the world. About society itself." I still haven't gotten rid of his book. I recall a college professor talking about Thomas Mann's *The Magic Mountain,* asking what it might mean to view Hans Castorp's symptoms as "sharing in the sickness of the age." Delivered from economic necessity, Hans has no motivations, no ambition, but he has this softness inside him, a rotten spot. He allows himself to be absorbed into a tuberculosis sanatorium, despite being in fine physical health when he arrives, because it offers him a retreat from the working world he finds meaningless. My longing to get rid of things, to do away with the overwhelm, but also my shopping, even my retreat to a tiny mountain community once known for its tubercular sanatoria—perhaps these are all symptoms.

When I wake in the night lately, my hands are curled into claws, as though I'm trying to grasp or hold or maintain control with the strength of the tiniest muscles in my fingers, my wrists. Anxiety is my response, my nervous system's response, to excess stuff, news, information, stimulation. I enter into loops of hyperthinking, replaying conversations, dreaming up future scenarios, wondering in the night if I should return the pants I just bought.

Excess is a problem that can't be overcome by thinking.

The Purge

Deprivation may seem like the only alternative to all this excess. Eliminate, remove, empty. Cut it off, cut it out. We all feel the accumulation on some level, as Marie Kondo's popularity attests, as do cleanses, tech fasts, deprivation tanks. We seem to love to imagine our desert island choices: the thrill of not having everything, of not having to choose anymore. Defining lack by a select few items. On the Reddit thread r/minimalism, someone voices their "minimalist wish for the day":

> At this moment I wish my house was magically emptied, all my belongings in a room (not mine), and those I wanted would conveniently be just at the front of the pile so I could take them to my empty house, and I could walk away from the rest and guard my front door like Ceberus [*sic*] that nothing came in my house that I didn't truly want. Sigh! Despite having decluttered quite a lot in the last years, I'm feeling overwhelmed and my mind is cooking up fantasies.... The less I have the better and more focused I feel, please, someone, magic my things away....

The desire not to have to deal with your things. Not to have to see them, or touch them, or discard them yourself, but to have them whisked away by magic. The moments after the haul video, after Christmas morning, when my dad would gather up all the boxes and wrapping paper and stuff them into the trash can in the garage, ridding them from view. To clean up is satisfying, to tidy, to remove what is unwanted from the scene.

The house we bought is an 1,100-square-foot town house, another duplex, with a small backyard and a shed. I like the small footprint, convinced that it reduces our energy consumption, that we don't need tons of extra space like my parents' generation seems to think they do. But the closets, although they have doors, are tiny. They are all stacked to the ceiling, so that any new purchase requires a reckoning with everything we own. Our house is a grand, failing experiment with gravity, a long game of Jenga we always end up losing. It means I think about excess constantly, wondering what we don't need, what we can get rid of.

Everyone I know has their own puny human coping mechanisms, ways of dealing with the toomuchness. Merry puts a bucket in her shower to collect the excess water. Josh and Clarissa use only one piece of silverware each, one bowl, one cup, to cut down on the multiplicity of things. Thomas walks around at work in the Smithsonian archives turning off lights in empty rooms. Natalie's house has a hot tub, but she never fills or heats it. Susan and Dwight and Jenifer offer us their extra belongings: clothes, books, a sofa, a bike rack. We compost and recycle and kept collecting our glass bottles even when the glass recycling closed down during the pandemic. I have my water canisters, biding their time until they find a use. All of these amount to nothing on a global scale, but we do them anyway, we try to find ways to feel better, to diminish our relationship to excess. To reject it, to separate ourselves from it.

Minimalism is a privilege, and far more people live with lack that is unwanted. In acknowledgment of this, Simone Weil's approach was to starve herself, the ultimate deprivation. While others were subject to violence and to food rations, she couldn't bear to consume, to feed herself, to be nourished. Fixating on materialism and greed can lead to a Simone Weil approach: self-starvation, self-deprivation, can seem like a solution. While I was shopping in high school, spending money that wasn't mine, I was also starving myself, trying to go a full day eating no more than half of a granola bar. I was trying to make myself as small, as invisible, as I felt, while my closet grew. In some ways this is how I see our coping mechanisms and our conversations about what we can do for climate change: the desire to reduce one's footprint to nothing, to disappear, so as no longer to be complicit in it all.

I don't want anyone to die by my hand. Under capitalism, people die by my hand every day. The hand belongs to my second body, a hand of interminable violence that, by bringing me things, objects that do not fulfill but reliably fail to fulfill my fantasies, strikes others down, impoverishing and enslaving them to low wages and terrible conditions, a hand of mine that enriches some CEO somewhere while everyone below him is locked in fierce competition for smaller and smaller scraps, the competition depriving them of well-being and peace of mind and a happy life. How can I wish for all sentient beings to know happiness and the root of happiness, to be free of suffering and the root of suffering, while my second body's hand is out there strangling them, snuffing the life out of them for a pair of shoes?

The extremity with which we seek to purge ourselves of technology, sugar, belongings, speaks to a longing for status. In recent years it has found its design covalent in the aesthetics of minimalism. Many of those rooms I coveted on *Apartment Therapy* and *Design Sponge* were nearly blank, white walls and white surfaces housing only a single object. Large rooms with a couple of chairs or a single bed. Minimalism is a style that denotes status by virtue of excess space. All that space means you have enough room to put all your belongings away. Minimalist décor attempts to be neutral, to have no relation to anything outside it: pure geometric paperweights weighing down nothing. Food decanted into label-less containers. They allow a person to exert control over a space, over the visual environment. To curate and to discard.

The rhetoric of minimalist art was "domineering, sometimes brutal," art historian Anna Chave writes. In the 1960s, a time of war in Vietnam and police violence against protesters and students, and the rise of multinational corporations, civil rights, feminism, and gay rights, a group of white, mostly male, cis het artists wanted their art to own the space. They wanted to evacuate meaning from art. Whatever their muddled intentions, their work was taken to be "aloof from politics and commerce and above personal feeling." But such an evacuation is impossible, and when Chave digs deeper into their motivations, she finds, for example, an overly strong interest in Fascist architecture, an obsession with "purity, primacy, and immediacy," and the language of control and force. Not to mention a lot of straight-up dick art. She's talking about things like Dan Flavin's bare fluorescent light tubes. Writing in 1990, Chave suggested, "What disturbs viewers re: minimalist art objects may be what disturbs them about their own lives and times, the blankest steeliest face usually more attractively masked." Today, minimalist art objects seem desirable, pocketable, because technology's steely face is also our phone, our closest friend, and we have learned to love its plastic, glass, and metal body. Minimalism in design and minimalism in art suggest a kind of neutrality, a blankness, a freedom from referents, but neutrality is always a pose, a stand-in for something else. The whiteness of minimalist spaces, like the whiteness of an Apple store, has always unsettled me.

Perhaps people crave minimalism at home because it feels like it absolves them of guilt. If you don't have to see all your stuff, all your waste, you might not be reminded of consumer guilt, oil guilt, white guilt. Privilege guilt, survivor's guilt.

Clean white surfaces suggest universality, another word for apoliticalness. They suggest whiteness itself, the separate but neutral. I always wonder when I see someone's clean white space in person or on Instagram what they think and feel as they cut into a shipping box or unwrap something new and discard the packaging. How long do they let the box pollute their space before they need to remove it? Until someone comes over, or until they take its picture? Or immediately, right after unboxing? What do they see, what do they feel, when their eyes land on the brown cardboard polluting their curated universe? What do I feel?

I wonder if perceived blankness was part of the draw of New Mexico for me. The longing for space has been a lure for colonizers to the western United States for centuries, but the desire in me is not to conquer but to escape. The desire to escape—from consumerism, patriarchy, heteronormativity—is also what landed Agnes Martin here, and Georgia O'Keeffe, and many artists and writers, lots of them white, over the decades. It's the vision of an adobe house that Animal Collective sang about in 2009: "I just want four walls and adobe slabs / for my girls."

Spanish Pueblo Revival, also known as Santa Fe Style, was codified by the Museum of New Mexico between 1912 and 1916 as "a promotional image to attract tourists, and a romantic backdrop for Anglo-American newcomers," writes landscape architect Chris Wilson in *The Myth of Santa Fe*. In the 1950s, the city of Santa Fe adopted this architectural style as a code, requiring buildings downtown to maintain a low height, flat roofs, and plaster or adobe walls of certain earth-tone shades. When a local architect used a different-color plaster, slightly grayer than the traditional brown, he was challenged by the ferocious historical preservation board. The city buried its utility lines in order to make it seem older, a place out of time. Today, new buildings go up and conform to the style, so we have a faux-adobe McDonald's, a faux-adobe Home Depot.

The style is protected by the city to preserve this evocation of empty remoteness, of blankness. Homes the color of the earth that surrounds them. Surely that visual simplicity attracted me, coming from an Austin replete with giant metal-box condos, a skyline bedecked with cranes for all the years I lived there, the logos of Facebook and Google now looming down on passersby. Santa Fe's architecture mimics an architecture of necessity; it appropriates both Native and Spanish styles and tries to whitewash them. It's a mix of cultures that has displaced two of them, offering a sense, an aesthetic, of history evacuated of the brutal facts of that history. Some locals refer to it as Disneyland on the Rio Grande. What capitalism offers us: a stage set on which to live our lives without knowing whom we crush. In some ways it is the ultimate colonial insult, to adopt a bastardized version of an ancient cultural lifeway as an aesthetic to draw more white people. The city itself is a lifestyle brand.

As such, it is a fantasy. There is no outside to any of this; I haven't escaped anything by being here. I have chosen to be okay with the appropriation I live within, the tourist economy and the tourists, extracting what feelings of authenticity and misplaced nostalgia they glean from this city. Posting images of this landscape and this architecture implies a fantasy life that I don't wish for others to be hooked by—it's a lie, it's colonizing, but the visuals are potent and defying.

The same remoteness that attracted me to New Mexico, I came to find out, attracts people who want to escape with a different idea in mind: protection from some future apocalypse. During the pandemic, people have bought houses in Santa Fe en masse, sight unseen, to have "just in case" the worst happens in Dallas or Los Angeles. Our real estate market has become wildly inflated as homes sit empty or, worse, become Airbnbs, while renters and first-time buyers face competition from exorbitant cash offers. It strikes me as similar to reports of increasing numbers of interested buyers for underground bunker communities in remote parts of the U.S. and New Zealand. The bunker is an extreme version of this kind of escape, undergirded by rejection or minimalism, by a longing to shelter oneself from the toomuchness. Looking for a bigger space than our loft, we drove out to a house out in the Pecos that had a bunker of its own. It was an underground room, full of discarded building materials. No canned goods, nothing off which one might survive. Mouse traps. A bunker for mice. O'Keeffe had a bunker installed at her home, as did many in the region surrounding Los Alamos, a holdover from the Atomic Age. While visions of the world's end have existed in all times and places, we live in a time when people are actively imagining, preparing, and planning for the end of the world. They are storing up supplies and readying for apocalypse of some undetermined kind. Can you imagine the survivor's guilt after whatever the doomsday preppers are prepping for? Do they live with a projected version of that even now? What else could one do with that feeling, that self, but bury it underground?

But God, doesn't it sound amazing, to be wiped out? To be erased. The emptiness, the open space, the clean slate. No more mess. The planet has undergone a series of extinctions, from the Chicxulub asteroid that killed the dinosaurs sixty-five million years ago to the Great Dying, when megavolcanoes in Siberia poisoned and warmed the atmosphere. I have an ongoing fantasy that one day I will wake up and the internet will have disappeared entirely and we'll all go back to our own minds and immediate lives. The quantum lie at the heart of the longing for apocalypse: that we would somehow be able to observe or partake of this emptiness. When in reality the fact of our existence would necessarily fill, deplete, pollute it. But O! the desire, when a new volcano erupts, or something devastating like a global pandemic occurs, for us all to say, that's it, I'm calling it, the end—of civil society, of democracy, of human existence.

"There's a certain amount of hubris involved in imagining that we're all living on the edge of a great disaster," Bradley Garrett writes in *Bunker*, "that this age in which we happen to be alive will be that significant. A greater degree of hubris is required to see the possibility as an opportunity, to imagine that we will ride out that disaster into a new phase of history, profiting handsomely in the meantime." The bunker is a lie. It promises an escape from the systems in which we are enmeshed. When Chelsea and I inadvertently buy an excess of toilet paper or canned goods, the shelves stacked teeteringly, nowhere to put everything, we joke that we are turning into preppers, like all those toilet paper fiends during the early days of COVID-19. Rather than a way out, prepping is another way to consume, and bunker life has created a thriving real estate market. Buying a fantasy of an afterlife, an escape from this circle of hell, isn't anything new—it's another quasi-Catholic indulgence, a chance to invest in salvation. Then as now, the call of apocalypse, like the call to save one's soul, is coming from inside the house of capitalism, and capitalism has no problem owning its own end, too. Now we fear not our soul's demise but our body's, our way of life. Our *stuff*. Hoard it away for the end times. That hopeful lateness of late capitalism. How we long to mourn it, to let it go so we can miss it.

A less dramatic form of this longing for an ending, one that might feel familiar if you aren't a prepper: retirement. What is retiring but an attempt to exit? An escape. When we moved to Santa Fe we joked that we were retiring. I had just finished graduate school, and Chelsea had only technically been in the workforce for three years. The need for an endpoint becomes palpable immediately after you enter the labor market; it was palpable to me from the relative privilege of a teaching fellowship. But how does one ensure that such an end is possible, without hoarding something over the years, squirreling away some capital to spend out one's own demise? In *Having and Being Had,* writer and then-professor Eula Biss describes meeting with a financial planner at her university:

> I want nothing to do with [the stock market], I think. But I want to retire. The adviser is assuring me now that even if the market dips, even if it crashes, it will come back up again. Given time, he says, it always comes back. I ask him if he can imagine this system of investment coming to an end. No, he says, your money is safe. But that is not what I'm asking. I'm asking if there's any way out of this.

Most people I know long for a way out of this. I see them trying to buy a fantasy that looks like less work, more time off, space dedicated to repose, hobbies that become lifestyles. Purchasing a lifestyle, even a bunker underground, looks like a way out, but it's a mirage. A glimmer of water on the dusty highway to never being able to retire. When we joked we were retiring to Santa Fe, ages twenty-nine and thirty-six, we were pretending, or hoping, that it was as easy as a decision we could make. In reality we were underemployed for a stretch, until we each figured out jobs and started earning more than we ever had before. The surplus didn't buy us out of it, either. Instead, we eventually used Chelsea's W-2 job and my art writing prize to buy our house, so that we wouldn't have to contend with the skyrocketing rents in Santa Fe (from all the out-of-town panic-buying preppers). And the house, which provides a refuge from the precarity of the rental market, has become another thing to spend our surpluses on. A new roof, a heater for my garage office, paint, furniture. Even from the vantage point of what we're calling the Salad Days, it turns out you can't buy or acquire less, buy a smaller life or impact or a smaller set of needs and desires. Desires only compound one another once satisfied, breeding new wants, new exit strategies. Psychologists refer to this phenomenon as the hedonic treadmill. It's also perfectly described by the title of a Lydia Davis story: "I'm Pretty Comfortable, but I Could Be a Little More Comfortable."

Preppers exist in a psychological space of dread, which "differs from fear: both because it is about the future rather than the present and also because it stems from a danger not immediately present or even discernable. In other words, fear has an object. Dread does not." Is dread like desire, its gloomy cousin, its counterpart? Our desires technically can have no object, because once we land on an object we find the desires are unsatisfied, unsatisfiable. They are longings, and must preserve the distance, the space between two things—that's the "long" in "longing." The distance required for daydreams, imagination. Dread is a kind of daydream. An imagined future, a possible world other than this one. It can look like paint colors or apocalypse. Do we want against death? Do we want toward it? Does it matter?

More than dread or panic, my feelings swing toward despair. A feeling of having been born into a disaster that everything I do, every breath I take, contributes to, accelerates, makes worse for other people and creatures.

In the humanities archive where I interned, one of the book conservators installed a bug room. It had an elaborate entomological display of all the types of insects that had been found in the archives over the decades. Ancient beetles and moths, spiders and grasshoppers, under glass, each affixed with a tiny label. On the upper floors, signs near the elevators warned, "If you find a bat, do not touch it." The archive was meant to house objects, paper, books, clothing, and furniture in pristine, untouched condition, to keep them safe from the ravages of time. But masses of objects make ideal homes for critters. They're inevitable, they're in everything. Just as we ourselves are covered in bugs, all over our skin, in every one of our organs. We exist in symbiosis. On a cellular level, more of our bodies consist of bacteria than human cells. We are not impenetrable objects. We are multiple, plural within our very skin. It's our own ego trip that has us trying to get rid of it all, I muse as I down a probiotic, trying to rearrange my gut flora.

I cannot live in my closet. There's nothing to eat there (except candy). If we retreat into the bunker, nestled in stacks of toilet paper, we will be moth-eaten. The nutritionally sufficient foods stored up will taste eventually like nothing. We need more than material efficiency or comfort. We need complexity, which only comes from encounter. Exchange. The market, again.

How we dread and long for a new dark age, the safety of knowing, of boundaries, of limits, of smallness, of interiority, of our bubbles. Garrett writes, "We must first try and render boundaries around the incomprehensible. That's why preppers do what they do, whether it be stockpiling food or building a bunker: action provides solace." The term coined by philosopher Glenn Albrecht to describe this feeling is "solastalgia," "the sense of grief and existential dread caused by rapid environmental change." What can we do with this feeling? How can we contain it?

Objectification

Simone Weil defines "force" as "that x that turns anybody who is subjected to it into a *thing*." She's talking about the force and the violence of war in Homer's *Iliad,* and she's also talking about the force of Hitler's rise and the occupation of France that occurred while she was looking for a publisher and trying to get out of the country to escape death in a concentration camp. But when I think about the drive for profit that constrains every person's action and thought today, it is her words I hear.

> From its first property (the ability to turn a human being into a thing by the simple method of killing him) flows another, quite prodigious too in its own way, the ability to turn a human being into a thing while he is still alive. He is alive; he has a soul; and yet—he is a thing. . . . Who can say what it costs it, moment by moment, to accommodate itself to this residence, how much writhing and bending, folding and pleating are required of it? It was not made to live inside a thing; if it does so, under pressure of necessity, there is not a single element of its nature to which violence is not done.

Weil wrote this on the heels of working on the assembly line in a Renault factory in Spain and joining a workers' brigade against Franco. It was here, by stepping out of her bourgeois life, that she experienced firsthand "the dehumanizing effects of modern industrialism and war," writes Christopher Benfey. She could see the violence of work under capitalism, how the soul had to writhe and bend and fold and pleat itself to carry on. When people are objectified—by violence or by capitalism—and are doomed to live out the rest of their days as things, "their days hold no pastimes, no free spaces, no room in them for any impulse of their own."

The drive for profit makes objects of us all. This is easy to see in the day-to-day reality of an Amazon warehouse worker or a garment factory worker or a coffee farmer: people have been turned into objects, into machines that can produce goods, work that only remains because it is cheaper for a barely paid human to do it than a machine. But we are all in it. There is no place where capitalism's hand doesn't reach us.

When we bought our house I felt this objectification, as I learned more about the game of credit scores, the appalling fact of compound interest. On the first visit we made to the lender, they asked why I had recently canceled my longest-standing credit card. "It was a Chase card," I told them, "and Chase used slaves as collateral in the 1800s. When I learned this, I immediately called and closed the card." "That's too bad," the lender replied, referring not to this history but to my canceling the card. I was wary of homebuying from the out-set. I knew that owning property was the cardinal sin of colo-nization, that before the Europeans arrived, most Indigenous people saw themselves as stewards, as caretakers of the land. To own it is to make it an object, as I objectify myself in trying to improve the house, worrying that it may not be good enough or big enough. And yet, we had already left one city because the rents had become impossible and the home prices were far beyond anything we could afford. We felt that we had to buy to stay alive, to keep living in the place we had chosen. We both feared any sign of development in Santa Fe, certain that it spelled the same kind of squeezing out we'd felt when the tech industry ballooned in Austin. So we bolstered our credit scores, we followed the rules, and we bought the first house we could qualify for. Even that was a desperate game, after having been outbid on two other houses by out-of-towners paying cash.

When you're deep enough in it, when surviving is the task at hand, the possibility of escape disappears. Of life on the battlefield, Weil writes, "In the end, the very idea of want-ing to escape the role fate has allotted one—the business of killing and dying—disappears from the mind." A *business*, she calls it. The cold calculation of capital. It is hard to see the violence from the perch of a comfortable life, especially when the violence exists at some distance—the factories that make our belongings are far away, invisible to us. "To be outside a situation so violent as this is to find it inconceivable; to be inside it is to be unable to conceive its end," writes Weil. "Consequently, nobody does anything to bring this end about." Under the yoke, there is no opportunity for resistance. The suffering continues under this system because it has "deprived the sufferer of the resources which might serve to extricate him"—things like time, rest, reflection, an ability to take care of one's body, the capacity to care for others.

There is no still point, no end within capitalism, despite our desire to envision one, to see this moment as "late" in capitalism, as though on the horizon lies some other world. Graeber writes, "One of the defining features of capitalism: that it is a motor of endless production, one that can maintain its equilibrium, in fact, only by continual growth. Endless cycles of destruction do seem to be, necessarily, the other side of this." The treadmill of production "requires 'wastelands' from which resources are increasingly extracted and where (often toxic) waste is increasingly dumped," writes Traci Brynne Voyles in *Wastelanding*. No matter what it is producing—shoes, pajamas, nuclear weapons—the system needs to be fed and the system needs to deposit waste. Where do you extract? Where do you dump? Wherever you envision the wasteland. Value is a social construct. That goes for the value of objects, the value of land, the value of people, the value of moths.

New Mexico, my refuge, has historically been treated as a wasteland, a "sacrifice zone," by the U.S. government. In the twentieth century it was deemed expendable as a place for the testing of nuclear weapons and the mining of radioactive minerals. Whole swaths of New Mexico, in particular lands inhabited by the Diné and the Pueblo peoples, were designated sacrifice zones. The U.S. government decided to wasteland, to sacrifice, not only the land and the ecosystems therein, but "to wasteland, to render pollutable, the lungs, the cells, and the respiratory tracts of everyone involved." Needing more raw uranium to fuel the nuclear arms and energy race, and later, needing a place to put the radioactive heavy metals waste from the hundreds of mines opened and abandoned on tribal lands, the government tried to discard entire groups of people from the land they'd inhabited for thousands of years. It's a story of displacement we typically try to historicize, a genocide that happened hundreds of years ago during the settler colonial era. But it continues now: instead of cleaning up the Jackpile mine, the government suggested that the Laguna people simply be moved from their land. Trying to draw a boundary between ourselves and the waste we produce, we render the land and the animals and the people that live there objects that must be dealt with.

During the nuclear era, the U.S. government built bunkers to house the highest-ranking officials, trying to prepare for the end of the world they had made possible. Adding up how many people would survive in the bunkers, and how many would perish outside of them, "they calculated casualties of everybody else as 'megabodies': a totally inhumane term that denoted one million dead citizens," Garrett writes. Similarly, when trying to determine how to "reopen" the economy during a global pandemic, calculations were made by government officials to determine the dollar cost of the predicted loss of human life. Human beings became part of an equation, objects to be counted, to be discarded.

This is the problem with rejection, dispossession, minimalism. If we must cast something aside in pursuit of cleanliness or aesthetics or space, we objectify someone in the process of removal. A clean white space, that purity, brings with it the necessary ridding of pollution, an argument that undergirds genocide. And what are the preppers waiting for, longing for, but genocide that kills all but them?

In the hoard, we all become objects. We, like the preppers,

are entombed by our things. Earth's atmosphere is a container filling with carbon, gas fumes, methane. Overpopulation is one of the greatest threats to life in this container. Our political discourse centers around questions of immigration that render large groups of people expendable. We design elaborate containers for humans that have been discarded by the legal system and call them prisons, detention centers. All the while, on an overpopulated planet we build storage facilities that exceed the square footage necessary to house the entire unhoused U.S. human population and fill them with excess, unused stuff.

The city of Denver installed storage containers for the unhoused population to keep their belongings. When they found some of the people living in the containers, they took them down. This sort of displacement of unhoused populations dates back to the late 1800s, the early days of excess waste in the United States. Strasser writes, "During the forty or so years around the turn of the twentieth century, mass production and mass distribution created unprecedented quantities of trash that disturbed private citizens and plagued city administrations." Because poor people spent time searching the dumps for items of value that could be used or sold, they became associated with trash, called trash, and eventually treated like trash. When we begin to see people as stuff, we start to confuse the boundary, start to devalue human lives along with land, along with certain objects.

All of this can be traced farther back to the way capitalism as an ideology taught people to "see themselves as isolated beings who defined their relation with the world not in terms of social relations but in terms of property rights," Graeber writes. In America, slavery, the ultimate conception of a human being as property, came not from some internal desire within human beings to own other people, but from the way the founders framed the documents on which the United States was created. Built into their vision for the country was the concept of property and the system of wealth accumulation that supported it. James Baldwin argues,

> The idea of black persons as property, for example, does not come from the mob. It is not a spontaneous idea. It does not come from the people, who knew better, who thought nothing of intermarriage until they were penalized for it: the idea comes from the architects of the American State. These architects decided that the concept of Property was more important—more real—than the possibilities of the human being.

When the concept of property is more real than the possibilities of the human being—or the land, or the animal, or the plant—it is no longer possible to see human beings as more than objects, more than laborers or consumers to be bought and sold, to buy and to sell to. In a 1967 interview with NBC, Martin Luther King, Jr., said,

> You can't thingify anything without depersonalizing that something. If you use something as a means to an end, at that moment you make it a thing and you depersonalize it. The fact is that the Negro was a slave in this country for two hundred forty-four years.... This led to the thing-ification of the Negro, so he was not looked upon as a person. He was not looked upon as a human being with the same status and worth as other human beings.

To render a human being a thing that could be owned in a system that valued property above all else transformed the American idea of personhood and of work. While capitalism suggests that hard work is the way to freedom and humanity, it also built itself on the notion that hard work can be bought from others at the price of their humanity. When a capitalist country is founded on systemic racism, even when slavery has been abolished, hard work allows only some people to access some levels of freedom and humanity. It leads some people nowhere. And it leads no one toward full humanity or freedom. Work under a system that values property and profit above human life makes human beings into objects, makes them long to escape their own lives. The system is built to dehumanize.

Why is private property, accumulation, the only way to see our relationship with the world? Why is this inevitable? What if it isn't? Graeber asks,

> What, in fact, are the origins of that attitude toward the material world that allowed people in certain corners of Atlantic Europe to create these colonial empires to begin with? If we do not ask such questions, we are left with the tacit assumption that there is nothing to be explained here, that anyone in a position to massacre and enslave millions of people in the name of personal profit would naturally wish to do so.

It's important to watch who and what is being dehumanized in language, and what is being humanized. Dehumanization, thingification, continues to happen when land is destroyed, when animals are placed in containers barely large enough to fit their bodies. It is not the same as slavery, as Native genocide, but it is the same logic that allows the violence: the logic of profit, growth, and expansion that objectifies the living, that turns entire species and ecosystems into abstractions. It is not the only view. This attitude toward land and bodies was manufactured. It justified colonial expansion because everything, every creature, every person, became a thing.

To bunker is to make oneself a thing, an impenetrable object. Seeing oneself as an object, as capital in need of protection, leads to the bunker. Buying a house was our way of bunkering, of grabbing on to what we were told would be security, the safety of equity, as the world around us careened into pandemic and lockdown. To close ourselves off, to protect ourselves, we structure our lives and spaces to keep us from harm, what Garrett calls hardened architecture. We attempt to harden ourselves off, to become impregnable, to push away all the threats and burrow inward to safety. We are digging our own graves and snuggling down into them, surrounded by whatever capital we can accumulate. In an attempt to preserve our agriculture into the future, agronomists

> designed a Global Seed Vault in an Arctic mountain, an impregnable bank where they could save a million varieties of seed covering all the Earth's important food crops. Eight years after it opened, during the hottest year ever recorded on the planet, melting snow and heavy rain flooded the entrance to the tunnel and then froze. The seeds weren't damaged, but the builders were no longer confident that they'd constructed a stronghold that would last into deep time.

Doomsday preacher Bill McKibben writes, "Even our arks are leaking."

Making Use

Moths are on the rise because of warmer winters and because people have an excess of clothing, requiring them to store what they don't wear. The moths spend most of their lives burrowed, hunkered, cocooned in eggs and later in pupae of their own weaving, until they burst or eat their way forth, hungry and feeding or flying and reproducing. As caterpillars they molt, sometimes four or six or sixteen times, shedding a layer of skin to make room to store their expanding bodies. Moths are among the few composters on the planet for keratin, the almost indelible protein that makes up wool. They compost horns and hooves, undigestible, unbreak-down-able things.

Some caterpillars eat their own mothers. Some eat each other. Some eat sloth poop, or tears squeezed from the eyes of sleeping birds, or blood sucked from living creatures. They're just trying to make their way in this world. We shouldn't be so hard on them. Without their pollination, certain orchids and yucca would not exist. Moths are responsible for the existence of silk, which they weave around themselves as a cocoon, making their own clothes. They made the Silk Road, so they basically invented shopping. In some ways, we could see the moths in my closet as playing a long game that started there in ancient Indochina. They made the silk in the fabric I bought to sew into some kind of drapey silk noil top. The silk I bought came from China. Bury me in it.

Like humans, the moths are absurd and disgusting and beautiful and necessary. They're drawn to every flickering new brightness they see for reasons science still can't explain. They try to consume the light and it kills them.

Nothing we do matters. Our individual carbon footprints are too small to have any real effect on the crises the planet faces. But maybe my tiniest actions do have global consequences. Maybe each time I waste something, something vital leaches from me, depleting my use to the universe. Maybe the energy isn't so much quantifiable as accumulative. Psychological.

My therapist, C, texted me some dialectical behavior therapy handouts about "radical acceptance." With accepting reality comes sadness. I cannot fight the moths, I cannot fight my own desires, I cannot fight the forces of destruction that accompany life in a capitalist system. To accept these realities is to be met with a humbling sadness. We are all in some ways living with this tragic consciousness and must find ways to accept the tragedy of this moment—with lucidity and tension, we are aware of the thresholds we cross, our hubris as we cross them. We are beyond solastalgia, beyond the longing for another world. We know too much.

I finished my hat and entered it to live therein till my last days arrive. Each night I go to sleep under my piles of organic cotton money, hands clutched tightly around nothing, and wait for the sweet acquittal of death, when my last longing will be fulfilled: to be composted and fed to a tree, finally able to give something back. The moths can have the hat.

Crystal Vortex

Merián thought someone put the whammy on her. The pain in her neck just struck her one day. But who it was—and what was causing it—these weren't important. What mattered now, she said, was doing what she knew how to do: heal herself, move out of pain.

I met Merián Soto a few years ago at an artists' residency in Wyoming where we, a dance choreographer and a sleepy writer, shared a studio overlooking a creek. She was trying to write about her teacher, Elaine Summers, a choreographer with Judson Dance Theater who developed a technique called Kinetic Awareness. It's a somatic practice in which you move each part of the body on its own, with precise awareness of the muscles you are using and how much tension you are applying. Summers wanted dancers to feel and use every tiny muscle independently, and to recognize and engage the connection between their bodies and minds at all times. "She trained us to move every part of the body, every direction it could go, with the full range of tension and speed, from zero to one hundred," recalls Merián. "She had a marvelous exercise called bone hugging, where you apply three-dimensional tension to each bone in the body, you squeeze." Her training involves observing the body's changes and sensations while lying on a set of balls of varying sizes and shapes to develop consciousness of the body in the ever-changing now, a process that ultimately has healing effects. It sounds fundamentally akin to what many people I know, myself included, are seeking when they go to healing springs and spas, to the massage therapist, to yoga: a way to be in their bodies more fully, to move out of pain.

At the residency, Merián was becoming distinctly aware of the challenge of writing about a physical practice that could only be taught and passed on through the body, person to person, and that isn't recorded, possibly can't exist in language. How do you preserve it, maintain it, keep it going? It's not something that you can hire someone else to do for you, and it's not something you can buy. It's something you have to do, much like dance.

I used to dance seriously, from age three to eighteen, and spent so many hours training after school I barely had time to breathe. When I was injured in a *Black Swan*–esque fall my senior year, legs taken out from under me by another dancer, I had to stop for the first time. My back sent throngs of pain into my left hip every time I bent over, and I spent the rest of high school going to physical therapy at six in the morning, struggling to get in and out of my car. The physical therapist kept telling me that I had to do exercises at home, that it was the only way to heal, but I wanted so badly to *be* fixed.

In ballet and modern, I loved using my mind to push shapes into and through my body. It was an experience of flow, of connection between my ever-active mind and every tiny muscle, getting them to work together, to do impossible things. No room for other thinking. Most of the time I live in my head and snub my body, forget about it. In my thirties, suffering from chronic pain and migraines, Kinetic Awareness intrigues me, as my skepticism of alternative healing modalities wanes and my affinity for them deepens. I'll try anything.

We are in a woo renaissance. Practices we lump under the category "New Age," many of which were adopted or flatout appropriated from thousand-year-old Eastern traditions or Indigenous ceremonies—yoga, crystals, sage smudges, incense, astrology, meditation—are a booming business in America. Sage smudging has become so popular for cleansing one's space of perceived toxic auras that white sage has been overharvested, making it difficult to access for Indigenous people who have used it for centuries. Crystal mining is destroying the earth and miners' bodies just as coal mining does. Like our faith in supplements, in exercise, in dieting, our faith in woo is scientifically unsound and yet unshakable. We dabblers and new believers are in the process of colonizing spiritual practice, the mystical. A final frontier.

The global pandemic only makes our faith stronger, as our awareness of being sick or the potential for getting sick grows. When I say "our" faith, I include myself, studying the astrological forecast, wearing black tourmaline (to dispel negative energies), placing huge weight on the words of yoga teachers. All of which suggests we are looking to heal ourselves, to move out of pain, and we are looking for something to put our faith into, seeking some kind of meaning. Or at least, I am.

After I moved to Santa Fe—and wasn't I drawn here in part for the New Age bounty, the healing air, the woo paradise?—I began seeing a therapist named L. Her *Psychology Today* profile listed Enneagram coaching and something called "Eclectic," and her long, wild gray hair conveyed wisdom, something witchy. When I told her I wanted to be a writer but couldn't figure out how to make that a career path, she recommended *The Artist's Way* to me, mentioning she'd found it helpful in her own life. Despite the lure of some forms of woo, I was skeptical of L, as I am of all therapists at first, and skeptical of the Enneagram, and skeptical of *The Artist's Way*. I remembered it from working in a bookstore, where it sold regularly and I'd mentally filed it under "not for me" between *The Secret* and *Men Are from Mars*. As a writer, it's easy to be skeptical of self-help as a genre. I can smell manipulation on the page.

An early chapter of *The Artist's Way*, the 1992 self-published bestseller by current Santa Fe resident Julia Cameron, discusses the importance of "filling the well." "As artists," she writes, "we must learn to be self-nourishing. We must become alert enough to consciously replenish our creative resources as we draw on them—to restock the trout pond, so to speak." After reading a few pages, I got sick to my stomach. My well felt bone-dry. I didn't like admitting it, but I felt totally depleted creatively, as if I had nothing to say. "Any extended period or piece of work draws heavily on our artistic well," she writes. This had never occurred to me. I had recently written my first book, a process that took six years, and somewhere deep down I feared that I might not know what to write next. My first book had not been published yet, but that didn't stop the premature panic. More realistically, I was overwhelmed by teaching, freelance writing, and finding my groove in a new life, figuring out how to (barely) support myself after grad school without full-time employment. I was busy trying to learn how to be a person, how to live, and writing about that life didn't seem possible in any determined way that I was used to.

The next day I tried Morning Pages, the best-known technique from the book: "three pages of longhand writing, strictly stream of consciousness." Cameron warns that the process of writing them is "apparently pointless." Groggy from sleep, pen in hand, I had no idea how I was going to get through all three pages. Possibly the notebook I was using was too large. Chelsea brought coffee to me in bed and, seeing how daunted I was, gently said, "You don't have to do it all." "Yeah, I do," I said, all my overambitious, overfunctioning baggage strangling the words.

I wrote the first three pages and continued to follow the protocol, week by week, for twelve weeks. I had checked the book out from the library, too embarrassed to actually own something like this, and took the library copy with me to Wyoming. In Cameron's view, by doing the pages (and you "do" them, you don't "write" them), you listen and hear the currents of your own ideas, and then you transcribe them. Listening is a form of acceptance, yielding. Writing, creating, becomes a mundane act. The pages operate as a habit like brushing your teeth—or maybe more honestly like flossing. A little painful, a little messy, but a vital form of maintenance. For me, and I imagine for many other overachieving, hyper-educated millennials supporting themselves after graduating into a world where full-time employment, let alone benefits, is hard to come by, Cameron's emphasis on creativity as a daily habit, an ongoing process, a subterranean space within your own consciousness, can be a real relief. It's a neoliberal relief to think that creative practice can occur when you're working on something else, when you're too busy striving to think. But the bigger relief was also a threat: the idea that creative practice could be a life, a world of its own, with values and rules not determined by familiar metrics of productivity or financial gain.

I was starting to think of myself as a writer, working to support myself, but what would I write, how would I keep writing, what was there to say? I have always written from my own life: intermittent diaries when I was a kid; notes passed obsessively between my friends in junior high and folded into origami envelopes and decorated with secret code names; and then later long letters to my girlfriends, more journals, so many college papers, annotated playlists. I had spent six years writing all through grad school—seminar papers, journal articles, a dissertation. But once I started Morning Pages, I realized that my ideas come slowly through living my life, not through directed attention. I couldn't plow my way through this writing, like I'd done as a student. I had to surrender to time and wait for it to come.

After a few years of adjuncting, grading, and editing, my mind consumed by the demands of others' writing and thoughts, I found a job that allowed me time and space to do the waiting that my writing demands, working twenty hours a week as an archivist for Bruce Nauman, a visual artist. Early in his career, after finishing art school, he started teaching and had a lot of free time. In interviews from this period, he describes his creative practice in terms of waiting, wondering what an artist does.

> That left me alone in the studio; this in turn raised the fundamental question of what an artist does when left alone in the studio. My conclusion was that I was an artist and I was in the studio, then whatever it was I was doing in the studio must be art. And what I was in fact doing was drinking coffee and pacing the floor. It became a question then of how to structure those activities into being art, or some kind of cohesive unit that could be made available to people.

His work from this period, the mid-1960s, includes photographs like *Coffee Spilled Because the Cup Was Too Hot* and *Coffee Thrown Away Because It Was Too Cold* and now-famous videos like *Dance or Exercise on the Perimeter of a Square* and *Bouncing Two Balls Between the Floor and Ceiling with Changing Rhythms*. In these videos, a lanky young Nauman paces the studio on camera, giving himself an assignment, like walking around a taped square on the floor, bouncing balls, or playing a violin. He says, "At this point art became more of an activity and less of a product. The product is not important for your own self-awareness. I saw it in terms of what I was going to do each day." These activities, these non-products, are now owned by places like MoMA. His most recent videos sell for millions of dollars, an irony of the art market: that creative practice, pursued for its own end, can also be valued as a form of capital to acquire. That the market is hungry for your creative endeavors, your spiritual reckonings.

Art, a category that includes writing, is a practice that doesn't necessarily need a product. Rather it is a way of thinking or being, one that I had previously only allowed myself in spare moments at my retail job at the bookstore. All the notes I was writing to myself and shoving in my pockets while on the clock at $7.25 an hour were the seeds for my first book, but I didn't discover this until years later. The permission I needed to allow myself the space and time and apparent aimlessness of a writing practice, what Cameron calls a flow of consciousness you can dip into, was sitting right there on the shelves at BookPeople, but I hadn't found it yet.

Becoming aware of oneself, turning inward, is uncomfortable and can alert us to pain we didn't know was there. Many of our activities exist to numb us to this discomfort. Yet self-knowledge is the gateway to insight: quiet reflection is the space where insight can occur. Often such reflection is viewed as recursive, navel-gazing, self-indulgent. Self-care is a new perversion, a neoliberal project of caring for the body and mind primarily to make them more productive, useful in the marketplace. Employers encourage it. But what about taking care of yourself, healing through time and awareness? Who has the luxury? And lurking a little deeper under this scarcity, for me, an iceberg of white guilt: What right have I to take care of myself, my mind, my body, when mine is the body of the colonizer? Of course self-help feels indulgent to me. Everything does. Existing does.

I balked, but was also intrigued, when L suggested that what I sought wasn't a career but a spiritual path: to know my own mind and to rely on it. To find inner wisdom and follow it. She pointed me to an online Enneagram test, which indicated that I am a type 6: the Loyal Skeptic. Deep down I do not trust anything, including and especially my own heart. The Enneagram struck me at first as another bullshit personality test, two ticks removed from Scientology, but I couldn't deny that it was disturbingly accurate, pinpointing qualities of myself I'd never been able to name. I *am* afraid and worrying and anxious. I'm always strategizing and grasping for control, and being a 6 explains why I constantly poll the people around me when I try to make any decision. Wondering how to be an artist, I looked to the artists I've worked for, and to books with clear instructions and activities.

At L's suggestion, I completed an entire "Life Design" module from the 1979 self-help book *Wishcraft,* which involved making detailed lists of the attributes of my ideal environment, my ideal day. I made a chart of the activities I find most enjoyable and rated them along the axes of "Mind, body or spiritual?" "Alone or with someone?" "Planned or spontaneous?" "Fast or slow-paced?" I learned that what I most wanted was time, hours and hours of it in which I could read or walk or have deep, meandering conversations with others, with myself. I wanted to be an experiential sieve, filtering experience through me without trying to direct it. For me, this is what it meant to be a writer, to make writing the center of my life. While art is often framed as a business, a career path, or a series of accomplishments with external rewards, I remind myself that my real work is to be less oriented toward specific goals and more open to whatever moves me. To yield, over and over. To accept that I must continually indulge the universe.

Once I decided my purpose was to find meaning, I began to Google that purpose. Logotherapy is a type of therapy to help people find meaning in their lives: the lifelong quest for self-reliance, inner guidance, that I realized I was looking for with L. I found Chelsea's copy of *Man's Search for Meaning: An Introduction to Logotherapy* on our bookshelf, in the section I'd labeled "Self-Help/The Cosmos," which housed my Enneagram book and books on astrology and mindfulness. The author, Viktor Frankl, was imprisoned in a series of concentration camps during the Holocaust. In a setting where human life was treated as if it had no value beyond work, he gained insight into the importance of finding meaning in your actions under the most nihilistic conditions possible. Unlike Freud, who believed humans to be driven by "the mere gratification and satisfaction of drives and instincts, or in merely reconciling the conflicting claims of id, ego and superego, or in the mere adaptation and adjustment to society and environment," Frankl believed that every human life and decision has meaning, and that human beings are driven by a desire to find that meaning or sense of purpose.

Yet at the time of the book's writing, the 1940s, he found his patients suffering from "the feeling of the total and ultimate meaninglessness of their lives. . . . They [were] haunted by the experience of their inner emptiness, a void within themselves." I can relate to this void, this inner emptiness, this sense of meaninglessness. Frankl's patients were responding, presumably but not exclusively, to the violence and horrors of the Holocaust. For me, meaninglessness arises out of a sense that the world is being destroyed by human-made climate change, that the violence of white supremacy ravages the lives of people of color, and that as a white woman in an affluent country my existence contributes to both the destruction of the planet and the violence of white supremacy—my writing is an example of this. Not to mention the ultimate threat to meaning: the bare fact that death comes for us all. So what meaning or purpose could I possibly find? Why should I spend my time reading self-help books, meditating, writing about both, while the world burns?

L encouraged me to meditate and sit with the tension of searching for meaning in a cruel world. After listening to Pema Chödrön's *How to Meditate* on my walks, I found myself drawn most often to tonglen meditation. I say to myself, on each inhale, that I am breathing in suffering, and on each exhale, I am breathing out a release from suffering. It is intentionally the opposite of what you might automatically do when confronted with pain, either your own or someone else's. Instead of trying to dispel or dissolve suffering, I mentally take it in, suck it in, breathe it into every cell. I specify the suffering. I breathe in my headache and all the headaches of the headache sufferers of the world. I breathe out a relief from my headache and all the headaches of the world. I breathe in my irritation and all the irritation of the world. I breathe in my anger and violence and all the anger and violence of the world. I breathe in my exhaustion and the exhaustion of every tired being. I take it in, and I give something else back. What is this if not prayer?

Unless I engage in magical thinking, I know tonglen does nothing for other people. Their suffering does not decrease when I imagine myself breathing it in, and it is not released when I imagine releasing it on the exhale. But, if I understand the intention behind it, it does make me a more compassionate, empathetic person. I feel my own headache and think of all the people who have headaches, people who might not have the chance to rest and try to recuperate. I feel my own exhaustion and relate that to the people all around the world who are overworked and tired. I find an inner awareness of my own pain and then turn my awareness outward, remind myself that I am not the only one suffering, that indeed suffering is part of human life.

Suffering is like a gas, according to Frankl. It expands to fit any space, even if it is a small suffering, and it can also be highly concentrated, as in a concentration camp. But to compare suffering is ineffective, as Brené Brown, a sociologist and pillar of the self-help universe, argues. The suffering of another does not diminish my own. Awareness of another person's suffering can help put mine in perspective, but it does not make my pain a less valuable tool in the search for meaning, Frankl would say. Pema Chödrön wrote, in the late 1990s,

> Times are difficult globally; awakening is no longer a luxury or an ideal. It's becoming critical. We don't need to add more depression, more discouragement, or more anger to what's already here. It's becoming essential that we learn how to relate sanely with difficult times. The earth seems to be beseeching us to connect with joy and discover our innermost essence. This is the best way that we can benefit others.

In other words, self-help is a way of helping others. To avoid self-help, to avoid this search for meaning and purpose in your own life, to ignore your own pain, is to make yourself unavailable to others and to causes beyond the self. Selflessness, then, is a hindrance to compassion, to a recognition of our embeddedness in relations with others. For Frankl, responsibleness (this is the word used in the English translation, not "responsibility") is a fact of human life. "In a word, each man is questioned by life; and he can only answer to life by *answering for* his own life; to life he can only respond by being responsible. Thus, logotherapy sees in responsibleness the very essence of human existence." We are responsible to others for our actions and inactions. The purpose that I seek might be an awareness of this responsibleness, the permeable boundary between me and the world. How all my decisions affect other people, affect the Earth, affect all sentient and nonsentient beings.

If, in the face of human cruelty and destruction, we come to believe that there is no justice, that everything is random, then it follows that our own actions have no meaning. But the recognition of injustice undercuts this kind of nihilism. To recognize injustice, to witness pain, is to long for justice, for a more just response or action to be taken. That longing gives us purpose. Thus our lives have meaning, and they can be either working for justice or not working for justice, i.e., allowing injustice. There is no neutral stance. There is no meaningless life or action. Every action entails responsibility to another, or a refusal to acknowledge your own responsibility. Crucially, these positions are not stagnant or stable but change every time we make a choice, speak up, stay silent. Like art, or faith, they are practices, not identities.

It would be easier if we could simply adopt a stance or belief system that rendered all of our actions meaningful and moral. Religion has been used this way throughout human history: plausible deniability. As long as you believe yourself to be following the tenets of a particular faith, you're off the hook. There's no need to consider the meaning of your choices as they arise. Just follow the protocol. The dangers of religion and self-care are the same: consumerism. Things with ostensibly good intentions are so easily co-opted into malignant or degrading things. They become indulgences, false but tangible mercies you can buy. But the work of compassion for others, of compassion for the self, of finding meaning and purpose, is ongoing. It's the practice that matters, not the objects; it's the doing, the action, the activity, the yielding. Like indulgences, the practice is more important than the thing, but we want to buy it, to achieve it.

I've seen four or so therapists over the years, and each of them has, without my asking, offered me numerous book recommendations. One of them introduced me to the work of Kristin Neff, who wrote the book on self-compassion. Like many other researchers in the field of empathy, Neff has demonstrated, scientifically, that we cannot feel compassion for others without first having compassion for ourselves. But in a world where time is commodified, self-compassion, like self-care, becomes a form of work or labor.

To have compassion for oneself requires awareness of one's internal life. Self-awareness, that primary activity of the artist, has in recent decades morphed into self-making, a kind of work. The self has become a product, a brand, a thing to put our faith into. We use work as the route to a meaningful life, a purpose, but work is fundamentally bereft of meaning under global capitalism. In her book about working as a seasonal associate in an Amazon warehouse, Heike Geissler writes about being asked to become less and less of a human being at a job centered around increasingly meaningless objects and actions. Longing for any kind of reprieve, Geissler retreats to the restroom, "a place that belongs at least a tiny bit to you, here in this gigantic hall. A place that's not transparent, where no one checks on you, where it's quiet and the light's not too bright." She finds a space to be herself, fully human, unsurveilled, off the floor. A way to be a body, what Amazon notoriously denies its workers, so that their truck drivers end up peeing in water bottles, their distribution staff going into labor or dying on the warehouse floor. One in one hundred and seventy Americans works for Amazon. In recent months, the Amazon Labor Union has attempted to unionize Amazon warehouses around the world, so far succeeding only once. The forces that keep work dehumanizing are powerful and not easily dismantled or resisted. Geissler begins to write on the job as a form of resistance, a way to be "rescued." Her job at Amazon asks that she cease to be human, or at least become less human, in order to fulfill her duties. Work asks the same thing of each of us, to varying degrees, and the artist's role might be to resist that. And so my quest for meaning is a matter of life and death for me, but it is also my work as an artist (and the work of all artists, or, as Frankl might suggest, all humans).

On the one hand, I was taught that work is drudgery. My dad took the train downtown to Chicago every day, in winter leaving before the sun was up and coming home after dark. He's an accountant. His work sounded terrible to me. But that was what work was: terrible. My parents have said all my life that work isn't supposed to be fun. All work sucks. Micki McGee, author of *Self Help, Inc.*, quotes self-help writer Marsha Sinetar:

> Perhaps [the idea that work is drudgery] evolved out of the puritan ethic, which kept people's noses to the grindstone, grimly slaving away from sunrise till sunset. A respite was needed—not so much from the work, as from the attitudes behind the work, which were based on a deep antipathy to joy and playfulness.

The early American Puritan work ethic McGee describes cannot be disentangled from the elaborate system of oppression on which the nation was built: slavery. As Matthew Desmond writes in the *New York Times*' 1619 Project, in America, enslavement is a more accurate origin of our idea of what "real" work looks like. "Slaving away" is understood as a virtue, a sign of true effort and enterprise, to be pitted against laziness or sloth. Working as hard as you possibly can is one way to be sure you are using your time on Earth well. As the motto over the gateway to the concentration camps where Viktor Frankl was imprisoned put it, *Arbeit macht frei:* work makes you free. Because our ideas of work evolved from a system of human enslavement, the subtext implies that as long as working conditions are better than enslavement, better than a concentration camp, we're doing great, work is easy and pleasant by comparison, and don't you forget it. It could be worse.

Maybe the artist's work is to figure out how to be human without defining humanity in capitalist terms, in terms of labor and product and consumer. Nauman says, "An artist is put in the position of questioning one's lifestyle more than most people. The artist's freedom to do whatever he or she wants includes the necessity of making these fundamental decisions." While other types of work have requirements and lists of objectives that the worker must accomplish, for the artist, all of these tasks are self-generated. It is never clear what one ought to be doing. I am still haunted by the Richard Scarry book *What Do People Do All Day?* I ask myself this all the time. When I am doing my paid work, for Nauman, or my creative "work," or my household tasks, or trying to relax, I am wondering if this is what I am supposed to be doing, if this is how other people fill their time. In the various jobs I've had over the years—bookseller, barista, adjunct professor, dance teacher, receptionist, archivist—I've never known if I was filling the time properly.

I struggle with this notion of work as drudgery when I work from home. Some of my so-called work is writing, and the practice of writing involves much more than sitting at a keyboard and typing away. To write I need to be reading, an activity I find pleasurable, and thinking, which can look like doing nothing. I need to do mundane things to take my mind away from the writing, as that seems to be the only way I can write. I sew, I garden, I walk, I bake, I clean and tidy, I stare into space. None of these looks like work as I imagine it. In the afternoons, I do what I call my paid work, which is mostly data entry. Typing the same information sometimes hundreds of times into a database. This is more like the drudgery of labor that feels correct. But it requires so little mental attention, I can listen to audiobooks or podcasts while I do it. Then I am doing two types of work at once: I am reading, which means I am writing, and I am also doing my paid work. Like when I walk and listen to a Pema Chödrön book, I am getting my cardio, but I am also learning how to be a person. The cleaning and cooking and sewing are types of labor that we traditionally view as unpaid, non-labor, because a) they occur in the house, b) the sphere associated with women, and c) they haven't been valued or compensated by our society in the West for a long time. These are activities of caretaking and maintenance that people now are more inclined to view as work, as labor, but they are also the necessary ablutions and mendings and makings of being human. Even these feel, to me, self-indulgent.

I asked Harmony Hammond, the last artist I worked for and a friend, if she felt like her work was selfish. Like taking the time to focus on her artwork was somehow self-indulgent. She replied,

> "Selfish" isn't the word that I would use. Of course I protect my time. I'm very structured about my time, or I wouldn't get anything done. . . . I think what I'm more aware of in relation to time (other than that there is never enough of it), is "privilege." I have an awareness of privilege. To be able to work, even as a single mom, or when I was commuting and teaching, to somehow be

able to do my work, to be able to do what my passion is, and be recognized for it, is a real privilege. Yes, I have to set boundaries; yes, I have priorities, and the work is the major part of my life, for sure, but other things, like teaching or the martial arts that I did for so many years, they're part of the work too. I don't separate what I'm doing outside and what I'm doing inside, or what I do in the house from what I do in the studio. For me, they just kind of flow together and feed each other. And normally it feels pretty good, unless I get too anxious about something. The multitasking can get out of hand.

Time is a privilege, and the way we use it can be privileged. (Time can also be a curse. Interviewer: "Who is your art for?" Nauman: "To keep me busy.") And Hammond's work as an artist isn't separate from her hobbies or her paid work or making her home. I feel deep kinship with her last sentence here, about multitasking. I also relate to and remember vividly how she told me most days she works in the studio and around the house until she "collapses."

The blessing and the danger of life as an artist—of life for many working people in the era of the internet, of what Jonathan Crary calls 24/7 capitalism—is that we have trained ourselves never to stop working, to see nothing as separate from work. Crary writes,

Because one's bank account and one's friendships can now be managed through identical machinic operations and gestures, there is a growing homogenization of what used to be entirely unrelated areas of experience. At the same time, whatever remaining pockets of everyday life are not directed toward quantitative or acquisitive ends, or cannot be adapted to telematic participation, tend to deteriorate in esteem and desirability.

This past Memorial Day, Chelsea and I planned to take the day "off." But instead, I spent all morning writing about work, and she worked on art books for her job. After a while, she looked over at me from across the bed to say, "It's eleven thirty and all we've been doing is working." We are choice examples of what Micki McGee refers to as the artistic work model for the postindustrial labor force, in that we "are accustomed to working without supervision"; "find ways of motivating [our] selves even in the absence of compensation" (hand-raise emoji); "typically work out of [our] own workspace"; and "blur the distinction between work and pleasure." This blurring has become the reality for many more office workers since companies shifted to remote work at the beginning of the COVID-19 pandemic. Rather than reducing the amount of time working or making more space for reflection, working from home maximized the productivity of many people. Without a commute, they were able to—and felt obligated to—begin working immediately upon waking, work through meals, and work while trying to care for their children. The space for the nonworking self became smaller and smaller, as the space for working took over the space for living.

My friend Eliza Naranjo Morse is an artist, and in a talk the other day she said that her life is busy and full, so she spends much of her time doing other things besides her art: growing things, building things. Her art is a place where she can go to process the rest of her life and the world beyond it. In other words, it's a way for her to be unbusy. She sees art making, what could be termed work, as a refuge and space of reflection, digestion. The talk was with two of her friends and fellow Indigenous artists, who see their art as a form of friendship, collaboration, and community. It accompanied a show called *Working with Kin,* curated by Heidi Brandow, that demonstrated how the artists are connected to one another and influence one another's work, and you could feel the personal intimacy in their conversation, in their recollections of meeting each other years ago and watching one another's artwork grow alongside the person. I was moved by this expression of art as a relationship with others. I've always written about my friends, and many of my essays arise from conversations with friends. Other people are part of my thought process and the emotional process of writing for me. The more I write, the more important it feels to bring other people into the practice and to share it with them as I work through ideas. The essays change as my friends read what I've written about them and offer their own reactions, interpretations, and new directions.

When your life is the material for your work, it's harder to discern where your nonworking self exists. Essayist Pam Houston writes, "Sometimes I feel like a cannibal. Sometimes I wish there were five minutes of my life I didn't reinvent as I went along." When I find myself rereading a notebook I wrote in six months ago, unable to remember the self that wrote the words, I feel like a cannibal, like I am devouring my past self to feed my current self. Houston's friend Jane quotes Adrienne Rich to her in response: "*What kind of beast would turn its life into words?*" It's hard for me to realize that every experience I have, every thought I have, will eventually be written down and mined for use in an essay like this one. That in order for my writing to be true to my life, nothing can be sacred, or rather, everything must be. Writing, what Eileen Myles calls "living twice," is empowering, a chance for reinvention, for changing the narrative, and it is also hollowing. What is left of me off the page?

And yet this is what I desire, for the writing to contain the fullness of my life. Nauman says,

> I struggle a lot with those issues. It seems as though more of my life is concerned with things I care about that I can't get into my work. It is important to me to be

able to get these things into the work so that the art isn't just something I do off in the corner, while going hiking in the mountains remains separate. I want there to be more continuity; going hiking isn't doing art, but I want the feelings that I have there to be available in the other parts of my life. I don't want the art to be too narrow.

Nauman often uses his body in his work, and in recent films, he's returned to his early video pieces as a much older man. In the *Contrapposto Studies* series (2015–2017) and *Walking a Line* (2019), he wears jeans and a white T-shirt, like he did in the videos from the sixties, but shows the shakiness of his limbs as he learns how to walk again after nerve damage in his feet and legs from chemotherapy for bowel cancer. Sometimes you can see the outline of his colostomy bag. Harmony makes paintings with straps torn from the tatami mats on which she practiced martial arts, materials she says are "charged with body contact." Eliza incorporated bushels of flowers from her garden into her most recent artwork, and grew flowers and vegetables with the residents of a nearby retirement community as part of the project. Still, when I write about people I know, when I write about my life, I wonder if I am navel-gazing, focused too much on myself. When Chelsea and my friends and family read my writing and see the major scenes and minutiae of our lives on paper, do they feel cannibalized? Or do they feel seen and reflected? What do I feel? Self-reflection can be self-indulgent, narcissistic, but it is also the only way to know the self, to write the self.

L assigned me some homework two years ago, and I still haven't done it: an aimless walk. "Go park on Garcia Street and wander aimlessly for thirty minutes, then write about it." I didn't know how to take an aimless walk when she gave me this assignment, and I still don't now. And I'm still thinking about it, and still feeling guilty that I haven't done it. She's not my therapist any longer, but the assignment hangs over me. (Perhaps that conjunction should have been "because.") What is the point? *Not having a point is the point,* I remind myself, unable to put on my shoes. L once asked if I ever played hooky, and I said, "Oh, last Sunday we stayed in bed and watched *The Crown.*" She laughed and said I didn't know what hooky was. And maybe she's right. Maybe when I'm not always working on a bunch of things I don't know who I am or what to do. When I started *The Artist's Way* I hadn't actually gotten to the point of what could be called writer's block. Instead, I panicked that I *might* experience it at some point in the future and set about solving a problem I did not yet have. I forgot how to be aimless—or I only knew how to be aimless when I was paid to be doing something else, like selling books or interning at an archive or guarding the computer lab. Even now, I feel I can work on this essay without guilt only when I am simultaneously scanning photographs for my paid work; the archival-quality scans take forever, the hum in the background reminds me that I am not just focusing on my own stuff. My best ideas arise in my freest time, which is the time I've sold to others. It's easier to feel free when my time has already been paid for. Only then can I feel sure there isn't something else I "should" be doing.

Aimlessness is not something I was taught to value, not something our society values or recognizes as a thing. It becomes laziness. Self-care, Audre Lorde wrote, could be a political tool: "Caring for myself is not self-indulgence. It is self-preservation, and that is an act of political warfare." Simply existing, especially existing as a part of a marginalized group, is a form of resistance. But of course, self-care as Lorde envisioned it has been commodified, Goopified, and sold by white women back to white women. It is championed by companies who seek not to care for living beings but to optimize the human machines of their labor force. I do not know that preserving my body is a political act of good. I am taking up space when I publish a book. I am using up valuable natural resources.

The "Artist Date," the other tool Cameron offers in *The Artist's Way*, is way less popular, based on my experience and a cursory survey of my artist friends. Many readers don't recall the date. Cameron asks that once a week, you find an hour to do something for your "inner artist," who is a version of your inner child. Go to a museum, go to a garden: basically, go on an aimless walk. Every way I tried to do this task, it turned into an errand. As with the aimless walk, which kept turning into a good chance to get some cardio in, I couldn't get in my car without figuring out how I could also swing by the library or the grocery. I ended up wandering the aisles of Big Jo Hardware for a full hour, looking around, taking it in. The hardware store employees kept asking if I needed help. And I did need some chicken wire for our garden, which they cut for me. Errand accomplished, somewhat inefficiently. In his book about millennials, Malcolm Harris writes, "Free time can always turn to productivity, so when productivity is properly managed, there is no such thing as free time." The Artist Date became mercenary. And it was another pressure, obligation, task. The whole point was open-endedness, freedom, aimlessness, wandering, and what comes of it or doesn't. As I try to cultivate aimlessness and find the ability to play, what am I doing but enhancing my productivity as a writer?

For a stretch of time after we moved to Santa Fe, when I wasn't sure how to make money, I turned all of my hobbies into enterprises. Sewing turned into a clothing business. My little garden became our vital food source. Everything had to become "productive." If I didn't have a full-time job as a professor, I would have to make up for it in side hustles. Some might have told me that the months following my dissertation defense could have been an opportunity to rest, to transition. But I would have told them, "I have to pay rent." "There has ceased to be any internal necessity for having rest and recuperation as components of economic growth and profitability," Crary writes. "Time for human rest and regeneration is now simply too expensive to be structurally possible within contemporary capitalism." I didn't know how to rest, and I still struggle on weekends not to spend the whole time creating new projects for myself. Self-help is a real wellspring for projects.

This is feeling like an old realization, a re-realization. In Sheila Heti's book *Motherhood*, a book outwardly grappling with the decision to have kids or not, but which I read as a kind of self-help and a manifesto for the creative process, she writes,

> I want to take up as much space as I can in time, stretch out and stroll with nowhere to go, and give myself the largest parcels of time in which to do nothing—to let my obligations slip to the ground, reply to no one, please no one, leave everyone hanging, impolitely, and try to win no one's favor.

Embracing these ideas—doing nothing, abandoning obligations, pleasing no one—and practicing them has the result of making me more and more of a weirdo, less and less of a "healthy normal." Less and less "well-adjusted." And I don't want to have kids, I don't want to have a career, I don't want to proceed on some well-worn path toward accomplishment. Chelsea and I left Austin, left the academic job market, and moved to Santa Fe in rejection of these paths. The lives we sought were slower, less directed, more aimless than the ones we'd been living. All things an industrial world doesn't want us to be. We've both changed since moving to New Mexico, leaving the university. We talk about how we "got away" and how living in this small, somewhat isolated place offers the freedom to be however we want to be.

Eventually Chelsea quit her publishing job and now we both work part-time, just enough to meet our needs. People keep asking her what she plans to do next, what it is she's working on, as though existing weren't enough. Friends introduce her as a writer, and she gets weird about it, their need to put a title on her life. By her own account, she's become more selective, less organized, preferring the company of cats and plants to art world folk. I try to preserve mornings as times to write and be aimless, but every few months I find myself filling that time with appointments, meetings, obligations. Even in a slow, small place it's easy to get caught up in a certain perfunctory busyness. It's easy to feel like aimlessness is a kind of failure, a not-enoughness.

Up the stairs of a ramshackle house on top of a mesa in El Rito, where the toilet was composting and the water had to be trucked in from below, Chelsea and our friend, a painter, and I each took what was supposed to be a microdose of LSD. We'd spent the afternoon swimming and were planning to go to dinner for Chelsea's thirty-ninth birthday, and had gotten to talking about the Michael Pollan book on LSD that had just come out. Lately all our friends seemed to be experimenting with acid or mushrooms, a Trump-era yearning to expand or contract one's consciousness. I had never done acid and have little practice with drugs, too busy in my youth getting straight A's and refusing to have fun as a matter of principle. I immediately got a migraine. Chelsea, who did a lot of acid as a teen, must have taken too much and had an intense, terrible trip. For several hours she was sure she was dying. We had to leave the restaurant because the floor was opening up beneath her, and all the waitresses were wearing white face paint, she told me in a whisper in the bathroom. After driving for another hour through the already hallucinogenic northern New Mexico June landscape, with Dr. Seussian plants and striated cliffsides, we found ourselves sitting in the car outside a restaurant in Española for two hours. The painter was on his own trip, blithely eating tacos in the backseat, while we watched a chain-link fence, and Chelsea saw time unfolding rapidly, the sun setting and rising and setting in a matter of minutes in the field beyond.

Not familiar with mind-altering drugs, I tried to think of what to say to help her ride it out. I talked about how she was now like our cat, Gary, for whom every second is a new world, a birth, everything that happens a great new discovery. I was unwittingly channeling Chödrön, or maybe Gary was: "To live fully is to be always in no-man's-land, to experience each moment as completely new and fresh. To live is to be willing to die over and over again." Or, as Pollan writes, "The great gift of the psychedelic journey, especially to the dying: its power to imbue everything in our field of experience with a heightened sense of purpose and consequence." Perhaps people are drawn to psychedelics, and to astrology, crystals, because we live at a time when things seem especially without purpose or consequence. LSD disrupts the default mode network, causing us literally to lose our sense of self, our autobiographical narrative, which is why so many people describe their experience as one of merging, becoming one with the world around them, with people and plants and objects. Some find this comforting, others exhilarating, others terrifying.

Later that night, I stopped the car at Chelsea's insistence to watch the moon rise behind a mountain ridge, first a sliver of bright light, then a larger and larger slice, with the shadow of the ridge carved into it. "What is happening?" Chelsea asked, eyes wild. "I've never seen anything like this before! Have you?"

"I saw a moonrise like this in Wyoming last summer," I said.

She was adamant. "No, no way, this has never happened before. Nothing like this has ever happened." Technically, she was right. The temptation to see each moment in relation to those we've already experienced is a function of our default mode network, a way of situating every thing that happens according to how it reflects on us and on moments we've experienced before.

In an interview, author Lauren Groff talks about time and how humans "expend so much energy trying to deny the passage of time and its necessary changes." They try to understand it, shape it, while animals allow it to pass, and there are so many signs in the seasons that show the rightness of its passing. It's a comforting way to think about it. Time is passing always at the same pace; there's nothing for us to do but accept it, go with the flow. Yet I am so deeply impatient. I can't off the top of my head think of something I do lately in which I'm not waiting to do the next thing. Writing can be a comfortable way to occupy or exist in time. I don't watch the clock, I forget to eat, certainly I forget to get up and move my body. Hours float by, I've forgotten what they are. Yet starting that timeless process requires me to be willing to take a step out of time, to forgo my impatience, and so it's often hard for me to get there. Because to lose the impatient feeling is to lose a sense of control over my life, my day, my place in the world. Even if the voiding of ego is a pleasant loss, the ego fears it. Easier for the ego to make a plan, a list, a strategy, to come up with a rationale for writing or not writing, for writing while scanning, for reading while walking. All the little paths and trajectories we make up give us end products, or we become the end products, linear narratives with pre-scribed ends. Living in time as Groff suggests is much harder, murkier. Aimless.

A few Septembers ago, for our third anniversary, Chelsea and I decided to hike to Nambe Lake, a longer trek than our usual one- or two-hour trails. We packed sandwiches and apples and started up between the yellowing aspens. The creek our guidebook said to follow rushed alongside us, full of moss and plants like a jungle. Creeks and rivers and water-falls in New Mexico usually appear utterly dry, running only deep beneath the ground. Later we learned that snowmelt had flooded the path, erasing it and creating a series of new streams in its place, each of which we tried, dutifully, to follow to the lake. We laughed, half enjoying the outing and half terrified, not knowing where we were headed. We had alternating melt-downs. We kept asking each other, "Is this the stream?" until at a certain point I yelled, "NOTHING IS THE STREAM!" When we finally got to the lake, exhausted from wondering for three hours if we were totally lost, the lake was really more of a pond. This was a deep disappointment for me as a Mid-westerner. An object lesson. Now when we hike, we try not to get so hung up on getting to the end of the trail that we lose sight of ourselves completely. But the endpoint is always so tempting. That sense of purpose.

In Wyoming, I found myself avoiding the short bike ride to the studio I shared with Merián, working instead in the house where I slept and ate, listening to people come and go making their breakfasts and lunches, watching someone tend to the vegeta-ble garden, my writing surrounded by mundane activities. One morning, I came into the kitchen after writing for several hours out on the porch. The fridge door closed and there was Mer-ián, gathering eggs and greens. "Do you want an omelet?" she

asked. As she cooked and we ate, we talked about how capitalism encourages us to move our bodies less and less, to be more
confined, sedentary, folding in on ourselves. She remarked on
how it felt for her to spend the day in our studio writing, such a
shift from her usual practice as a dancer. As I milled around my
office in the afternoon, trying to find new ways to avoid writing,
periodically I would look out my window and see her by the
creek, poised on one foot with a seven-foot branch in her hand,
balancing there. Following her lead, I started venturing into the
creek, wading up to my knees. Once I found the entire spine of
an animal, another time a skull.

As an anxious person, I often feel trapped inside my brain.
I am only thoughts, cycling through a series of fears and worries. It's easy enough to dull them. Begin the cycle of checking, the choreography of apps. As we scroll, our bodies hunch,
curl, we become closer and closer to what Merián called "eyes
with thumbs." They want us to keep scrolling. If you stop
scrolling, as I try and fail and try again to do, with timers
and app limits and deleting apps and creating a folder named
"Ludic Loop" in which to hide the apps, you might snap out of
it, get up. Maybe take a walk. When retyping my first book in
a kneeling desk chair sparked a chronic and debilitating ache
in my midback a few years ago, I saw a naprapath in Santa Fe
who would demonstrate a strange movement—lying on his
back and flailing his legs in the air, swinging his arms rapidly
from side to side—and ask, "Do you ever move like this? Like
this? You should." When I remember, I try to move in some
new way, shake things up. Anxiety is a form of being caught in
self-reflection, which is how I become unaware of my body or
my immediate surroundings. Conscious movement is the only
exit route, what I used to find in dance and now find in yoga,
walking, water aerobics, bodywork.

Sometimes I wear a black dance unitard while I write, convinced this will remind me to move, to be conscious of my

body as I go through the day. When I danced, it was about putting on and taking off tights, sheaths of elastic covering my legs and feet and hips and groin. The waistband of the tights pressed deep lines into my hips and stomach. In a leotard, you're constantly aware of your butt as the fabric slides up over the tights. My shoes were full of wool and gel and tape over toes taped so many times they had no skin but a gray layer of adhesive opening a blister, tearing off a toenail. I would roll all my pliable, naïve joints, unaware of the bunions forming on my feet. I still have toes so strong they can each pick up a marble, even the pinkies. Occasionally I use them to pick up a pen. I tried a ballet class after we moved to Santa Fe but found I can't do anything physically competitive without going back to that place of perfectionism. I pushed myself so hard the old injury crept up. Now I feel the connection with my body, the freedom I once had in dance, only in the warm-water exercise pool at the community college. I never use the lap pool but instead join a few senior citizens as we tool around the body-temperature water with foam weights, noodles, and kickboards. Underwater, I can move without feeling competitive or critical. I can feel my body from within.

At the basic level, Kinetic Awareness asks you to engage individual muscles with as little tension as possible in the rest of your body. In practice, it can look like lying almost completely still. Like doing nothing. Elsa Gindler, who trained two of Elaine Summers's teachers (one of whom, Charlotte Selver, also taught Erich Fromm), writes, "For us relaxation is that condition in which we have the greatest capacity of reacting. It is a stillness within us, a readiness to respond to any stimulus." Gindler called her technique *Arbeit am Menschen,* or "working with human beings," and she focused on ordinary movements: sitting, standing, breathing, walking. In Nazi Germany, Gindler, who was not Jewish, housed, fed, and

taught Jewish students, offering somatic practices to help them
cope with fear and maintain physical strength in the face of
extreme persecution. One of her students at the time wrote,

> Without compromising her students or herself, she also
> made extensive use of her classes for the purposes of
> resistance. It was known that new arrivals in the con-
> centration camps were often ordered to stand erect
> whole nights through, and if they could not, were mis-
> treated. In consequence, Elsa Gindler often did stand-
> ing exercises with us. Without mentioning the purpose
> of such exercises, she helped us find out how we could
> stand longest and with the least strain.

She understood that the basic movements of the body, and a
person's ability to sense her own body, could offer a form of
relief from the most dire circumstances. Gindler claimed to
have healed her tuberculosis this way in her twenties, by breathing with her healthy lung and resting the one that was diseased.
Her work went on to influence Wilhelm Reich, as well as contemporaries of Nauman experimenting with slow movement.

I found a student of Elaine Summers, Ellen Saltonstall,
through a book Merián lent me and recently looked her up
online, in search of a class I could take to begin Kinetic Awareness practice. The tension that has built up in my neck and
shoulders from years of typing, from stress, from the weight of
the world, perhaps, has become a migraine trigger. Saltonstall
developed her own version of Kinetic Awareness and renamed
it, hilariously, bodymind ballwork. The balls are meant to help
you sense the body from within, as opposed to observing it
from outside yourself. After trying out one of her videos on
YouTube for neck and shoulders with some tennis balls I found
in the cat toy box, I ordered her book and my own set of ten
balls, all different sizes, shapes, colors, and textures. I lie on

the floor, place the balls under different parts of my body, and move as slowly as possible across them, trying not to enlist any extra muscles in the movement. It is excruciatingly hard.

Before and after using the balls, I am supposed to lie on the floor and simply feel my body, from the inside. I can't explain how difficult this is for me. First of all, I usually forget the lying still part and go straight to rolling on one of the balls. Then I remember and take the ball out, and I can last maybe thirty seconds lying there, but I can't feel my body. I can only think about how I'm lying there not doing anything.

Why do I need all of these gimmicks to learn how to be still, to relax? Perhaps it doesn't matter what it takes, what corny book or yoga wisdom or round inflatable ball or amethyst face roller. Maybe we crave the gimmicks, the balls and the platitudes and the crystals, to remind us we are bodies, to remind us of something beyond the clock, of our existence and its meaning. Like the breath in meditation, they are objects that connect to our being, our existing, rather than our needing to do, to figure out. They call us to our senses, to embodiment. They help break down the boundaries between us and the world, between us and time. They could be anything. Bruce Nauman: "This is just another instance of using what's already there." Pema Chödrön: "Everything that occurs is not only usable and workable but is actually the path itself. We can use everything that happens to us as the means for waking up. We can use everything that occurs." How can we use what's already there, instead of seeking something outside of ourselves? Connecting with the deep boundarylessness between ourselves and the world beyond the self is overwhelming. It can seem to make all our lives into a messy, meaningless chaos, but it is also a way to situate ourselves in meaningful relation with others, with the world, with the impacts of our own actions and choices.

—

A crystal vortex is a place on Earth where significant geologic events have resulted in a congregation of crystals deep in the Earth's crust that have special, palpable currents of energy. This is the best definition I can find online, on websites that use the word "metaphysical" liberally. It is safe to say that most non-Native millennials are using crystals in ways that do not reflect their traditional healing and ceremonial use for Indigenous peoples in the Americas, like Spencer from the reality TV show *The Hills* covering his body in "hundreds" of crystals to free himself from his sister's drama. The locations of crystal vortices throughout the Southwest, places where people claim to feel the vortices most strongly, often coincide with sacred Indigenous sites with long cultural histories—mountains, rock formations, bodies of water—but these locations continue to be sites of colonization and appropriation as tourist attractions for mostly white visitors and transplants. When we tried to camp in Sedona, Arizona, one of the best-known crystal vortices, passing through from Joshua Tree en route to Santa Fe, every possible campsite and forest road spot was full, and it did feel like a vortex to me, sitting in a line of cars snaking through the canyon, a tourist vortex, a human sinkhole.

No patch of ground is anything but sacred. No patch of ground is anything but soaked in blood. Everything is part of the path. The vortex is in us and around us and has nothing and everything to do with us. People have always cried out that the world is ending, that this must be *it*, the last straw, the final days, and now more than ever, and so on, but we just keep going, don't we, the survivors, from one piece of scarred and holy ground to the next, picking up the glinting shards to carry in our pockets or place on a shelf to remind us of stone, of energy, of powers greater and longer and older and wiser than we'll ever be. To remind us we are merest flesh. To whisper to us as we fall asleep the only words that bring us comfort in this godforsaken world: "I will outlive you, too."

The Meaning of Life

Witches

After the plague killed 30 to 40 percent of Europe's population, the feudal system really went to shit. Lords couldn't get anyone to harvest their fields. The surviving laborers worked until they had what they needed, then they stopped working. Workers had the upper hand. The pandemic had given them a lot to think about, so they came up with new ideas, new visions for how to live. The lords called their new ideas heresy. They needed everyone to stop starting their own societies and staging uprisings left and right. It was all very tedious for the lords. They insisted the violence was a threat to their wives, the ladies—they might be kidnapped. The heretics, working class men and women, weren't interested in the ladies, they just wanted to live in a fair society. "Confronted with death and the possibility of sudden death," writes Silvia Federici, "people no longer cared to work or to abide by social and sexual regulations, but tried to have the best of times, feasting for as long as they could without thought of the future." Some were egalitarian, some what we would now call queer, some protosocialist, some all-out communist. Some refused to work, or worked only to satisfy their needs, or demanded compensation.

But now the lords had a real reason ("We need some laborers") and a pretend reason ("Gotta protect the ladies") to get rid of the troublemakers. They got the leaders of the Catholic Church on board, bishops who were mad that all these heretics weren't paying their tithes or buying indulgences. Together they teamed up with the bourgeoisie, the beloved middle class, who were frankly sick of all the messy violence and unrest and people questioning their morals and values, and they started to hunt and burn the heretics.

The heretics weren't their only problem, alas. The lords still needed more workers to plow fields and make textiles and colonize the rest of the planet so they could accumulate some real unearned capital gains. In other words, they needed babies. Babies grow up and become laborers or wombs in which to produce more laborers. Babies came from women, but in the thirteenth and fourteenth centuries, women were busy! They "worked as smiths, butchers, bakers, candlestick-makers, hatmakers, ale-brewers, wool-carders, and retailers," Federici writes. They made silk, they were schoolteachers, they were doctors and surgeons and midwives. They raised children in villages, sharing what we consider household labor in a communal, public setting. The lords needed women to stop leaving the house and doing projects and talking to one another and sharing remedies for birth control and abortions—that above all—so they came after the healers with especial vengeance.

They turned every meaningful part of these women's existence—their skills and communities and independence—into the mark of a WITCH in a massive terror campaign to scare all the rest of the women out of their lives. They crafted an entire state surveillance system to make sure women didn't terminate their pregnancies, and cast those who did as child-murdering, devil-worshipping monsters to encourage everyone to support their efforts.

Burning heretics had been so much fun that they started to

hunt and burn other wayward women, too. And the women-hunting really took off, because frightening women was in the interest of their goal of increasing the labor force, i.e., producing more babies. I'm cribbing and embellishing from Federici's incredible book *Caliban and the Witch*, a Marxist feminist history that reminds us the witch hunts "occurred simultaneously with the colonization and extermination of the populations of the new world, the English enclosures, the beginning of the slave trade, [and] the enactment of 'bloody laws' against vagabonds and beggars." It doesn't get a lot of airtime, but the witch hunts were one of the foundational events in the construction of the society in which we live and complain today.

Amazing, how easy it was to get everyone to believe the women were witches, to go along with it. It didn't hurt that Eve was Adam's downfall, that women had been suspect since the Judeo-Christian creation myth. Unmarried, childless women stood in the way of getting capitalism off the ground, so unmarried, childless women became people to fear. If a woman wasn't married to a man, people were happy to believe, surely she had married the devil! And was hoarding penises in the woods. In birds' nests. (The newly invented printing press made it possible to spread the word about devil worship and conveniently recorded these details for posterity.) Witches were often old women who lived alone, some of them on public assistance, some of them widows. They were also midwives, childless women, and women made utterly precarious by their unmarried status. They were women who embraced sexuality outside of marriage and family. They included queer and gender-nonconforming people, who have existed for all of human history. The rituals attributed to witches bore the marks of subversion, of turning the known world upside down: eating human flesh, mass celebrated backward, counterclockwise dances, gathering at night and outdoors, "contrary to the new capitalist work-discipline."

They burned women for growing vegetables. They burned them for living alone. They burned them for gathering together. They burned them for drying herbs. They burned them for angry looks.

This went on for about four hundred years.

They burned them for using birth control. They burned them for performing abortions. They burned them for aging. They burned them for infertility. They burned them for being queer. They burned queer men, too, and trans people, and anyone not conforming to gender expectations. They would have burned me. They would have burned my mother.

Witch hunting ended in much of the world by the 1700s, though it still goes on in countries where capitalism is trying to take hold. "The definition of women as demonic beings, and the atrocious and humiliating practices to which so many of them were subjected left indelible marks in the collective female psyche and in women's sense of possibilities," writes Federici. The legacies of the witch hunts have been deeply ingrained in what is expected of a woman's life. The witch is a mirror we hold up to her at every age, and the alternative to the witch is the life we condition her for from birth, if she is assigned a female gender: motherhood.

When a baby person is born, despite the spectrum of both gender and biological sex, they call it a girl if it looks like it will have the ability to become pregnant. This occurs even if the baby's sex is difficult to ascertain, which happens quite frequently. As long as the potential to be pregnant is present, writes Anne Fausto-Sterling in *Sexing the Body*, the baby is called female. Medically speaking, a woman is a womb. A vessel for something else. And from its earliest days they give that baby womb other babies to take care of and call it play. The being's selfhood is tied up in bottle feeding and diaper changing, care for others, while the being itself is still in diapers. They give it a Fisher-Price kitchen and some fake makeup to play with. They never let it be itself, have a self.

If you grew up in a progressive family and never played with gender-specific toys, they still got to you. You were steeped in it with every movie and TV show and ad you ever saw: that to be alone, to be childless, to be old, to age without makeup or hair dye, to have cats, to be surrounded by other women, to have any kind of interior-directed project not intended to improve your appearance and your ability to mate with the opposite sex and have more babies that you mysteriously but genuinely so long for—well, you'd better stop all that and get busy, because the baby-having is the only thing that will give your life meaning. And value. You are worth nothing to this world without a baby. Even better with two.

While I cooked dinner in my Fisher-Price kitchen, while my mom cooked dinner upstairs, while my dad worked in the city, did my brother have a tiny toy briefcase, did he ride an imaginary train to imaginary work? No, he played video games. Whole other universes opened to him to move through as many different beings. I say this not because I resented it or envied it—I had no interest in other universes. I was content to act out my future confinement as caretaker over and over again.

The idea that a woman without children is worthless and dangerous has a wide reach. During the witch hunts, the word "hag" came into the English language. A hag was a repulsive old woman. Calling an old woman a hag transformed her from a font of knowledge, cultural memory, and medicine into a force hostile to life—specifically, new life. Because she was no longer fertile, the old woman was stripped of her sexual identity and agency, an effort to vilify and demean all sex outside of procreation, i.e., most forms of female plea-sure. Old women's living conditions deteriorated as "family life"—meaning babies—"gave priority to child-raising at the expense of the care previously provided to the elderly."

Folklore worldwide is replete with the image of the hag, from the Slavic Baba Yaga to the Japanese Yama-uba. Chelsea and I saw an exhibit on depictions of Japanese demons and ghosts at the Museum of International Folk Art in Santa Fe and delighted in the images of the Yama-uba, their long, scraggly hair, sagging bellies, wrinkled skin. The other demons all had tentacles or claws or wings or sharp weapons. The Yama-uba were simply old women. Across cultures, the hag is unkempt, aged, childless and/or threatening to children (rumored to eat them, to kill them). Her features are seen as repulsive, she lives alone at the margins of society, she's frightening. Today we might call her a cat lady.

In manufacturing the figure of the witch, thirteenth- and fourteenth-century scholars drew on philosophy and cursory knowledge of anatomy to assert "that the female body was so toxic that it might poison those around it," writes Brenda Gardenour Walter in *Toxic Airs*. A witch's toxicity came from "her uterus and the poisonous by-product of menstruation." Isidore of Seville and other theologians at the time claimed menstrual blood "was toxic enough to cloud mirrors, rust metal, and dissolve glues." The witch's "pestilent breath" was considered a toxic miasma and the source of infection, disease, and even the plague. Old women were particularly dangerous, able to "poison the eyes of children lying in their cradles" when "noxious uterine vapors" infected their gaze; the "evil eye" was an academic, medical theory.

To send the point home, when witches were executed, officials required entire communities to gather in public and witness the event. These spectacles were intended to terrify the rest of the community, including the "witches'" children, "especially their daughters who, in some cases, would be whipped in front of the stake on which they could see their mother burning alive." Putting women on trial in public during the witch hunts laid the groundwork for them to police one another and eventually themselves. The word "gossip" changed meaning at this time from "friend" to an insult meant to undermine female friendship. Sexualities outside of heteronormative, property-owning families were persecuted, including homosexuality, which "in several parts of Europe was still fully accepted during the Renaissance." (Indeed, the word "faggot" comes to us from the Italian word "*fagotto*," meaning "a bundle of sticks," which referred to "the kindling for the stakes upon which the witches were burned." Heretics who renounced their beliefs were made to wear an embroidered *fagotto* on their sleeves.) Restricting sex to the family allowed the smooth transfer of property from one generation to the next. The witch hunts turned our healing powers into cosmetology, skin care! Rather than caring for our own interiors, our focus turned to the surface and to our most crucial role, in which we learned to enclose ourselves and each other, until we could no longer see beyond it: Caretaking. Existing only for others.

At the time of this writing, a different plague is decimating the world's population and the United States is in the midst of a labor crisis, in part because so many people have died. Women have been driven out of the workforce in great numbers to stay home and care for children, demonstrating capitalism's continued subterranean reliance on women's subjugation despite decades of so-called progress. Because underneath it all, women were doing the bulk of the labor, women were doing the bulk of childcare, and most of all, women felt the internalized pressure to have children.

"Being able to say no makes yes a choice," writes adrienne maree brown in *Pleasure Activism*. This summer, the Supreme Court struck down *Roe v. Wade*, the legal decision protecting women's "privacy" that allowed them to obtain legal and safe abortions, making it less possible for people with uteruses to choose not to have children. And in conservative U.S. states, new laws are being passed every month that strip more people of their ability to say no to an unwanted pregnancy. Yet, as Jenny Brown writes, the euphemism of " 'choice' loses the deep feminist truth that women must be able to determine the use of their reproductive organs." It's not so much a choice as the basic ability to control one's own body, one's own life. We talk about having or not having children as a personal choice, but it's always political, always overshadowed by a set of power structures that alter what choice is even possible. One could argue that using the language of choice and consigning women's reproductive autonomy to the realm of "private" and "personal" decisions are some of the reasons *Roe* could so easily be overturned.

The notion of reproductive freedom has faded from view and yet also come into sharper focus. As many more people are being forced to carry pregnancies to term, forced to have babies, the need to imagine the possibilities for lives without children is paramount. What would it mean to live in a truly pro-choice society? What would it mean for the lives of those raised as girls to be theirs to choose? We have to be able to imagine what a happy life without kids looks like before we can desire it. We could be heretics, witches if we wanted. We might finally be free to make our own world or to learn from those who have tried. Imagining these alternatives is the only way I know to cope with the current retrograde reality, where I can't stop seeing it: all of us whipped in front of the stake on which we can see our mothers burning alive.

Baby Fever

As a child, I wanted babies. "What's a woman to do?" Joy Williams asks. "She gets to want to have a baby." What else could I have wanted?

I remember the first time I picked up a child, not exactly a baby, more like a toddler, on the back deck of a neighbor's house one summer. I was too young to babysit, but the plan was already in the works for me to start as soon as I was old enough. What was I, ten? I asked to hold him, knowing that this was what I was most meant to do, and his mother said yes. I remember reaching down to pick him up, and he was so monstrously heavy, his lower half dangling like a lead weight below, as I tried to heave him up to my hip. There kept being more of him, and my arms gave out, he slipped and fell down with a meaty thud, several thuds, and he started crying, and so did I, and I went home and can still feel the shame turning to acid in my mouth when I remember it. As though even then, I felt the pressure to prove that I had some mothering instinct or ability, and I tried to demonstrate it, and I failed, and it gave rise to so many unspoken questions about whether or not I was fit.

For years I babysat kids in our neighborhood, feeding them, playing with them. A dress rehearsal for the future. I found myself easily overwhelmed by the kids and their needs in the few short hours I spent with them before putting them to bed. Once I was asked to make four kids scrambled eggs for dinner. I had never eaten an egg before in my short life, let alone cooked one. I was happiest when the kids were asleep and I had the house to myself. Then I would clean the kitchen, tidy each room, and organize messes as I found them. I knew I was doing something to help the mom who couldn't manage it all. The image of myself as a mother must have become less appealing to me with these firsthand glimpses of the reality of life with small kids, though I would never have said so if anyone asked.

Instead, when the subject inevitably came up, I would focus on a new desire that had manifested. As a teen what I wanted, what I was curious about, was pregnancy. How amazing it would be to be pregnant! I wanted to attach myself to the image of the mother without going so far as to imagine myself as a mother. I wanted her power. Pregnancy sounded like an adventure, an undertaking, a project. I loved projects. A project to affirm my personhood, when I spent much of my time feeling an unfitness I could not articulate or truly acknowledge. I envisioned pregnancy the way Adrienne Rich describes it in *Of Woman Born*: "As soon as I was visibly and clearly pregnant, I felt, for the first time in my adolescent and adult life, *not-guilty*. The atmosphere of approval in which I was bathed—even by strangers on the street, it seemed—was like an aura I carried with me, in which doubts, fears, misgivings, met with absolute denial. *This is what women have always done.*" Who wouldn't want that? Who wouldn't want to be met with approval for your own body, your own self? To find yourself comfortably bolstered by the history of your gender. To fill the role that is expected of you, that you've been training for all your life.

I wonder if my mom felt this way when she was pregnant. She had her kids at thirty-five and thirty-seven, older than I am now and relatively late for her generation. Her dad wouldn't pay for either of his daughters to go to college. They were just going to get married. What was the point? (Right before I left for college, he pulled me aside at my family graduation party. I assumed he was going to ask me to get him a plate of cheese and crackers, but instead he told me, "Don't read too many books, now, Jennie, or the boys won't like you." I went on to get a PhD in reading books.)

My mom was determined to get out of the framework in which her dad tried to confine her. She left home after high school, which was unheard of for women in her Catholic community, and put herself through secretarial school. Before kids, when she was single and working, she lived with a friend for eleven years. My mom cooked and Karen did the laundry, a division of labor they found equitable. This exercise in independence made my mom a witch in her own family. Her parents barely spoke to her, as she was living outside their house unwed. She spent her twenties single, without kids, and then she married my dad and three years later had my brother. What led to that decision? Was it simply what was expected of her or what she expected for her life? It never occurred to me to ask her about her life before kids or about her pregnancies.

In the 1980s, when my mom got pregnant, the pressure to have kids came as a national mandate. Feminist ideas circulating in the 1960s and '70s, along with bestsellers like Ellen Peck's *The Baby Trap*, had made aging baby boomers less inclined to have kids. Sociologist Kristin Park, citing an earlier study by Laurie Lisle on the stigmatization of childlessness, describes a campaign in the 1980s to "nudge" the "ambivalent" into procreation that drew on "projections of population decline's negative effects on the economy and the nation." Pronatalism, or the encouragement to have kids, aims to "slow declining fertility rates while also bolstering the 'family values' social and political movements," according to Andrea Laurent-Simpson. These campaigns sought to reaffirm what psychologist Nancy Felipe Russo called the *motherhood mandate*: the fact that "the expectation to bear children and enact the mother identity is inseparable from femininity in the United States." To fill your gender role and your social role as a woman, to affirm to others that indeed you are fully a woman, is to bear children. Is this my mom's story? From *The Baby Trap* in 1971 to the birth of my brother in 1984?

Pregnancy sounds like a way to feel colossally embodied. Perhaps it appealed to me because I wanted to be big. When I was a teenager I tried to make myself smaller and smaller, as thin as possible, because everything I saw and read suggested this was a route to power. Pregnancy would be my one opportunity in a lifetime to be big and eat and eat with impunity and take up space in the world. Motherhood is women's only unimpeachable expression of power. Some would say my desire to be pregnant was an instinctive, natural, maternal drive. But these drives don't exist without the institutions that reinforce them. They are cultural. And as such we can examine them, change them. Maybe if more options were presented to me, if there were more types of narratives portrayed than just kids or career, I would have been able to imagine a different life for myself. Maybe if my mom had known more options, she would have, too.

I had a prodigious model of motherhood at home. By the time I was in elementary school, my mom had become the ur-mom, what Chelsea described to me once as the "*Leave It to Beaver* mom." Girl Scout troop leader, gingerbread house decorator, softball coach, catechism teacher, organizer of countless fundraisers for our school's music department. She was the producer of the high school talent show for two years. She was responsible for the annual school phone directory. In a community where moms were excessively involved in their children's school and activities, she stood out for her investment and her dedication to committees and projects. It's as if, after working for a decade, she had so much energy, such a high capacity and need to be engaged, that she poured all of it into our school. She wasn't a helicopter parent—she paid little attention to whether or not I did my homework. But as a stay-at-home mom, she was at school nearly as much as I was. I didn't resent her for this, except in a few instances where I felt she overstepped her boundaries, like when she called my teacher to say she thought I was spending too much time on the yearbook and was going to burn out. I did so many activities, so many projects, without ever seeing that I was imitating her.

Now I'm familiar with the limits of my own patience, my need for quiet, how easily I become overwhelmed, snap. My mom snapped from time to time. I can vividly recall how overworked she was, on top of all that she did at school—shopping for groceries; cooking, then having us (usually me) reject or criticize what she made; trying to keep clean what we continuously made a mess of. Her own mother died when she was thirty-nine. We were little, two and four, and she was caring for us through her grief, something I only recently realized. She never talked about it. For several years she was doing all of this while undergoing extreme and debilitating cancer treatment, but I never saw evidence of a symptom. Only this year did I learn that during her chemo, after we went to school, she would get back in bed. I still can't picture it. She kept so much from us, shielding us from the effort it took to fill her role, as mothers are expected to do. But from time to time I sensed how motherhood pushed her to the brink. I can hear the exhaustion in her voice as she beseeches, "Could someone else make a decision for once?" "Could someone else empty the dishwasher?" She seemed so sick of us, sometimes, and sick of motherhood, or the parts of it that asked her to be a household servant, and I felt this, and knew I was in part to blame—simply for existing. My mom's expression of her anger gave the lie to it all. "Female anger is a threat to the institution of motherhood," writes Rich. Yet that's exactly what this institution does. It pushes people to the edge, and then it silences them.

It's no wonder my mom felt angry. She did everything. And this continues to be the case in a majority of straight households for cis women. Kate Manne writes,

> Around the world, women average between two and ten times more of this work than their male counterparts. The global value of this work is estimated at $10 trillion

annually.... Studies show there is but one circumstance
in which men's and women's household work will tend
to approach parity: when she works full-time and he
is unemployed. And even then, the operative word is
approach. She will still do a bit more.

I don't know how not to be infuriated by this. It describes the
house I grew up in, my dad commuting an hour in and out
of the city to work all day, my mom making our lunches and
driving us to the bus stop when it was below zero and picking
us up from soccer practice, ballet. It describes the white, suburban households that surrounded us, every one of my friends'
childhoods, including the few in our community whose
mothers worked. When I talk about motherhood, I am talking about the motherhood I witnessed, a model of privileged,
often white motherhood isolated to a single-family unit and
dwelling. The nuclear family. I knew nothing as a child about
motherhood in the context of an intergenerational household
or a community that supports one another with mutual aid.

In the 1970s, the years when my mom was working and
childless, a group of radical Italian feminists, including Silvia Federici, began a movement called Wages for Housework.
The premise behind it—that women should be paid for their
work raising children and maintaining a house—was based in
the realization that capitalism is undergirded by the unpaid
labor of women as childbearers, childcarers, and homemakers.
That capital can only be earned in a society in which women's
labor is valued at zero. Federici writes,

Wages for Housework means that capital will have to
pay for the enormous amount of social services employers now save on our backs. Most important, to demand

Wages for Housework is to refuse to accept our work as
a biological destiny, which is an indispensable condition to struggle against it. Nothing, in fact, has been so
powerful in institutionalizing our work, the family, and
our dependence on men as the fact that not a wage but
"love" has always paid for this work.

Needless to say, the movement didn't take off. (Every time I am
frustrated by a chore, I shout, "Household labor, no wages!")
Instead, motherhood remains naturalized, a condition of loving care that women are born for. When I ask my child-having
or child-longing friends, who are queer or straight, cis or non-
binary, why they wanted or want to have kids, some will cite
this so-called maternal instinct. It's a desire that simply arose
in them, they claim. Which implies that by not having kids, I
am denying or devoid of such natural maternal instinct. That
I am lacking something.

Several tell me this maternal instinct arose at age thirty-
five. Their "biological clock" went off and suddenly they had
to have kids. However, while our bodies do have "biological
clocks" that determine our sleep patterns, hormones, and the
years in which we are fertile, there is no biological factor that
kicks in during your thirties to tell your body to have kids,
nor is there an innate "maternal instinct" that arises when a
woman becomes a mother. There is, however, a powerful cultural clock. At what age do you become a witch? Thirty-five,
forty? Your time is running out. The call to motherhood is
external, but it is powerful, and naturalizing that call—calling
it an instinct that just kicks in—helps keep the structures of
heteronormative society intact. What is a biological clock? A
euphemism for mortality? Or worse: a fear of no longer being
a "viable" woman?

This is the catch-22 at the heart of feminism: that by pointing out, in this case, the systemic imperative to have kids, by detailing the pro-natalist culture in which we are raised and continue to live, I imply that none of us is really acting with agency. Not because of some biological clock, but because of the structures that reinforce motherhood as a norm for female identity. Those who refuse motherhood are also reacting to these systems. There is no free place from which to decide. It places us all on shaky ground. And yet if we don't revisit the history, dissect the structures in which we are entangled, the long trajectory that brought us to the reversal of *Roe*, they have the power to prescribe not only our desires but our reality.

The witch hunts created the role of the fit mother and encouraged women to fill it by hunting down and murdering those who did not conform to a solitary, housebound version of motherhood. Federici writes, "A new model of femininity emerged: the ideal woman and wife—passive, obedient, thrifty, of few words, always busy at work, and chaste. This change began at the end of the 17th century, after women had been subjected for more than two centuries to state terrorism." Tens of thousands of women died so that we would all learn our place.

This story has been repeated over and over throughout history, as Jenny Brown recounts in *Without Apology: The Abortion Struggle Now*. In the U.S., abortion was legal until 1873, when it was outlawed, along with contraception, not "for religious reasons or to prevent female promiscuity," as many assume, but to "'guarantee a steady flow of increased population, as soldiers, as breeders, and as future consumers.'" Between 1800 and 1900, writes Brown, the birth rate in the U.S. declined from eight children per woman to four. More than lawmakers or the church, it was doctors who sought to put an end to abortions, especially for married women. Concern about population decline coincided with the desire to replace midwifery and women doctors with a largely male "scientific" medical profession. Banning abortion put the midwives out of work or sent them underground. The Comstock Laws made it illegal to distribute "any knowledge of contraception and abortion."

It happened again in 1976, three years after *Roe* was decided, when the Hyde Amendment went into effect, banning federal funding for abortion. The cost of an abortion became prohibitive for many pregnant people in the U.S. as the number of abortions paid for by the federal government dropped from three hundred thousand a year to three hundred by 1995.

And in the 2010s, a series of alarmist articles about the declining birth rate in the U.S. led such conservative luminaries as Paul Ryan and Ross Douthat to plead in news conferences and the pages of *The New York Times* for "more babies please," warning that a declining birth rate "will lead to economic stagnation and national decline," writes Brown. It's too simple to say that men in power got together and decided it was in the best interest of the workforce, the military, and the economy to control women's reproductive abilities by forcing them to have children, then forcing them to stay home by failing to provide them with adequate childcare, healthcare, and wages. As with the witch hunts, a variety of motives and interests coincide in the desire to coerce people with uteruses into having—or not having—children.

In recent decades, more women began to work outside the home, and some men in hetero relationships began to take more responsibility for household labor, but, Manne writes, women are still "likely to feel guilt and shame for holding a male partner accountable—and . . . to feel an excessive sense of gratitude toward him, even for falling far short of fairness." In a queer, childless relationship, Chelsea and I both catch ourselves doing this. I have a Midwestern mom's impulse to let her get her food first and take the second portion. To take less than what I want, in case she wants more. Our relationship shorthand for this tendency is "coconut cream pie," because once in a restaurant I told Chelsea to order the coconut cream pie for us to share as dessert, knowing it was her favorite and not telling her that I can't stand it. As much as I've learned about my own boundaries, there is nothing easier for me than finding subtle, insidious ways to diminish myself, my needs, and my desires in any relationship. To make myself smaller. Manne writes,

> Part of the problem here, then, may be *women's* sense of entitlement—or lack thereof. Some women may not feel entitled to equitable domestic arrangements and leisure time for themselves, on par with that of their husbands. Or they may feel entitled in theory but be unable to insist in reality, given the social forces around them that tell them *not* to insist and to "take one for the team" in perpetuity. Jancee Dunn even writes, in *How Not to Hate Your Husband After Kids,* of not feeling entitled to eat whole, undamaged crackers from the box. Instead, she eats the broken ones, saving the good ones for her husband and daughter.

How sad, our broken-cracker lives. Deeply ingrained in the institution of womanhood, deeply ingrained in our social structures, is the entitlement to less and the imperative to sacrifice your own desires. Manne herself, the author of a book about male entitlement, falls prey to the same trap. In the acknowledgments section, she ends a paragraph devoted to her husband: "I can only hope to someday go some way toward deserving him." The person who wrote a book about male entitlement doesn't feel she deserves her own husband? Make it stop!

Childfreedom

Adrienne Rich radicalized me. Reading through my annotations in *Of Woman Born*, I can see my anger materializing, my life shifting direction under my feet. I was in my early twenties when I read the book in a grad school class alongside a viral *Atlantic* article by Anne-Marie Slaughter called "Why Women Still Can't Have It All," with a picture of a baby in a briefcase at the top. The professor assigned the essay thinking it was uncontroversial. Slaughter makes an economic point: women still face discrimination in the workplace. But I was livid. I sat in my chair sweating, an until-now-unformulated rage boiling up from my stomach. I raised my hand and asked, "What if I don't want the baby or the briefcase? Why is that *all*?" This was not the conversation we were meant to be having. Aren't there other things beyond careerism, work within a narrowly defined framework of productivity? Other relationships to nourish and cherish besides a legal spouse and dependents?

I was in a heady moment, reading Rich and Audre Lorde and bell hooks and Gloria Anzaldúa for the first time and trying to choose the life of a queer woman, despite the strictly heteronormative storybook community in which I was raised, despite my lifelong training. I was reading sentences like, "Institutionalized motherhood demands of women maternal 'instinct' rather than intelligence, selflessness rather than self-realization, relation to others rather than the creation of self." I wanted self-realization. I wanted to create myself. What did that look like?

My desire began to shift again. Suddenly I longed to be old. More than anything in the world, I wanted to grow up, to be not a messy twentysomething but a woman in her sixties, her seventies, with long gray hair, wrinkled and worn and

leathery skinned. I wanted to be a woman from whom nothing was expected. Again I didn't articulate what lay behind
that desire, but now I see a connection to the pregnancy fantasy. Pregnant or old, I would be momentarily enough. I was
onto something here. Without really being able to know what
I was embarking on, I sensed that between pregnancy (that
moment of female omnipotence, godliness, Virgin Mary
holiness) and old womanhood (when a woman is free of the
expectation to bear, to make herself desirable for a man) lies
a gulf of life unknown. An undiscovered country. Another
planet.

By twenty-eight, when I'd found my footing as a queer
woman and a partner who knew she didn't want kids, I grew
more certain I wanted a different life than the one I'd been
raised to imagine. I was certain this was something I could
make for myself. Whatever loss I felt in knowing I wouldn't—
oops!—find myself pregnant one day (barring a violent encounter), I had to grieve it early. I knew immediately that I
would never be a "natural" mother. Having kids as a queer
woman is an endeavor that requires planning, determination,
and in most cases a large financial investment. Being queer
made it easier for me to say no.

At the same juncture where I found certainty, most of my
friends and peers, even those who had long vowed never to
have kids, gradually became uncertain. They didn't want kids,
exactly, but they voiced concern they might someday regret
not having them. Might miss out. One by one I watched my
friends fall like dominoes. Seeing this hurt. I thought we
were on a path together, the group of friends I had made in
grad school, at the bookstore, at writing residencies. They all
wanted to be writers or scholars or artists. Now it seemed that
my friends had been doing what I was doing on the way to
being mothers. What I had believed was a life we were all

creating together was just a phase for them. As if, suddenly, the life I was building wasn't enough. A creative or intellectual life doesn't exclude the possibility of a life with kids; having kids just makes it a hell of a lot harder. Hadn't they seen the numbers? Why were they making their lives harder? Why were they leaving me behind?

Like women in the 1970s and '80s, some millennials are "delaying" having children or choosing not to have them at all, an anomaly the media obsesses over. Silly millennials, with their plants and pets and roommates and gig-economy jobs without benefits! They'll get around to it eventually. Viral tweets like "PLANTS. ARE. THE. NEW. PETS. / PETS. ARE. THE. NEW. KIDS." seem to have been interpreted by the media as a cry for help. Millennials, they said, are the saddest generation, graduating into a recession, and now look! They can't buy houses or have kids or anything. Articles about the declining birth rates in 2019 and 2020 seemed designed to encourage us all to get on board, to get our shit together so we could finally "start a family." But I wonder if the millennials were onto something.

In 2021, preliminary CDC data states that the birth rate went back up for those ages twenty-five to forty-four. And if my Instagram feed of late is any indication, the campaign to shepherd us all back into the isolated, politically convenient container of the nuclear family is working. But for anyone out there in my generation who has their doubts, who is curious about alternatives, there's still time for us to do something different.

I read an editorial in *The New York Times* about why it's okay, even ethical, not to want to have children. The essay's main argument, told through a variety of anecdotes about childless people, is that the world is unfit for children.

In other words, it would be wrong to bring a child into this broken world.

In other words, this argument against having children is speaking *on behalf of children* who have not been born.

This same logic pervades some environmental arguments against procreation. In another *Times* piece a few weeks later, I read that couples are making their choice not to have kids a political stance on climate. They know that having kids now will negatively impact future generations, so they are making a sacrifice.

For whom?

For the children.

This is exactly the logic of the antiabortion movement, the so-called pro-life. Unborn humans are where we should focus our political energy. Why can't we not want children for ourselves? I don't want them for my own sake. Not because I think kids are terrible—it's not about them!—but because I want my own life. Not because the world isn't good enough for them, but because they actively make the current problems of the world I live in worse, with the pitter-patter of their little carbon footprints. It's not the future I'm trying to preserve or protect. It's now. It's me. It's my life.

Saying this, writing the words, feels like breaking a taboo. I sit at my desk and watch through the window for the lighted torches and pitchforks to march toward the front door. Refusing motherhood is at once a failure and a crime. The deep-down guilt of it. Like abortion, the crime is stopping something that never started, ending a life before it begins. Thwarting possibility, potential, unfulfilled futures. But no one talks about the possibility, the potential, the futures thwarted by having kids. Eileen Myles writes, "I think women are supposed to open their legs to time and let it pass through them."

When I watch my friends become mothers I feel a terrible loss. When my friends stay with disappointing boyfriends and say they just want to get married someday and have kids someday, I'm bereft. When the best minds of my generation spend all their savings on IVF treatments, only to lose each precious embryo and say that now they will never have a life that feels complete, I long to tell them: Darlings, we are free! Throw out your syringes, thaw your eggs, scramble them! You are enough! You are a whole person, on your own, without the baby, without the husband. It makes sense that a person raised as a girl wouldn't think of themself as whole or complete on their own. The foundation of our culture is the idea that they aren't. I can see how important it is to them, the baby. How badly they want it. And when they get the baby, I see their joy. Usually on Instagram, because they no longer have time to talk or text. I rarely hear from them much again, as they are, presumably, swept up by the tide of blissful selflessness, or the onslaught of unpaid labor under bad reproductive working conditions. Why does having a baby feel so important, so necessary, to them? Is it truly what they want, or is it what they've been made to feel will fulfill them? No one can answer this question objectively.

Of course, I'm getting carried away. I cannot voice any of these concerns. I can't respond to someone's ultrasound photo with a screed about the way the motherhood mandate oppresses us or the ramifications for the climate. (I can't even mention that posting an ultrasound photo is in direct contradiction with their professed political stance on abortion!) Not only am I not supposed to voice my anger or my disappointment, but I'm supposed to be thrilled. I'm supposed to treat this as an unmitigated source of joy for their life and mine. No other decision a person can make demands such reverence, such unconditional positive regard. I am talking not about the child itself but about the decision to have it. In her novel *Either/Or*, Elif Batuman writes,

> Nobody ever explained what was admirable about having the kids, or why it was the default course of action for every single human being. If you ever asked why any particular person had had a kid, or what good a particular kid was, people treated it as blasphemy—as if you were saying they should be dead, or the kid should be dead. It was as if there was no way to ask what the plan had been, without implying that someone should be dead.

All I can think about as I describe my own anger, frustration, and disappointment at the millennial pandemic baby boom's coinciding with the dismantling of *Roe* during the sixth great extinction is what my pregnant friends, my mother friends, will think reading this. How it will make them think I hate their kid, that I don't support them.

If you go far enough down the road questioning the value of having kids in an era of environmental and social collapse, things get pretty dark. On the website StopHavingKids.org, you will find a list of reasons not to have kids, each accompanied by its own terrible and detailed graphic. A crying, shirtless child beside a bleeding, one-eyed dog behind bars: "Existing Life in Need of Help." A person breastfeeding a child while working on a laptop with a phone pressed to their shoulder, on the floor of a room strewn with toys: "Parenthood Regret." (My favorite of these graphics comes on the page for childfreedom, labeled "No Kids Due to Circumstances." It pictures a naked person on a leather sofa reading a book, with a stack of pancakes beside her.) The home page states, in all caps: "THERE IS AN UNCONSCIONABLE AMOUNT OF NEEDLESS SUFFERING AND DEATH IN THE WORLD. BIRTH SERVES AS THE CATALYST FOR IT ALL."

Most of the ideas on the website derive from the arguments of anti-natalist philosopher David Benatar, who writes, "Those who never exist cannot be deprived. However, by coming into existence one does suffer quite serious harms that could not have befallen one had one not come into existence." Benatar emphasizes that choosing to have a child denies agency to that child, because you have decided for them that they should exist. His philosophy centers around the desire to prevent suffering. Because all human life contains suffering, the only way to prevent it for others is not to create more humans. Funny how this extreme argument for childlessness is still somehow centered around the children themselves, their hypothetical lives.

A more palatable, less human-centered version of this position comes from Les Knight, who founded the Voluntary Human Extinction movement. His bid for humans to "live long and die out" has proven to be a balm to many similarly minded people who are horrified at the losses to other species and ecosystems human consumption has wrought. But even the gentle humor in his slogan "Thank You for Not Breeding," or in the Center for Biological Diversity's free condoms featuring endangered species that say things like "For the sake of the horned lizard . . . slow down, love wizard," can have an ominous echo for those familiar with the history of forced sterilization in the U.S.

Childlessness hasn't always been possible for everyone, and it continues to be impossible for many. For most people with uteruses around the world, their default status is involuntary motherhood. ("Nearly half of all pregnancies worldwide are unintended," according to a United Nations Population Fund report. Unsafe abortions resulting from unwanted pregnancies are one of the leading causes of maternal deaths.) The ability not to have children throbs at the center of U.S. politics, and decades of Republican strategy went into bringing down *Roe*. As Angela Davis wrote in *Women, Race and Class* in 1981, "women's desire to control their reproductive system is probably as old as human history itself."

Long before Roe, before the birth control movement, white American women found a way to decrease the number of babies they were having. In the late nineteenth century, a steep decline in the white birth rate "implied that women were substantially curtailing their sexual activity," writes Davis. This was not something to be celebrated. Instead "the specter of race suicide was raised in official circles." Naturally, then-president Theodore Roosevelt freaked out and declared that "race purity must be maintained." Davis writes, "In his State of the Union message that year Roosevelt admonished the well-born white women who engaged in 'willful sterility—the one sin for which the penalty is national death, race suicide.'" The president linked women's ability to say no to forced motherhood with anti-nationalism and aligned the nation with whiteness. The presumptive caretaking that women took on extended farther than their own families. Now they were tasked with maintaining the birth rate for their (white) nation.

The birth control movement took Roosevelt's warning to heart. As Davis describes, birth control advocate Margaret Sanger went on to "define 'the chief issue of birth control' as 'more children from the fit, less from the unfit.'" In order to get powerful people on their side, they had to frame birth control as a way to elevate the lives of white women while "controlling the population" of people of color. In addition to wanting to increase the number of white pregnant women, groups of people viewed as nonwhite or "inferior" for other reasons (as

Sanger horrendously put it, "morons, mental defectives, epileptics, illiterates, paupers, unemployables, criminals, prostitutes, and dope fiends") posed a threat, flooding the market with workers who might eventually rise up against the powerful. Population control was a more palatable idea for the state and for the general populace than people with uteruses' having control over their bodies.

So popular were these ideas in the early twentieth century that "by 1932 the Eugenics Society could boast that at least twenty-six states had passed compulsory sterilization laws and that thousands of 'unfit' persons had already been surgically prevented from reproducing," writes Davis. Rather than granting more agency to people with uteruses to decide if and when to have children, the federal government intervened directly with their bodies for decades. In a single year, 1972, the U.S. government paid for somewhere "between 100,000 and 200,000 sterilizations." (For comparison, in the twelve years of Hitler's reign, 250,000 sterilizations were carried out in Nazi Germany.) In America, sterilizations focused on lower-class people and people of color, in particular Native American women. "By 1976 some 24% of all Indian women of childbearing age had been sterilized," writes Davis.

As with the antiabortion movement, forced sterilization sought to control certain groups of people and to prevent their continued existence. The legacies of these policies are still with us, and they inform the medical establishment, policy debates about choice, and the impervious motherhood mandate. "While women of color are urged, at every turn, to become permanently infertile, white women enjoying prosperous economic conditions are urged, by the same forces, to reproduce themselves," Davis writes. Perhaps the pressure I feel to reproduce comes from whiteness itself.

Reprogenetics technologies like IVF often involve embryo selection, when a parent chooses which embryo to implant from their own or from a set of donors'. Sociologist Dorothy Roberts quotes an ad for an IVF clinic in *The New York Times Magazine* that offers "Doctoral Donors with advanced degrees and numerous other donors with special accomplishments and talents." Craigslist ads solicit egg donors, "specifying 'WE HAVE A VERY HIGH DEMAND FOR JEWISH, EAST INDIAN, MIDDLE EASTERN, ASIAN, ITALIAN, and BLONDE DONORS.'" Roberts describes this as a form of "benign eugenic thinking." It allows parents to choose trait markers like sex, race, and ability—the very categories that stratify our society. How benign can that be? She writes, "Fertility clinics' use of race in genetic selection procedures may help to reinforce the erroneous belief that race is a biological classification that can be determined genetically or that genetic traits occur in human beings according to their race." However, race is "an invented social grouping," not a genetic or biological category. Those who have children because they want someone who looks like them, who has their eyes, their features, and those who choose the gender of their children are engaging in a form of eugenic thinking not unlike the mentality that gave rise to forced sterilization. Those who had "good" childhoods and want to bring "good" people into the world, people like them, people who will act and vote like them, are also engaging in this type of thinking. They want to control who gets to exist. What do they mean by "good"? What work is "good" doing here?

If the birth control movement privileged population control over the empowerment of people with uteruses, and if IVF has its own sinister set of implications, what alternatives might grant full personhood, and the ability to control their own reproductive capacities, to people with uteruses? In her book *Full Surrogacy Now: Feminism Against Family,* Sophie Lewis considers the radical possibility of wages for pregnancy. After outlining ways that the international surrogacy industry and the various groups that mobilize against it impact surrogates, she arrives at a desire for "incentives to practice *real* surrogacy, *more* surrogacy: more mutual aid." Increasing and bolstering the industry of gestation and childbirth, she argues, and paying more people to be pregnant, could ultimately diminish the "supremacy of 'biological parents'" in favor of communal families and "nongenetic investments" in future generations. All of this sounds, to me, fantastic, if a bit vaguely imagined. At the same time, it reveals the flattening effect of capital: everything becomes a way for some to be bought and sold, others to buy and sell.

I'm all for pregnancy and parenthood in a different world from ours. In a world where pregnant people have care, support, where moms aren't totally on their own. Where having babies isn't the be-all, end-all of a woman's existence, the only route to human fulfillment. Where we live in a sustainable society that can support new members of its population without exploiting the resources of other countries and species. Lewis asks, what if we looked at pregnancy, gestation, and birth as the labors they are? Surrogate mothers who have been paid to carry and deliver babies "retroactively reimagine their prior pregnancies as undervalued services." Only then can they see the difference in how their role is "valued." Putting pregnancy into the context of capitalism—the context in which it already exists—makes clear that child production and care are forms of labor that merit compensation. We would not have a workforce without pregnancy. But then, I keep asking: Why must we have a workforce?

The unborn child is a hypothetical, a thing not real or true, a Schrödinger's cat who can't matter but who has so much power, more power than most uterus-having people to choose their own lives. Abortion bans make it clear how radical this idea—the full personhood of people with uteruses—still is. Regardless of the health of the pregnant person, their desires or needs, and the circumstances by which they became pregnant, antiabortion activists value the embryo over the pregnant person. "If a man chooses to put his sperm inside a woman," writes Myles, "inside her it must stay. It's like she's Tupperware." Her value lies in the life she could possibly contain. The expectation to caretake begins in the womb, when a fit mother is scrutinized for how well she eats, how she cares for the life within her. I see this same expectation at work throughout my life. I could have a hysterectomy and my painful periods and migraines might cease, but I know how difficult it is to convince a doctor to do this. It is seen as a last resort because, more than a person living my life, I am primarily a woman of childbearing years. Even if I tell them I do not want children. I am a vessel, a machine to be optimized, Tupperware, not a living being who deserves care, deserves to experience less pain because I exist unto myself.

I choose my body. I choose my life. Still, when asked if my partner and I plan to have kids, I am made to feel a unique combination of disappointment and condescending knowingness—"Oh, give it a few years. You'll change your mind." I make a crack about our three cats, falling on my sword, and try to move on. This kind of comment is coming from a place of love. The person just wants us to be happy, and they believe that kids are the way to happiness. Perhaps they believe that since we aren't straight, we should especially be inclined to have kids, to have a "normal" family. But what if my happiness, my family, is a life they've never envisioned, never known or considered? After reading the opening pages of my first book, which is about the queer life of writer Carson McCullers, my grandma told me on the phone, "I like it, but I don't know anything about that life."

A few years ago, an artist I met in Wyoming had the gall

to tell me that having kids was the most meaningful, nay, the *only* meaningful, thing a person could do in life. Several others agreed with him. Do they realize, I wondered idly, not aloud, that in casual conversation they have called my full humanity (the fullness of my humanity) into question? That by choosing not to have kids, in their equation, I have willingly forgone an experience—*the* experience!—that makes me human and complete? And legitimate and generous and sustaining? Do they understand that by saying genetic parenthood is the only route to a full and meaningful life, they eject queers and trans people and single people and sterile people and anyone who doesn't choose what they chose from the spectrum of humanity, of full human experience? Do they have any idea what they're saying, when they casually suggest it matters more than anything else they've ever done, anything I could ever do?

It's an odd flip: what is technically a purely biological function is now seen as the one authentic higher human experience you can subject yourself to in pursuit of purpose. As with the idea of career as a path to fulfillment, this turns a form of labor into a peak experience, an identity and life-defining aspiration.

To treat motherhood as a peak life experience is a form of gatekeeping that excludes those who parent but cannot be pregnant from accessing a "full" life. It excludes anyone without a functioning uterus, and it defines those who have one as fundamentally unfulfilled unless they make use of it. My friend Tara has been single for a long time, despite wanting a partner. She went to a baby shower and had to endure friends and mothers swooningly repeating the phrase "From maidenhood to motherhood!" Where was she in that conception of womanhood? Nonexistent. "How can I be the only one in the room who notices this?" Tara asked me. I understand the desire not to miss out on a fundamental human experience. The longing for completism. But I also know that no life is complete, and every life is complete. Sorry, fellow millennials. There aren't metrics here, ways to optimize and perfect. Life is on its own terms. I suspect this is a queer sensibility, or one brought to me by choosing a queer life. I had to give up all the things I learned to want, the legible futures that would make my life "complete."

The alternative to finding meaning through children is far scarier, but to me more exciting. If having children is what humans have done since the beginning of time, if for most of human history motherhood has been involuntary, perhaps it's high time to try absolutely anything else at all. In *Motherhood*, Sheila Heti writes, "In a life in which there is no child, no one knows anything about your life's meaning. They might suspect it doesn't have one—no centre it is built around. Your life's value is invisible. . . . How wonderful to tread an invisible path, where what matters most can hardly be seen." Defining your own path can be terrifying. And it can be seen as threatening to those who have chosen the route that is most visible, that is considered normal. It is also lonely, I am finding. Lonelier by the year.

The English language doesn't have a word for people who don't have children. In the past, researchers used the word "childless," but people without children found that term a bit dire, so they changed it to the more optimistic "childfree." Subjects in studies of childfree cis women from 2003 and 2019 express longing for "a positive feminine identity separate from motherhood." This suggests that there is no term that embodies a woman's life without motherhood. What, I ask, is the term for a man who doesn't become a father? I think we just call him a man. "Man" and "woman" are equally fraught terms, pigeonholing people into genders that may or may not fit their identities. For the childless, the childfree, the issue remains: Why must we be defined, named for what we do not have, what we do not want, what never enters the picture? Get this child out of here!

In recent studies of the childfree, you find people who had very happy childhoods and people who had unhappy ones. The subjects attest that they value their freedom above all: the freedom to choose, to decide how to spend their time. To eat pancakes in the nude, say. Some seek to preserve the intimacy they have with a partner by not introducing another person into the relationship. Others enjoy solitude. Some prefer to devote their time to other relationships with family or friends. Having kids, the cliché goes, changes everything. Often those who don't have kids simply did not want everything to change, like me—I built my life this way on purpose. I had the privilege to do so. I look at my life and I don't want everything to change. Many fear a "loss of the self" with motherhood, having witnessed it in other mothers around them. If I were to lose myself, I'd lose one of the major bodies of source material for my writing. To have a baby and keep writing about my life would require a type of compartmentalization, of boundaries I've never been capable of maintaining. I say this not from experience but from having watched others attempt it.

When asked about their "long-term satisfaction" with the choice not to have kids, childfree people's reports are "overwhelmingly positive." No regrets, some said. No second thoughts, others said. "Phenomenal." "More than satisfying—it's just been great." They report their lives as "superlative." How obnoxious, this satisfaction! Surely there must be some underlying deep-down disappointments or more people would be doing it.

I braced myself when I got to the section of the study on negative outcomes. Here come the regrets! All the big looming fears that we will be let down by our lives without kids! In fact, participants noted only two negative outcomes: "Otherness in Community" and "Difficulty or Loss in Friendships with

Parenting Women." Feelings of otherness and exclusion arose
for those who took part in religious groups or extended families that did not accept their choice. And many of the subjects
lost friends to motherhood, as I have. The studies are imperfect, focusing on straight, white, cis women. More research
is needed beyond these studies to understand childlessness,
childfreedom as a choice, as a community, as a manifestation
of agency and a way of living. But the negative outcomes stick
with me. The things that stigmatize this choice—being cast
out by your community, losing your female friendships—are
the very same things the witch hunts threatened.

On phone calls with two of my friends about why they
wanted to have kids, they each informed me, unexpectedly, that
they were now currently pregnant, one with her second child,
the other with her first. During the calls, listening to their reasons and asking occasional follow-up questions, I found myself
rolling my forearms along my desk with a small, spiky blue rub-
ber ball that I use to break up the tension in my muscles from
typing. After we had talked through her reasons, my friend
asked what was new with me. Suddenly my big, beautiful,
happy, full life shrank before my eyes. "The tulips are coming
up," I croaked. What's the point of living? What's the point of
me? I'm not growing a tiny lizard inside me who will become a
whole person and take over my entire life course. What could
I say to match that, to show we were still aligned? None of my
projects, including this book, seemed to rival the scope of hers.

This is what the institution of motherhood does. It
makes anything I do—climb Mount Everest, find a cure for
diabetes—small by comparison. Less meaningful, less generous, less self-sacrificing. When I called my parents to tell them
I was a finalist for the National Book Award, they followed it
up by telling me someone I went to high school with had just
had a baby. I can see how a single conversation like that might
push me to change my mind, if all the circumstances of my

life were different. Out of—what? Competition? A desire to keep up? To stay aligned?

Hours later, I rolled up my sleeve and saw purpling bruises all along the outside of my forearm. The tulips are a great joy in my life right now. The fact that a dirty old bulb goes underground all frozen winter and then in late February, when the hours of daylight increase, decides it's time to poke a green shoot out of the ground and fill my bleak late-winter serotonin-deprived heart with hope? Talk about the miracle of life! I read a whole book on seeds and I still have no idea how a bulb brings a plant to life.

The cultural fear or rejection of barrenness, of childlessness, reminds me of the way some people react to the desert landscape. They assume that it's blank, lifeless, that nothing grows here. But if you know what you're looking at, it's a really life-affirming place.

I wonder what would change if procreation were just a weird hobby, like ceramics or CrossFit, instead of the ultimate key to human significance. Child rearing narrows to a pretty specialized interest set: education, human development, youth athletics. It feels desperate to make a pregnancy, a child, your last bid for meaning in this life. I mean, what if it doesn't pan out? What if your kid is terrible, like *We Need to Talk About Kevin* bad? But it also makes sense. We are alienated from our labor, we are exploited, so work does not provide meaning or value. Where else can meaning and value come from? If not work, it must be kids. What other values, what other sources of meaning, could there be? This is my question. I want to see more people trying to answer it. Why does it bother me so much that everyone is having babies, why does it get under my skin? Because each time one of them gets pregnant or says they felt the call to motherhood arise within them, I feel my personhood diminishing. I feel I am less of a person in their eyes. Having kids is still the default, the norm—even for queer people now. To normalize not having kids would require that we normalize abortion (not to mention make it legal everywhere), normalize infertility, normalize singledom, normalize eldercare, normalize healthcare for bodies with uteruses, normalize healthcare, period.

When people with kids say that I'll change my mind, that eventually I'll see, they are presuming the fact of my regret, that without kids I'll miss out. They clearly haven't read any of the studies. (Imagine if I responded to the next friend's announcement of pregnancy with "Oh, give it time. You'll change your mind.") The common desire on the part of those who have kids to pressure others into having them isn't doing them any favors. It makes the whole thing seem an awful lot like a cult. A multilevel marketing scheme at best. What dark-sided queer theorist Lee Edelman called "the Ponzi scheme of reproductive futurism." But in the concern over what one might miss out on without kids, I wonder if they consider what they miss when they have them.

When you take children out of the equation, it costs much less to have a life. Children are part of the system that entrenches us in capitalist striving and labor production and endless competition. Children and wealth accumulation are in a positive feedback loop. If you don't have kids, you need to earn far less: a smaller living space; fewer mouths to feed, medical bills, clothes; no childcare, schooling. I'm not saving for anyone's college tuition. Our culture would have this as my *irresponsibility*. Always the emphasis is on some future moment. Capitalism defines the realm of home and family as separate from the realm of work, while hiding the fact that the home is meant only as a place to prepare oneself for more work. What if the home could be something more than a recovery zone or a realm of reproduction? What if life could be something more? Take away that one element, the child, and the possible paths are utterly different.

I know my writing requires solitude, long stretches to think deeply, space and time, and a kid removes solitude from the picture. With Chelsea I can have my solitude and our love, and this is so much more than I dreamed, so much more than "enough" or "it all." Nurturing as a practice is still there—in how I care for myself, my cats, my tomato plants. But it's only one part, not all-consuming. I can put it away if I want to, go in my room and ignore the meows and demands for attention and do no real harm to anyone. The cats don't need me at all times and neither do the plants, and I can choose the times (especially with noise-canceling headphones and a closed door). I can grow and change and have moods and not scar anyone. I don't need to make anyone understand the extent of my sacrifice.

I could follow this statement the way many childless people do, by reassuring the audience and myself of my love for children. I could say, Don't get me wrong, I love kids! I just don't want kids of my own. I adore being an auntie! I'm the godmother to my friends' kids! I love to babysit! Kids are wonderful! But then I'd be pantomiming the idea of womanhood as child-oriented, child-loving at all costs. I'd be reaffirming, reinscribing, the idea of a good woman, a fit woman, as one who cares for children. I think this idea is damaging, toxic. I want to see beyond it.

What Is Life?

Or, A Vindication of the Rights of Cat Ladies

To see beyond the idea of a woman as a vessel, of any uterus-having body as a means to produce new life, requires that we see such a body as a body, one that requires basic resources and care. Laws that require a pregnant person to carry an embryo to term and give birth to it regardless of its impacts on that person's health promote the rights of the fetus above those of the person carrying it. A legal brief proposing fetal personhood came before the Supreme Court to make this into law in 2022. If such a law had been enacted, which didn't seem beyond the realm of possibility at the time, pregnant people could be charged with homicide for miscarriages and abortions (multiple states have already introduced "homicide by abortion" bills, including Arizona, North Dakota, Mississippi, South Carolina, and Louisiana). Rather than establish that women, that anyone with a uterus, is a full person, anti-abortion lawmakers want to grant personhood to fetuses.

The distinction between a human and a person was made clear in the New York Supreme Court case *Byrn v. New York City Health & Hospitals Corp.* in 1972. In arguing a later case on behalf of an elephant's bid for personhood, Stephen M. Wise, president of the Nonhuman Rights Project, cited Byrn as precedent. He writes, "Byrn made it clear that being a person and being a human being are not synonymous . . . the Court said that while she was still a human, a fetus was not a person. It made it clear that personhood is an issue not of biology, but it has to be a matter of public policy." If we had an adequate, functioning healthcare system, and if our legal system affirmed that people with uteruses have the right to go on existing and to be given proper medical care throughout their lives—i.e., that they are fully people—abortion would by necessity be legal and readily available to anyone whose body, whose life, whose very vision for that life might be threatened by producing a child.

During the AIDS crisis in the United States, marchers chanted, "What do we want? Healthcare! When do we want it? Now!" The fight for gay rights was intimately entwined with the fight for healthcare for all, the belief that any person has the right to adequate medical care. But not long after, that goal shifted. As when the fight for contraception aligned itself with a eugenicist form of population control, the fight for gay rights embraced something more useful to the state than healthcare for all: marriage. To fight for healthcare is to fight for present, extant bodies and their well-being, their value and right to go on existing, thriving. To fight for marriage is to fight for the reproduction of ideal nuclear family units, in which property and generational wealth are contained and passed down, in which relationships find public sanction and legibility. If the political movement had stuck with the fight for healthcare, maybe the primacy of normative, i.e., married, relationships and the dependents they are intended to produce would also have lessened. Perhaps we would have more models for other ways to live, outside of marriage and biological families. (Or, take it back a tick farther: if the midwives, if the so-called witches, had been able to continue their work, maybe we'd have a functioning healthcare system today.)

"What do you have when you don't have a future?" asks Paul Lisicky in an essay about not having kids. He refers to government inaction to protect gay people during the AIDS epidemic as well as the ongoing attempt to rid society of non-heterosexual, non-procreative relationships and sexualities throughout history. For those who feel their lives are invalidated, who are not seen as valuable in the present, futurity, in the form of children, can be either a tempting lure—fulfilling a desire to have all the things that straight people have—or a slap in the face. Sometimes it feels this way to me. Like, how can queers have swung so quickly from "They want us dead" to "Let's make a baby"? Shouldn't there have been a moment somewhere in there when we rejoiced and enjoyed the lives we were given, the present, the possibility of surviving and thriving? Lisicky writes, "A reclaimed childhood was not something to waste—we knew that much—having spent so much of our actual own childhoods repressed, depressed, waiting to get out."

It isn't easy to find cultural precedents for other ways to live, other ways to make a meaningful life. Instead of clear answers, at thirty-five I find myself afloat in a sea of juicy questions. I gravitate toward any alternate way of living that I find in my reading or watching and hold it close like a talisman against a world that would rather I not be able to imagine any other kind of happiness. In her 2019 book *Notes on Fundamental Joy; seeking the elimination of oppression through the social and political transformation of the patriarchy that otherwise threatens to bury us,* artist Carmen Winant gathered found photographs made by women who left their homes in the 1970s and '80s to form lesbian separatist communes. As a historical model, the separatists aren't a great one. Many of these groups excluded trans women, and some were overwhelmingly white and privileged, though not all, and not the ones Winant celebrates in her book. But their attempt to make a new world for themselves captivates me. I love to look at the photos of them cutting each other's hair, dancing, chopping wood, and photographing one another. To see what their lives look like without a shaping gaze.

The photos prompt Winant to ask, "Is it possible to leave everything behind? [Is it] possible to begin again, outside of and beyond every system of living that you've ever known, reinventing what it means (and looks like) to exist, as a body and its soul, on the land?" She asks her students, "Can feminism actually exist within capitalism? Can you in fact imagine occupying a non-patriarchal world?" And she writes,

Increasingly, I find that students do not recognize the very premise of these interrelated prompts. They do not know what I mean, really, by the suggestion that there are other ways to organize and validate their lives. This cannot simply be the result of that which they do not know—after all, lesbian separatists were raised within a similar, if not more crushing, system of lopsided power and influence five decades ago. It is something deeper and more specific to our generation: a foreclosed sense of optimism (the decisive tool of radical action, the very engine of this work). In order to attempt to change their world, one must be able to believe, unseen, that they have collective agency to change the terms that organize their lives.

I keep looking back to women in previous eras because I can't see it either, a way to change the terms that organize my life. What do you have when you don't have a future? The separatist answer isn't the one I would choose, but I admire them for asking the question: *How else can we live?*

Overturning *Roe* is a grisly opportunity to recognize that we are not now, nor have we ever been, on a path of progress to dismantling patriarchy. That our work remains, will always remain, to affirm the idea that people with uteruses are full human beings. While this ensuing confinement forecloses reality, it also beseeches us to look back and learn how we were first made to see ourselves as less than fully human, to learn how women have found ways to be whole unto themselves in the past.

Reconsidering the meaning of personhood opens up a range of possibilities for what it might mean to care for ourselves and one another. We could raise bees, if we care so much about other beings, if we want something to nurture. We would in that case be nurturing the whole world. The bees are actually helping us. They keep many other ecologies and beings afloat. Faith in the human race seems small-minded to me, when there are so many other forms of knowledge we barely understand—elephants! Mushrooms! Trees that talk to each other underground through their roots! I don't think this is, as some would have it, a nihilistic stance, or a pessimistic one. I think it's the most hopeful thing imaginable. That something we can choose might help or support the planet itself, but let's make it less abstract: might help the bees, the mushrooms, the trees that sustain all life.

I want to decenter motherhood, to normalize and celebrate interspecies bonds, other kinds of love. Relationships with nonhumans remind us that human thought and language and emotion are not the only ones, the only society that is worth caring about, preserving. It's the feeling I had when I filled out the Arbor Day Foundation survey and was told they would plant one hundred trees in response. I'm alight with the possibility of planetary stewardship! Those trees clean the air! This is where I can easily be accused of romanticism, my own delusions of grandeur. Not because I believe some new person in the United States will "save us," later on, in the future, when they grow up and find a techno fix for global warming or unilaterally solve the voting crisis. But because I believe we can do things to help and not harm. To lessen our harm. And we know what we can do. I learned about it when I was sixteen, in my first environmental science class, and it was obvious even then what my generation was being called to do. Environmental researchers did the math. The first thing, the biggest thing, we in the United States (and Europe and Japan and Russia and Australia and Canada) can do for every other creature on this planet? Not have kids.

The bar graphs of how we can alter our own carbon footprints all have something in common: at one end, the bar for having "one fewer child" has a break in it, and then the Y-axis shifts its scale. While for things like not driving a car, not eating meat, and not taking cross-country flights, the footprint is measured in single tons, when it gets to having one fewer child in the United States, they can't fit the bar in the graph. They change the increments just for that one bar and measure it in tens of tons. Because otherwise the graph would look outrageous: everything on it would be reduced to almost nothing so that you could see the full extent of the impact of a single child. No one wants to see that.

In fact, this data comes out of a study of science textbooks and government resources about lessening your ecological impact that all diminish the most significant category and highlight those that are much less impactful. So I asked my friend Rhiannon, a rhetorician, to make me a more realistic chart. As though maybe what we all need to make the biggest decision of our lives is a better infographic?

Reducing your individual carbon footprint isn't everything. It isn't even much. But if more people did it, the results would

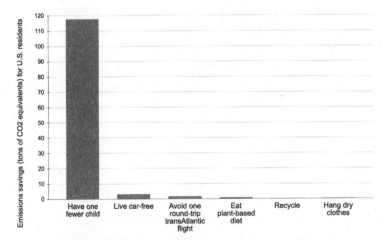

Source: Supplementary data from Seth Wynes and Kimberly A. Nicholas, "The Climate Mitigation Gap: Education and Government Recommendations Miss the Most Effective Individual Actions," *Environmental Research Letters* 12 (2017).

be staggering. While we wait and vote and hope that our legislators make changes to reduce the impact of industries, which are much larger than individuals', there is technically something those who have the option not to have kids can do to help.

Climate change threatens the ability of the planet to sustain life, period, in addition to threatening human survival. What does it mean to survive? When we talk about climate change and prevention, we are often talking about basic subsistence, or the maintenance of "mere life," according to political theorist Bonnie Honig. Lida Maxwell builds on this idea in her writing about Rachel Carson to suggest that what is lost through climate change is not just the ability to survive but relationships, multispecies entanglements, the richness of the world itself that makes life worth living. Not just our access to clean drinking water but our ability to be outside (without melting), to immerse our bodies in a cold stream without worrying about runoff, all the emotions and relationships we might access with the nonhuman world.

Rachel Carson knew the importance of "more life," of a life imbued with wonder in the nonhuman world, and her relationship with Dorothy Freeman was built around and in that space of wonder, the space that climate change and massive species die-off threatens and forecloses. Confronted with myriad expectations on their personhood, these women found in each other a kindred spirit when they met on Southport Island, off the coast of Maine. After sneaking a kiss in the woods when they parted, the two spent the rest of their lives in conversation, writing letters and talking and visiting each other throughout the year, and wresting away from their obligations as many weeks as they could have together on the island each summer. They listened for birds in the woods, crawled along the shore looking for fairy caves at low tide, and watched for phosphorescence from the beach in the middle of the night.

Their relationship didn't allow them to completely escape the limits of their heteronormative families: Dorothy's marriage to Stanley Freeman, Rachel's responsibility for her mother, her niece, and her grandnephew. (When they wrote to each other, they often enclosed two separate letters in each envelope: one was for sharing with their families, another, which they referred to as an "apple," was meant only for the other's eyes. Many of the letters were written while they sat under the dryer at the hairdresser. They carved out a space in which to exist. And later, they burned or destroyed many of the apples.) In Maine and on paper, they made a different kind of family, just the two of them and the world of plants, animals, and tidepools.

Carson didn't write or even conceive of her groundbreaking book *Silent Spring* until she'd met and fallen in love with Freeman. Her political self arose out of the world they built together. Lida Maxwell reads *Silent Spring* "as a work of love . . . on behalf of the human affects and pleasures (in particular, wonder and love) that are made possible by a vibrant multispecies world." Carson's writing asks us: What are we surviving for? And Maxwell describes her answer as "an environmental politics of desire," which fights for the "preservation of a multispecies world through and on behalf of human pleasure." This, too, is a human-centric approach to the environment, one that longs to preserve on our behalf, for our enjoyment, rather than considering the sentience of nonhuman creatures and entities and their value in their own right. But as an argument for reversing climate change at all costs, for finding other modes of human existence during our lifetimes, it's a potent one. One of the major catalysts for the environmental movement as we know it wanted to preserve her own pleasure—selfishly?!—in her own life. I bet she ate whole crackers from the box, too.

When Carson presented her readers with the prospect of a spring without birdsong in *Silent Spring,* they couldn't stomach it. The potential loss of their entanglement with birds was enough for them to lobby to regulate chemical companies and begin to build the EPA. What are the other affects and experiences in nature that will call us to make change, to change our own behaviors, to reconsider even our long-held desires? To preserve meaningful and pleasurable human lives—in particular, to preserve queer lives like Rachel and Dorothy's, which couldn't have existed elsewhere or without the ethereal call of the veeries—demands we preserve a nonhuman world to be entangled with. In the last fifty years, as the human population has doubled, wildlife populations declined by 70 percent. An environmental politics of desire, according to Maxwell, "reframes the practices named by 'frugality'—for example, a turn away from fossil fuels, the slowing of economic growth, the regulation of chemical use and pollution—as part of a democratic politics of pleasure and fecundity." Often critiques of capitalism and calls to be "greener" feel "against pleasure," critical of "a comfortable, easy life." While not having kids might be seen as a sacrifice, a form of frugality, it can also offer new ways of embracing pleasure and fecundity, the richness of our ongoing relations with what's left of the multispecies world. The richness of possible relationships with extant beings, with the world as it is.

To say that we on planet Earth are one big family, the birds and the bees, the forests and the trees, is pretty cheesy. But it's that kind of cheesiness—what Rachel Carson called "wonder"—that is missing from our thoughts and actions and beliefs and discussions about climate change. In the face of emergency, it's easy to grit your teeth and fight for mere survival, or throw up your hands and accept defeat, believing that your individual choices don't matter. So many people have made this argument to me. But more life demands that we access emotions beyond fight, flight, and freeze.

I spent a week at Rachel Carson's house in Maine, which has been preserved as it was in the 1950s and '60s: the wood paneling; books on tides and lichen; the big picture windows facing Sheepscot Bay, where seals and dolphins played and I watched them through Carson's binoculars. Brushing my teeth at Rachel Carson's sink, I wondered why I was back here again so soon, living in the house of some mid-twentieth-century woman—named Carson, no less. I needed to learn something more from her.

Each morning, Emily was out on the beach at dawn reading *The Edge of the Sea* and scanning the water for activity. We all became totally absorbed in the immediate environment, learning what we could from the books on the shelves about the unfamiliar intertidal zone. Brad found millions of blackberries just down the hill from the house, and Em used her eagle eyes to spot birds. The cottage had no television or Wi-Fi, so at night we cooked and looked at the moon and talked. I had read so much about Rachel Carson, and suddenly Chelsea and my friends wanted to know everything about her and her books and Dorothy Freeman. One night Chelsea read aloud to us from the beginning of *The Sea Around Us,* when Carson describes how the moon was created from the ocean by a tidal wave. Later, after the others had gone to bed, I reread her letters with Dorothy as the moon rose over the bay, waxing golden in the sky through the pines beyond the porch. I realized that the woods between Rachel's cottage and Dogfish Head, the point of the island where Dorothy lived, were what the two women had referred to as the Lost Woods. Rachel tried to preserve these woods during her lifetime. She wanted so badly to maintain the space between her house and Dorothy's, a place they had found together, that connected them. Ultimately, she couldn't afford to buy the land, and since her death the woods between their houses have been developed to make way for more people.

One morning I tried to find their path through the Lost Woods myself, but I kept getting spit out onto other people's driveways and private roads. I hid behind a tree for a solid ten minutes as a man with a cane walked to his mailbox and then back up his endless drive. As I dove into the underbrush between homes, I tried to look nonchalant, recording dozens of birdsongs on the Merlin app, nestling my feet several inches into the deepest green moss with each step.

At the end of the island, I made my way toward the shore at Dogfish Head, to see the view that the two women shared there, but was called back when a middle-aged woman in cerulean L.L.Bean lightweight down arose from her Adirondack chair and demanded to know who I was, where I was going. She informed me that Dogfish Head is now "his," gesturing to several large SUVs parked in a driveway, and the land between it and the Freemans' house is "hers." I explained where I was staying and my interest in Rachel and Dorothy, that I was trying to follow the path they took through the woods and along the shoreline, for research. At first, she wasn't going to allow me to walk down to the water, to even glimpse the view. Finally, when pressed, she told me I could "peek" at the shore along her property, and she "wouldn't tell." Tell whom? I looked down at the little cove and saw our very own family of eider ducks whom we'd been watching from the cottage all morning floating as if in a spa. Traitors. I turned around and walked back along the road, angrier by the minute at the enclosure of queer spaces, the encroachment of property values on a place once held sacred.

Seeing how Carson and Freeman found "human pleasures and counter-conventional desire" in nature, I wonder again, what is the meaning of life? What life is life? Whose life? Preserving your own pleasure isn't easy, though. After her niece died, Rachel adopted her five-year-old grandnephew, Roger, and raised him until she died seven years later at the age of fifty-six. Perhaps because he wasn't a child of her own, because she didn't decide she wanted children, but rather took on responsibility for one, there is an unusually frank response in her letters to the change in her life that Roger represents.

The frequency of her long, almost daily reflections to Dorothy declines immediately, all but ceasing in 1957, as does her ability to spend time with Dorothy in Maine. Work on her books, the kind of dreamy roaming it requires, becomes impossible. A part of Rachel's identity and the family she was building with Dorothy is lost, temporarily, and displaced by Roger and Rachel's ailing mother's needs. She shares with Dorothy what it all does to her mentally, physically, emotionally. "The poor child's demands on me have increased to the point where—even though understanding or trying to— I think I'll explode! He will scarcely let me out of his sight," she writes while trying to finish an article in December 1957. "And even while hating myself for it, I can't help thinking, 'Why did this have to happen to me?'" Though she has the chance to share wonder in the natural world with Roger—and eventually would write a book about this called *The Sense of Wonder*—she loses the sanctity, the privacy, the otherworldliness of her relationship with Dorothy in the process. Their world is harder to maintain.

The secretary of agriculture responded to *Silent Spring* by asking "why a spinster with no children was so concerned about genetics." But it wasn't a future world that Rachel Carson was fighting for. It was the world in which she existed, it was the world she'd found with Dorothy.

We talk about a carbon footprint as if it were quantifiable, like the graph, something we can strategically reduce to no impact at all. We talk less about the type of footprint we want to leave. Carson wanted to leave the woods unoccupied. When she couldn't do this, her attention shifted to a new project, research and writing that became *Silent Spring,* a text that encouraged citizen brigades to advocate for preservation and protection of their own local environments like the Lost Woods. We can leave other things behind besides children. Other forms of longevity exist, even if they are unquantifiable.

Researchers like Andrea Laurent-Simpson have begun to study what they've termed "multi-species families," in which adopted pets take on the role of family members, kin. Maybe this is what people feared from queers, the childless, all along: the slippery slope! But when you begin to consider "interspecies subjectivity," or the idea that we can care for those who are not human the same way we care for humans, this type of family has existed all along. I mentioned multispecies families to my acupuncturist, Kelly, and her face lit up. "I have one of those! I've always thought that the coolest thing about human beings is our ability to have intimate relationships with other species." We communicate with animals and plants, we care for them, we find friendship and love and mutual understanding with them. Kelly's response reminded me what a marvel this is.

Rachel Carson and Dorothy Freeman each had cats that they considered family. When I first came across a reference to Jeffie in one of Carson's letters, I thought he was a person. Elliott, Lou, and Gary are a part of my family as much as Chelsea is. When we first started dating in Austin, I knew that Chelsea would be a welcome addition to my household (me, Elliott, and Lou, at the time), because each morning Lou would leave her toy mouse on top of Chelsea's backpack or in one of her shoes. Laurent-Simpson writes of "a theory of mind" that animals' caretakers employ, which "allow[s] them an understanding of the animal's thoughts, emotions, desires, and intentions." We do this with animals, we do this with babies, and in the most recent research about empathy, it becomes clear that we do a version of this with other humans, imagining what they might be feeling, thinking, wanting, or intending. The mechanism for relating to an animal is, on a psychological level, the same as that for relating to a human. Humans grieve their lost pets as family—as Rhiannon says, riffing on George Carlin, "buy a dog, buy a tragedy." Animals grieve one another as well as humans with whom they've had close relationships.

A picture of me, age two or three, shows a blond bowl cut in blue zip-up pajamas, smiling broadly and holding a little plastic bottle, with a small pink buggy beside me. Inside it is nestled my favorite Cabbage Patch Kid doll (the one with the freckles, whose head got run over in the cul-de-sac, leaving skid marks across her face), alongside my E.T. doll. My child self already understood something about interspecies love. What if we looked at other creatures with the same awe and wonder with which mothers look at their babies? Why should a baby be any more miraculous than a tiny bird drinking water, a tulip unfolding, the tadpoles whose breaths make ripples across a pond?

My friend Adeena calls her late dog, Ruby, her best friend. I've never seen anyone with a closer relationship to a pet. When Adeena was twenty-five, her younger sister died, and I always saw Ruby as sort of a surrogate sister for her. When my first girlfriend and I broke up, I felt utterly friendless. But I got to keep our orange tabby cat, Elliott, who was for a while my main support system. He offered me a routine, a schedule, and companionship when I was most alone. And when it became obvious that he was lonely, I adopted a tiny gray kitten to be his friend. Lou changed Elliott's personality completely. Rather than a rambunctious ankle biter, he became a gentle, amiable presence at every social gathering. Adeena started calling him the mayor, because he's always looking out for his constituents.

A few months after we started dating, Chelsea adopted an orange kitten from our friend, who had found him in a cave outside Dallas, and named him Gary. Even though we were just getting to know each other, my mind flashed forward and saw the future: we were going to have three cats. We were going to be those women. Now that all three are under one roof, they have complex interpersonal dynamics that we witness and comment on. Gary is obviously in love with Lou, but Lou hates him. The drama never ends. In our multispecies family, we have closeness and mutual nurturing, but Chelsea says, "I wouldn't call it maternal. The cats are our friends. They keep us company. They communicate with us without words. They're part of our ecosystem."

In the morning Elliott runs out with me into the garden and smells every plant while I water. We are each letting the plants know someone is there. The cats intuit when one of us is upset. Elliott butts his head against my face to say he can tell I'm sad. They come and sit by our side if one of us is sick in bed. Each night all three of them sleep on Chelsea in a pile, and she lets them. Lou curls in her arms like a tiny person, with her head beside Chelsea's on the pillow. I've learned that even though they don't speak our language, keeping them apprised of what's going on always seems to help a situation, like when we go out of town. At first it felt crazy to talk to them, but now I see it as a form of respect, of consideration. The cats aren't children, nor are they a replacement for them. They're just beings we choose to cohabit with and care for.

The personhood of nonhuman entities like animals, plants, bodies of water, and land formations is a growing field of law that aims to protect beings that cannot defend themselves. In *Personhood*, Thalia Field writes, "Brussels, France, New Zealand, Quebec, Switzerland, Slovakia, Austria, and Egypt have all redefined animals as *sentient beings* and not things or property." Sentience, or the ability to perceive the world with one's own senses, demonstrates intelligence, emotions, and awareness. Granting animals legal personhood allows them to have rights that they do not have when treated as objects. It enables people to litigate on behalf of those rights, which the animals are unable to do for themselves (because we don't share their language). In 2017, New Zealand named the Whanganui River a legal person "after its headwaters were diverted, its bed was mined and straightened, its rocky falls flattened, its fish populations killed, and the water polluted." In Colombia, the Supreme Court made part of the Amazon rain forest a person. Granting legal personhood is one way that environmental activists are trying to unmake our conception of the bright line between human beings and other entities.

This kind of unmaking can be seen as disturbing. A river is a person now. What next? The idea threatens and challenges the basis of our individuality, our own personhood. Merlin Sheldrake, a mycologist and part of a wave of research on fungi and mycorrhizal networks, writes, "So much of daily life and experience—not to mention our philosophical, political, and economic systems—depends on individuals that it can be hard to stand by and watch the concept dissolve. Where does this leave 'us'? What about 'them'? 'Me'? 'Mine'? 'Everyone'? 'Anyone'?" To begin to see the nonhuman world as equally intelligent, equally sentient, equally valuable to human lives, radically alters our position in relation to everything around us. It changes fundamentally what we think of as a self. " 'We' are ecosystems that span boundaries and transgress categories. Our selves emerge from a complex tangle of relationships only now becoming known," writes Sheldrake. Expanding our notion of personhood changes our perspective on other species and entities. It offers a way to perceive ourselves as beings in a much larger web. It suggests ways we might live more gently, and with a wider lens of consciousness and interconnectedness.

These ideas about interconnectedness, about sentient animals, trees, and rivers, may be new to the legal field and to scientists, but they are among the oldest ideas in the world. They are shared by many Indigenous and ancestral peoples across the planet. "Our belief was we are part of the earth. We're of the earth. Not that we own it," Marian Naranjo told me. Scientists keep proving what they've known for thousands of years: that everything we encounter is a form of life, a being worthy of respect. Animals can't defend themselves and neither can rivers, until we can deign to learn their language, to try to listen. Mallery Quetawki, a Zuni artist and trained pharmacist I interviewed for "Thin Skin," paints the systems of the human body using animals, landforms, and the symbols of fellow Indigenous tribes and pueblos. She merges Western medical understandings of the body, Zuni philosophies, and images of disrepair and healing to communicate with fellow Pueblo people about environmental contamination and its impact on their health. A strand of DNA becomes a beaded necklace, broken apart by environmental exposure to uranium and stitched back together with zinc treatments. She describes her art as a form of record keeping, preserving the history of the knowledges she herself contains, passing them on to others. Surely we can conjure more images like hers to show ourselves what life really looks like, how it is entangled, how we fit.

On the phone, a mother friend tells me she knows many people like me, who "chose not to have a family." But kids aren't the only way to make a family. They aren't the only way to connect to life. It is of value, in any walk of life, to pause and ask, "What is my family?" Any person can question the expectations and norms of what a family is or should be and define it for themself. What expectations of a full and meaningful life am I trying to fulfill? Where do those expectations come from? Whose definition of family, of fullness? Who is enforcing it and how? Like when Dorothy and Rachel expanded their own relationships, negotiated the bonds of being a wife and a daughter (respectively), broadened their definition of family to accommodate each other.

I see in my own queerness, and in my relationship with Chelsea, something of what Rachel and Dorothy found sixty years ago. When we got together, we longed to live somewhere we could hike, garden, and be outside. We longed for space where we could build our own world together. We moved to a place where the sky literally feels higher.

Chelsea's certainty that she didn't want kids from the beginning of our relationship opened a space for me to begin to articulate my own desire, to shape the life I wanted. Because in our relationship there was no pressure or expectation for kids, I was free to see a new horizon for my life. I realized I could be an old woman, the way I'd longed to be, right now! Envisioning our relationship, the possibilities of it, was a big part of our falling in love, our foundation, and kids never had any place in the lives we imagined for ourselves. Those lives had everything to do with limitlessness, with the way time seemed to become infinite when we were together.

Like many queer women I know, I tried heterosexuality for a number of years. I always found it wanting—the pressure, the expectations, the swift movement toward climax/disappointment. The fear of pregnancy was boring, staid, played out over and over again in every movie, every show. Expressing this now, my frustration with straight relationships emerges as a narrative frustration. I felt trapped in that story. The options were all laid out, like doorways, when what I sought was an open field, an expanse in which to be, to become. Queer relationships offered this: no rules, no timeline, no expectations. Open-endedness. Something that I also find true about queer sex. It's never clear when it's over. It kind of keeps going, when it's good. I think of queerness now as something I chose. I considered the alternative, I gave it an honest effort, I chose something else. It's not a choice for everyone—for some it's part of their identity from birth, for some it's not an option they're aware of. And given my skepticism of agency within the social structures of the world as it is, perhaps it wasn't really a choice for me. But once I knew I had the option—to abandon the doors, to run into the field—I ran. I also fell in love. In one of her letters, Finnish writer and creator of the Moomins Tove Jansson describes falling in love with a woman for the first time as "like finding a new and wondrous room in an old house one thought one knew from top to bottom."

Not everyone falls in love on an island, or moves to a place where the sky feels higher, or finds a queer life that offers them a way of resisting. I've become fascinated by the life of science fiction writer Octavia Butler, whose 386 boxes of prolific journals and diaries at the Huntington Library archives offered Lynell George the source material for a book about making a life as a writer. An only child in Pasadena, where her mother cleaned the houses of wealthier white people, Butler found her island between the covers of a pink and tan leather notebook. "I made a universe in it," she writes. "There I could be a magic horse, a Martian, a telepath. There I could be anywhere but here, any time but now, with any people but these." Her notebook, writes George, was her sanctuary, the place where she could keep her dream of being a writer front and center, no matter what cruel comment she received from a teacher at school, no matter how many rejection slips she got from magazines for her stories. People around her told her to get a real job, to become a secretary, but instead she jumped from one mindless temp job to another, scrimped and saved, and refused to devote her mental energy to anything but writing.

With no clear model or possibilities for how to proceed, Butler spent her time at the public library, making lists of all the ways she might fashion a life for herself. She never married or had children, and some scholars speculate about her sexuality, though no official biography of her has yet been published. Ultimately she was able to publish her novels and offer the world Afrofuturist, multiethnic, and multispecies visions—including a story in which pregnancy is reimagined as a form of parasitism—though never a utopian one. "I don't write about perfect societies—utopias—first because they're boring, and second because I don't think they're attainable by imperfect humans," she said. "But I can visualize societies in which sex and race are interesting differences and not a mark of inferiority or superiority." She used other planets, fictional diseases, and nonhuman perspectives to think about personhood and to examine what we owe one another, what we can be to and for one another, as fellow species sharing a planet. Her early morning hours writing, walking, and taking in everything she could from the news, from books, and from people she encountered made it possible for her to visualize other ways to live, and to live otherwise herself.

My friend Jenny's partner of eighteen years died of ovarian cancer a few years ago, and she doesn't think she'll have another partner. She's okay with that, but people keep telling

her otherwise. Give it time, they say, don't close yourself off
to experiences, to intimacy. I don't see her closing herself off.
I see her opening herself up to this completely mysterious
life, that of a woman alone. To be partnerless is also to face
stigma, to hear from the world that you on your own aren't
enough, can't be or have a family made of your elders, your
friends, your pets, yourself.

It is difficult to choose something that's never been on the
table, that was never presented as an option, something you've
never seen. A truly pro-choice world would present everyone
with the option of a life without children, without a spouse or
partner. Would have as many cultural depictions of that life as
it did of married life or life with kids.

Toward the end of *Motherhood,* Sheila Heti lands on an
image of her life without kids that has stuck with me. "Since
my girlhood, I had been cautious about allowing myself to
imagine the beauty of being a woman alone in a house by the
sea. Yet now I saw the beauty a life could become." My life
feels like a woman alone in a house by the sea, though my
life at the moment is a woman in an 1,100-square-foot town
house with another woman and three cats in the high desert.
Why? Because as two women who don't want kids or marriage
or a certain kind of career, we can leave each other, and ourselves, alone. We can give each other solitude. When we are
at home together I feel free and unseen; I can inhabit myself.
Our love is not a spectacle or something to be witnessed from
the outside—one of the reasons we are adamantly against a
wedding. It is shared and interior. There's no pressure to be
anything to anyone, even to each other.

In her latest book, Sophie Lewis makes a radical argument for the abolition of the nuclear family. "Personhood,"
she writes, "was not always created this way, which means we
could, if we wanted to, create it *otherwise.*" In her view, the
family is a utopic ideal that in practice is the source of vio-

lence and trauma for many people, the opposite of the care it is supposed to provide. To abolish the family would demand an entirely new system of care for human beings not dependent on genetic relationships. Drawing on the Wages for House-work movement and cataloging a history of family abolition movements, from Marx and Engels to lesbians of color in the 1970s, she analyzes parenting as a form of labor and power.

> Parents, it is supposed, derive nothing so much as joy from the romance of this isolated intensity. Constant allusions to the hellworld of sheer exhaustion parents inhabit notwithstanding, their condition is sentimental-ized to the nth degree: it is downright taboo to regret parenthood. All too seldom is parenthood identified as an absurdly unfair distribution of labor, and a des-potic distribution of responsibility for and power over younger people. A distribution that could be changed.

As a self-professed communist, she believes the change lies in a total overthrow of the system of capitalism, from which she hopes the abolition of the family will follow. I admire Lewis's extreme position, her refusal to hedge, her adamant belief that our concept of family must be not transformed but fully abol-ished. But, barring the revolution she calls for, in the mean-time I take her work as a challenge to undermine the idea of family, to question it, to define it for ourselves.

Early in the book she offers a definition of love: "To love a person is to struggle for their autonomy as well as for their immersion in care, insofar [as] such abundance is possible in a world choked by capital." Perhaps family is as simple as say-ing to another living creature: I support your existence. I will go on supporting it as long as I live. The single people I know are all deeply connected to their siblings or their friends or their pets or their students (another realm in which women are expected to perform uncompensated emotional labor). I wouldn't describe any of them as not having a family. As having decided not to have a family. The LGBTQ community is credited with the invention of "chosen families," because queers are so often rejected by their birth families. For a moment, I was rejected by mine, but they came around eventually. I've always found the idea of chosen families a bit twee and unrealistic. Just because you reject or are rejected by your birth family doesn't mean they disappear from your life, your subconscious. They are still what formed you. But you do get to choose who you care for in this life.

If Chelsea hadn't been so certain, if instead she had wanted kids, what would I have done? Would I have been able to name my desires, to speak them, to assert what I wanted for my life, for our relationship, that my solitude, my writing, my sanity, was more important? Would I have been able to see beyond the prescribed desires, the prescribed reality in which I was raised, in which I still live? Would I have caved under the manifold structures built to reinforce naturalized motherhood? Would I have erased the vision of the house by the sea and filled it with children? Could it have happened so easily? I suspect it could have. I've spent so much time wondering why they, other people, are having kids, disguising from myself my own desire not to. A baby is a great apology to the world, to your parents, for being queer. It would be a good way to ask to be forgiven, to absolve myself of being queer and gain back some of the power and status I lose as a lesbian. Like, here, Mom, take this baby! Maybe that will make up for the rest of what you lost. Is it possible that I still hold myself to the standards of straight women, that I see myself as one deep down, or that some part of me longs to be a part of the group, even though I'm queer? A different flavor of having it all: my queer freedom and my hetero subjugation, both.

I still struggle with the impulse to mother, the social pressure to care for others. How often I want to mother everyone, how easily my boundaries slip and I am taking care of everyone in a situation but myself. Ordering coconut cream pie. How much harder it is for me to take care of myself, to prioritize my needs and wants, to even distinguish between something I should do and something I want to do. Maybe this betrays a longing to give myself up, to have an infant thing that needs my care so I can let myself go by the wayside. Instead I give myself up to/for writing, my muscles gluing themselves together in my neck, everything tightening and freezing in me so I can keep the words flowing onto the page. Perhaps this is why writing always feels selfish to me, like an illicit pleasure, something I am getting away with. Like being a person, like considering my life to be something of value on its own.

The art residencies I've been to, by and large, are roosting grounds for postmenopausal women in their sixties and seventies, women who have in all likelihood already accomplished marriage and children, maybe grandchildren, and now are embarking on the project of themselves. I see in these women everything I want to be now, a freedom from societal expectation. An invisibility, really. Their husbands may be extant, but the point of the residency is that their husbands are *not there*. And what do the women do with their long-earned freedom? Sapphic rites in the woods? Animal sacrifice? Orgies? Form Amazonian militias? They go into their rooms and they paint, or they draw, or they collage, or they dance, like Merián, making wild grunting noises from the studio next door; they write, they sculpt, they sit, they read, they nap, they take walks. They exist for themselves.

I joined a caravan of these women on a drive to a place called Crazy Woman Canyon in Wyoming, and I was amazed to watch them, their joy. They ran, they shouted, they sang, they whooped. After my parents moved to Florida, both in their late sixties, my mom sent me photos of her and my dad at Harry Potter World, standing beside a giraffe at Busch Gardens, at a Cher concert. Perhaps, I thought, trying to understand these frolicking women, trying to understand my mom's sudden exuberance, when they do not have children, or the burden of someday having them, or the need to prepare their lives to have them, they are at last free to be children themselves.

Coda

When I was thirty-four years old, as my friends were freezing their eggs or doing rounds of IVF or getting pregnant or miscarrying or having babies, my mom died. It happened without warning when an undetected aneurysm in her abdomen burst in the middle of the night. She was seventy-two.

The prior year had been an exodus of women from our family. We lost my grandmother, my aunt, and then my mother. At her memorial service, my dad kept telling people that what remained of our entire extended family could fit in the back of a Suburban.

To be without a mother is to feel constantly out of touch with something essential, as though I've forgotten or misplaced something at all times. A thousand times a day, something tugs at me and I have to remind myself, *I miss my mom.* She knew whole parts of me, of each of us, that no one else knew. Will ever know. When the matriarch of an elephant herd dies, in the immediate aftermath other members of the group will often starve. They don't realize they need to migrate for drought or to resources, they can't find food and water. The witch hunts, according to Federici, were "the

cause of the downfall of the matriarchal world. For the witch-
hunt destroyed a whole world of female practices, collective
relations, and systems of knowledge." It feels like that in my
family, that without her we are lost elephants. What we lost
was her wisdom, knowledge, warmth. After my mom died, I
watched the dog and two cats look for her, miss her, mourn
her. I watched them try to comfort my dad. Animal sentience
had never been so obvious.

Only when she was gone could I begin to see the shape of
my mom, the space she occupied, the extent of her labor on
my behalf, on my brother's, on my dad's. The way her labor
was made invisible all my life, naturalized as love, as a given.
Seeing the hole, the shape where my mom used to be, makes
me feel my rage about motherhood, and about the expectations the institution of motherhood places on me, all the more
acutely. Not only do I see the hole, but I feel a pressure to fill
it myself. At the same time that I'm blown open by grief, my
insides exposed, I find myself absorbing everyone else's sorrow, unable to distinguish mine from theirs. I'm taking it all
on, my dad's, my brother's, her friends', pushing mine below.
I don't feel entitled to my own pain. My own loss. My grief.

In the months following her death I read books on grief
and loss. I longed specifically for accounts of other people
who had lost their mothers, so much so that I reached out to
everyone I knew who had lost their mom, hoping that in their
experiences I would find some thread to help me see a way
forward without her. Losing my mother caused an identity
crisis I could not have foreseen. It was hard not to view everything I'd written as the pointless wonderings of a person who
has not confronted real loss. My big questions only multiplied.

In one book, forlornly titled *Motherless Daughters,* I found
solace in a chorus of women's refrains that losing their mother
was the hardest thing for them, too, whether it happened
when they were young or in midlife or late adulthood. This

offered justification for my sorrow. For many women, becoming mothers themselves was a new moment of crisis and validation, in which they said, "I have become what I once lost." Not wanting to have children, I realized with a start that I couldn't say what these women said. I will never become what I lost. In some way my mother's life will always be alien to me.

After I wrote her eulogy I wondered if I made her life sound too small. I kept wanting her life to be bigger, as though caring for and shepherding two entire people into the world is somehow insignificant. We've been made to believe it is, but it is massive. Huge. Heroic. It takes a village, but we expect it from one person. Why didn't my mom have more? What if motherhood, mothering, womanhood, wasn't this boundaryless, selfless, self-annihilating relationship? We were her life. Everything was for us.

In Zoom therapy I told C I was worried about what it meant to take a stance on childlessness, what it would mean to my mother. C had their baby on their lap, and the baby kept trying to close the computer and end the call. Pandemic single parenthood on display. They suggested that what I was describing had to do with differentiation. The process of separating myself from my mother. This boundary has always been hard for me to see. How can I want something other than what my mother wanted? How will I ever know what she wanted for me?

Jean, the nickname my friends use for me, was also my mom's middle name. Have I ever known where she stopped and I began? We are a merging. I'm wearing my dead mother's clothes. I am living the life she never could have, the life she made possible for me. Chelsea and I talk with awe about how she was starting a new life in Florida. When I cleaned out her closet, I found a whole fresh wardrobe, containing few of the clothes I recognized from her life in the Midwest. She had embraced an unfamiliar climate, a new world. How brave she was from the start, leaving home and working, those years I know so little about, stepping out of her expected paths and roles and seeking her own way, the unknown. Chelsea said that's why I was able to do it, because I had seen her do it. I knew it would be okay. She laid the groundwork for my life.

In my midthirties, I feel a closer kinship with death, with loss, than I do with babies. I feel like I'm living on a different planet from my friends with kids or those deep in their fertility journeys. As I feel like I'm living on a different planet from those who still have their moms. Instead of a gift registry, I'm writing a will. Kids are one way human beings soothe their minds about the impending loss of a generation. They are an attempt to grasp immortality, to try to pass on your values, your stuff. But relying on children as our legacy is what gave us generational wealth, laid the foundation of systemic racism. If we extend our idea of family beyond the individual to the wider world of creatures and ecosystems, we can begin to ask what we want for them. From them. We can begin to see ourselves in relation. Acknowledging and reckoning with death—with the limit on our existence, with the fact that we are temporary—can reframe what it means to live. What do we want to leave behind? What do we want to support, maintain, in the limited time we are here?

In Santa Fe many of my friends are aging, passing from their seventies to their eighties, outliving my mom. The population here is older than what we were used to in Austin, and I gravitate toward these friends. Their values make sense to me and reflect my own. It's been a rainy summer after many years of drought, and I go to Jenifer's to learn and help her gather honey from her bees. The profusion of flowers made five times more honey than she's ever had before—twenty frames instead of four. A vision of the way things could be.

Her husband, Dwight, shows me how to build a door for my office to keep the cats out. Friends like these understand what we've taken to calling gnome life, all the projects and hobbies and practices that fill our days. They, too, are interested in experiencing their own existence, relishing it, cherishing it. Living for pleasure and enjoyment. While to some people it might seem weird, to have more friends who are elders than who are peers, to spend so much time with people decades older than us, to me it feels like a place I can belong, where my own interests and ideas can be seen and cultivated, can grow, without being overshadowed by the pressure to procreate, to participate in one specific version of family life.

Maybe it doesn't dishonor my mom to consider a life without kids. Maybe I owe it to myself to let something new happen, for once. To make time for the bees and the aimless walks and the open-endedness of my days. Maybe I owe it to her. My mom didn't get to live out her dotage. So I'll live hers for her, starting now.

She used to tell me that if she had gone to college, she would have studied history. I keep turning back to women in the past, trying to understand what they knew about a life beyond mere survival, about envisioning another life. I keep gathering up images of alternate worlds, trying to see what it would look like if we—if I—felt really free to choose. I marvel at my aging body—the wrinkles around my eyes, the way my hands have begun to speckle. Sometimes at a glance I see my mom's hands. I write it all down in a notebook. I picture the years passing in my rocker on the back porch beside Chelsea, our hair growing long and gray, our faces relaxing into folds, our garden becoming ever more unruly. Each day is a question we ask ourselves—what is life?—and answer: *this*. I read back through the months that have passed, living my own life over and over until I can make some sense of it.

Acknowledgments

I live and write in Santa Fe, in what the United States government calls New Mexico, where I am a settler on the ancestral homelands of the Tewa people. New Mexico is home to the pueblos of Acoma, Cochiti, Isleta, Jemez, Laguna, Nambé, Ohkay Owingeh, Picurís, Pojoaque, Sandia, San Felipe, San Ildefonso, Santa Ana, Santa Clara, Santo Domingo, Taos, Tesuque, Zuni, and Zia; the Diné nation; the Fort Sill Apache Tribe; the Jicarilla Apache Nation; and the Mescalero Apache Tribe.

My deepest thanks to Marian Naranjo, Eliza Naranjo Morse, Johnnye Lewis, Mallery Quetawki, Melanie LaBorwit, and Manny Pino, for your time, your words, and your work to raise awareness about exposure.

I'm so grateful to have found an ideal editor in Naomi Gibbs, who is ever willing to dive into the depths with me. Thanks to everyone at the wonderful Pantheon Books, especially Lisa Lucas, Natalia Berry, Rose Cronin-Jackman, Sarah Pannenberg, Altie Karper, and Cat Courtade. And a big thank you to Tom Etherington for the beautiful cover design. Thank you to Bill Clegg, outstanding agent and true believer, and his team: MC Connors, Marion Duvert, David Kambhu, Lilly Sandberg, Nikolas Slackman, Simon Toop, and Nik Wesson. Thank you, Serena Solin, for your meticulous fact-checking.

Enormous gratitude to the staff at the foundations and residencies that supported me in the writing of this book. The Howard Foundation Fellowship funded my research and is a fantastic resource for independent nonfiction writers. Aspen Words and the Catto Shaw Foundation gave me a serene month in Woody Creek, Colorado, as I finished the book. And I first envisioned this set of essays as a book in 2018 at a Ucross Foundation residency in Wyoming. Thank you, Merián Soto, for sharing your practice with me there.

Thank you, Wendy Sisson and Roger Christie, for keeping Rachel Carson's house exactly as it should be, and for your generous permission for me to write about my time at the cottage.

This book would not have been possible without those writers whose work spoke closely to me as I wrote, including Sophie Lewis, who kindly shared an early copy of *Abolish the Family* so I could make my deadline. Writing workshops through the Work Room with Eula Biss and Sara Levine made a big impact on the final form of these pieces.

Each essay took new directions and shapes through conversations with friends and extended family. Thanks to Andy Campbell, Clarissa Colley, Josh Conrad, Cathy Cords, Stacy Dacheux, Jennifer Ling Datchuk, Jan Marie Du Bois, Thomas Edwards, Jenny George, Lynell George, Rhiannon Marge Goad, Natalie Goldberg, Andi Gustavson, Dwight Hackett, Jenifer Hackett, Harmony Hammond, Jenny Howell, Chris Kaiser, David Loh, Katie Loughmiller, Liz Lovero, Emily Margarit Mason, Nina McConigley, Julie McGilvray, Juliet Myers, Eliza Naranjo Morse, Bruce Nauman, Molly Patterson Flynn, Adeena Reitberger, Merry Scully, Shane Tolbert, Brad Trone, Laura Wallace, Liz Wyckoff, Susan York, and Natalie Zelt. Thank you, especially, Tara Kohn, my stalwart writing partner.

I'm grateful for Cash Ashby, Jandri Fernandez, Kelly Frith, Sarah Johnson, Kathrin Meyer, and Nikka Peralta, who made finishing this book physically and emotionally possible.

Thank you, Dad, Jeff, Virginia, and in fond memory of my aunt Carol. Thank you, Mom. I wish I could share this with you.

I'm ever thankful for Elliott, Gary, and Lou, my steadfast multi-species family. Thank you, Chelsea Weathers, for reminding me to keep digging, and for holding me up.

Sources

Thin Skin

Aleksievich, Svetlana. *Voices from Chernobyl: The Oral History of a Nuclear Disaster.* New York: Picador, 2006.

Atomic Energy Commission. *Manhattan District History Book VIII: Los Alamos Project (Y). Vol. 1, General.* December 1947, declassified December 1972. https://www.osti.gov.

Biss, Eula. *On Immunity.* Minneapolis: Graywolf, 2014.

Burns, Ken, director. *Cancer: The Emperor of All Maladies.* PBS, 2015.

Carson, Rachel. *Silent Spring.* New York: Houghton Mifflin, 1962.

Curie, Marie. *Pierre Curie.* New York: Macmillan, 1923.

D'Agata, John. *About a Mountain.* New York: Norton, 2010.

Ebright, Malcolm, and Rick Hendricks. *Pueblo Sovereignty: Indian Land and Water in New Mexico and Texas.* Norman, OK: Oklahoma University Press, 2019.

Eichstaedt, Peter. *If You Poison Us: Uranium and Native Americans.* Santa Fe: Red Crane Books, 1994.

Environmental Justice Atlas. "Chicago's Toxic Doughnut, USA: Altgeld Gardens." https://ejatlas.org.

Federici, Silvia. *Re-enchanting the World: Feminism and the Politics of the Commons.* Oakland, CA: PM Press, 2018.

Flavelle, Christopher, and Kalen Goodluck. "Dispossessed, Again: Climate Change Hits Native Americans Especially Hard." *New York Times,* June 27, 2021.

Freeman, Martha. *Always, Rachel: The Letters of Rachel Carson and Dorothy Freeman, 1952–1964.* Boston: Beacon Press, 1995.

Freinkel, Susan. *Plastic: A Toxic Love Story.* New York: Houghton Mifflin Harcourt, 2011.

Goldsmith, Barbara. *Obsessive Genius: The Inner World of Marie Curie.* New York: Norton, 2005.

Grunstein, Miguel, and Dale Kruzic, writers/producers. *Shadow on the Hill.* With Marian Naranjo, Suzanne Westerly, the Masters of Public Health Program at the University of New Mexico, Concerned Citizens for Nuclear Safety, and Martin Sheen. Thunder Road Productions, 2000. https://www.youtube.com/watch?v=zC0dZEvGsx4.

Hartmann, Ernest, Robert Harrison, and Michael Zborowski. "Boundaries in the Mind: Past Research and Future Directions." *North American Journal of Psychology* 3, no. 3 (December 2001).

———. "The Boundary Questionnaire." Ernest Hartmann: Selected Papers to 2013. https://ernesthartmann.com.

Hautzinger, Daniel. "The Chicago Woman Who Fought to Clean Up the Southeast Side." WTTW Chicago Public Media. February 4, 2020.

Jones, Suzanne L., and Frank N. van Hippel. "Transparency Measures for Subcritical Experiments Under the CTBT." *Science & Global Security* 6 (1997): 291–310.

Kroll-Smith, Steve, and H. Hugh Floyd. *Bodies in Protest: Environmental Illness and the Struggle over Medical Knowledge.* New York: New York University Press, 1997.

Lacey, Jennifer T. "Altgeld Gardens: Life in a Toxic Environment." Vimeo, September 21, 2009. https://vimeo.com/6688840.

Last, T. S. "Big Development on the Nuclear Horizon." *Albuquerque Journal,* May 26, 2021.

Lear, Linda. *Rachel Carson: Witness for Nature.* New York: Henry Holt, 1997.

LISA. "Nuclear Waste, Gold and Land Theft in Newe Sogobia." *Earth First!* 24, no. 6 (October 31, 2004): 40.

Masco, Joseph. *The Nuclear Borderlands: The Manhattan Project in Post–Cold War New Mexico.* Princeton, NJ: Princeton University Press, 2006.

McGilvray, Julie, and Robert Melnick. "Preserving the Pajarito

Site at Los Alamos National Laboratory." National Park Service, June 2, 2021. https://www.nps.gov.

Murphy, Michelle. "Alterlife and Decolonial Chemical Relations." *Cultural Anthropology* 32.4, 2017.

———. *Sick Building Syndrome and the Problem of Uncertainty: Environmental Politics, Technoscience, and Women Workers*. Durham, NC: Duke University Press, 2006.

Nuclear Watch New Mexico. "NNSA Finally Starts Overdue Los Alamos Lab Environmental Study for Nuclear Weapons Programs That Are Already Underway." Press release, August 18, 2022. https://nukewatch.org.

Price, V. B. *The Orphaned Land: New Mexico's Environment Since the Manhattan Project*. Albuquerque, NM: University of New Mexico Press, 2011.

Roberts, Sam. "Dr. Samuel Epstein, 91, Cassandra of Cancer Prevention, Dies." *New York Times,* April 15, 2018.

Ronda, Margaret. "Mourning and Melancholia in the Anthropocene." *Post45,* June 2013.

Sandia National Laboratories. *Expert Judgment on Markers to Deter Inadvertent Human Intrusion into the Waste Isolation Pilot Plant*. Sandia National Laboratories report SAND92-1382/UC-721, 1993.

Santa Fe New Mexican ongoing coverage of WIPP and Los Alamos and Sandia National Laboratories (2015–2022).

Saskatchewan Government Relations. "Northern Saskatchewan Uranium Sites and Neighboring Communities" map. 2015. https://www.saskatchewan.ca.

Singh, Neil. "Decolonising Dermatology: Why Black and Brown Skin Need Better Treatment." *Guardian,* August 13, 2020.

Stewart, Jane B., and Richard B. Stewart. *Fuel Cycle to Nowhere: U.S. Law and Policy on Nuclear Waste*. Nashville, TN: Vanderbilt University Press, 2011.

Tu, Thuy Linh Nguyen. *Experiments in Skin: Race and Beauty in the Shadows of Vietnam*. Durham, NC: Duke University Press, 2021.

United States Department of Energy. *Advisory Committee on Human Radiation Experiments Roadmap*. https://ehss.energy.gov.

U.S. Geological Survey National Water Information System Water-Quality Database. USGS 354855106312410 EAST FORK

JEMEZ RIVER-TRIBUTARY and USGS 354940106383610 EAST FORK JEMEZ R AT MOUTH NEAR JEMEZ SPRINGS, NM. https://www.usgs.gov.

Voyles, Traci Brynne. *Wastelanding: Legacies of Uranium Mining in Navajo Country.* Minneapolis: University of Minnesota Press, 2015.

Webb, J. H. "The Fogging of Photographic Film by Radioactive Contaminants in Cardboard Packaging Materials." *Physical Review* 76, no. 1 (August 1, 1949).

Weigle, Marta, ed. *Telling New Mexico: A New History.* Albuquerque: University of New Mexico Press, 2009.

Wellington, Darryl Lorenzo. "In the Shadow of the Manhattan Project." *New Politics,* Winter 2014.

Wenzel, L. Quoted in "Chicago's Toxic Doughnut, USA." Environmental Justice Atlas. https://ejatlas.org.

White House Briefing Room. "Fact Sheet: The American Jobs Plan." WhiteHouse.gov, March 31, 2021. https://www.white house.gov.

Strangers on a Train

Associated Press. "Huge Confederate Flag Flying High over I-65." *Decatur Daily News,* June 12, 2005.

Biss, Eula. "No Man's Land." In *Notes from No Man's Land.* Minneapolis: Graywolf, 2010.

Brooks, Libby. "Indigenous Women Speak Out at Cop26 Rally: 'Femicide Is Linked to Ecocide.'" *The Guardian,* November 10, 2021.

Castiglia, Christopher. *Bound and Determined: Captivity, Culture-Crossing, and White Womanhood from Mary Rowlandson to Patty Hearst.* Chicago: University of Chicago Press, 1996.

Deer, Sarah. *The Beginning and End of Rape: Confronting Sexual Violence in Native America.* Minneapolis, MN: University of Minnesota Press, 2015.

Denny, Frances. *Major Arcana: Portraits of Witches in America.* Kansas City, MO: Andrews McMeel Publishing, 2020.

Durston, Ellen Almer, Campbell Robertson, and Dan Simmons.

"Before Shooting, Highland Park Was Considered Chicago's 'Mayberry.'" *The New York Times,* July 5, 2022.

Equal Justice Initiative. "Lynching in America: Confronting the Legacy of Racial Terror." Third Edition. https://lynchingin america.eji.org.

———. The National Memorial for Peace and Justice and The Legacy Museum, Montgomery, AL. https://museumandmemorial .eji.org.

Federici, Silvia. *Caliban and the Witch: Women, the Body and Primitive Accumulation.* New York: Autonomedia, 2004.

Graeber, David, and David Wengrow. *The Dawn of Everything: A New History of Humanity.* New York: Farrar, Straus and Giroux, 2021.

Haile, Rahawa. "Going It Alone: Hiking the Appalachian Trail as a Queer Black Woman." *Outside,* April 11, 2017.

Lavery, Tim. *Chicago Crime Trends.* Vol. 1, issue 1. Chicago Police Department Research and Development Division, 2005.

Lewin, Katherine. "Interview with Lyla June Johnston." January 1, 2020. In *Reported.* Produced by Katherine Lewin. Podcast. https://www.sfreporter.com/

———. "Long Road Ahead: Data Among Challenges Facing New Mexico's Missing and Murdered Indigenous Women Task Force." *Santa Fe Reporter,* February 25, 2020.

Lorde, Audre. "Age, Race, Class, and Sex." In *Sister Outsider.* New York: Ten Speed Press, 1984.

———. "The Uses of Anger." *Women's Studies Quarterly* 25, no. 1/2 (1997): 278–85.

Lucchesi, Annita (Southern Cheyenne), and Abigail Echo-Hawk (Pawnee). *Missing and Murdered Indigenous Women and Girls* report. Seattle, WA: Urban Indian Health Institute, 2018.

Martin, Shea. "Wild, Fat, Black, and Queer: How I Became Free in the Mountains and Never Left." Autostraddle.com, November 12, 2020.

McMillan Cottom, Tressie. *Thick: And Other Essays.* New York: The New Press, 2019.

Medina, Eduardo. "Alabama Pastor Is Arrested While Watering Neighbor's Flowers, Video Shows." *The New York Times,* August 31, 2022.

Meraji, Shereen Marisol. "Outdoor Afro: Busting Stereotypes That Black People Don't Hike or Camp." NPR.org, July 12, 2015.

National Inquiry into Missing and Murdered Indigenous Women and Girls. *Reclaiming Power and Place: The Final Report of the National Inquiry into Missing and Murdered Indigenous Women and Girls.* Government of Canada, 2019.

O'Hagan, Sean. "Zanele Muholi's Queer South Africa: 'I Do Not Dare Shoot at Night. It Is Not Safe.'" *Guardian,* November 2, 2020.

Pachelli, Nick. "Stolen and Erased: Sex Trafficked in New Mexico." *Albuquerque Journal,* December 23, 2019.

Rankine, Claudia. *Just Us: An American Conversation.* Minneapolis: Graywolf, 2020.

Shapland, Jenn. "The Tracks." *The Lifted Brow* and *Literary Hub,* August 2015.

Simpson, Leanne Betasamosake. *As We Have Always Done: Indigenous Freedom Through Radical Resistance.* Minneapolis: University of Minnesota Press, 2017.

Smith, Bryan. "The Cluster Conundrum: Copycat Teen Deaths in Lake Forest." *Chicago Magazine,* June 18, 2012.

Smith, Jaune Quick-to-See, and Nadja Sayej. "'It's Like We Don't Exist': Jaune Quick-to-See Smith on Native American Artists." *Guardian,* July 29, 2020.

Vaselka, Vanessa. "Green Screen: The Lack of Female Road Narratives and Why It Matters." *American Reader* 1, no. 4. https://theamericanreader.com.

Walker, Connie. *Missing and Murdered.* 2018–2019. Produced by Marnie Luke and Jennifer Foster. Podcast. https://www.cbc.ca.

White, Evelyn C. "Black Women and the Wilderness." In *Names We Call Home: Autobiography on Racial Identity,* edited by A. J. Thompson. London: Routledge, 1996.

The Toomuchness

Associated Press. "Denver Removes Storage Units Lived in by Homeless People." *New York Post,* September 28, 2018.

Baldwin, James. *The Price of the Ticket: Selected Nonfiction, 1948–1985.* New York: St. Martin's, 1985.

Biss, Eula. *Having and Being Had.* New York: Riverhead Books, 2020.

Catalin, Claudiu Munteanu, and Pagalea Andreea. "Brands as a Means of Consumer Self-Expression and Desired Personal Lifestyle." *Procedia: Social and Behavioral Sciences* 109 (2014).

Chave, Anna. "Minimalism and the Rhetoric of Power." *Arts Magazine* 64.5, January 1990.

Chayka, Kyle. *Living for Less: Living with Minimalism.* New York: Bloomsbury, 2020.

Cohen, William A., and Ryan Johnson, eds. *Filth: Dirt, Disgust, and Modern Life.* Minneapolis: University of Minnesota Press, 2005.

Crary, Jonathan. *24/7: Late Capitalism and the Ends of Sleep.* New York: Verso Books, 2013.

Davis, Lydia. *Can't and Won't.* New York: Farrar, Straus and Giroux, 2014.

Didion, Joan. "On Keeping a Notebook." In *Slouching Towards Bethlehem.* New York: Farrar, Straus and Giroux, 1968.

Edson Escalas, Jennifer, and James R. Bettman. "Self-Construal, Reference Groups, and Brand Meaning." *Journal of Consumer Research* 32 (December 2005).

Fromm, Erich. *Escape from Freedom.* New York: Holt, 1994. First published 1941.

Garrett, Bradley. *Bunker: Building for the End Times.* New York: Scribner, 2020.

Graeber, David. "Consumption." *Current Anthropology* 52, no. 4 (2011).

Hall, Delaney. "Stuccoed in Time." February 2, 2021. In *99% Invisible.* Produced by Delaney Hall. Podcast. https://99percentinvisible .org.

Harris, Malcolm. *Kids These Days.* New York: Little, Brown and Company, 2017.

Hildyard, Daisy. *The Second Body.* London: Fitzcarraldo Editions, 2017.

Johnson, Ayana Elizabeth, and Alex Blumberg. "Is Your Carbon Footprint BS?" March 18, 2021. In *How to Save a Planet.* Produced by Kendra Pierre-Louis, Rachel Waldholz, Anna Ladd, Daniel Ackerman, and Hannah Chinn. Podcast. July 29, 2021. https:// gimletmedia.com.

Keltner, Dacher, and Jason Marsh. "How Gratitude Beats Material-ism." *Greater Good Magazine at UC Berkeley,* January 8, 2015.

Labarre, Polly. "Sophisticated Sell." *Fast Company,* November 30, 2002.

Lees, David, and Alberto Zilli. *Moths: A Complete Guide to Biology and Behavior.* Washington, D.C.: Smithsonian Books, 2019.

Lévi-Strauss, Claude. *The Savage Mind.* Chicago: University of Chicago Press, 1966.

Lowrey, Annie. "Why the Phrase 'Late Capitalism' Is Suddenly Everywhere." *The Atlantic.* May 1, 2017.

Magnusson, Margretta. *The Gentle Art of Swedish Death Cleaning.* New York: Simon and Schuster, 2018.

McKibben, Bill. *Falter: Has the Human Game Begun to Play Itself Out?* New York: Henry Holt, 2019.

Minter, Adam. *Junkyard Planet.* New York: Bloomsbury, 2013.

———. *Secondhand.* New York: Bloomsbury, 2019.

Murphy, Patricia L. "The Commodified Self in Consumer Culture: A Cross-Cultural Perspective." *Journal of Social Psychology* 140, no. 5 (2000).

NBC News. "MLK Talks 'New Phase' of Civil Rights Struggle, Eleven Months Before His Assassination." Interview with Sander Vinocur, May 8, 1967, https://www.youtube.com.

O'Connell, Mark. *Notes from an Apocalypse: A Personal Journey to the End of the World and Back.* New York: Doubleday, 2020.

Sanburn, Josh. "America's Clutter Problem." *Time,* March 12, 2015.

Shaer, Matthew. "Where Does All the Cardboard Come From? I Had to Know." *The New York Times,* November 28, 2022.

Siniawer, Eiko Maruko. *Waste: Consuming Postwar Japan.* Ithaca: Cornell University Press, 2018.

St. Clair, Kassia. *The Golden Thread: How Fabric Changed History.* New York: Liveright, 2018.

Strasser, Susan. *Waste and Want: A Social History of Trash.* New York: Metropolitan Books, 1999.

Subramanian, Samanth. "How Our Home Delivery Habit Reshaped the World." *Guardian,* November 21, 2019.

Trevino, Julissa. "This Swiss Town Is Protecting Its Glacier with a Blanket." *Smithsonian Magazine,* March 12, 2018.

Voyles, Traci Brynne. *Wastelanding: Legacies of Uranium Mining in Navajo Country.* Minneapolis: University of Minnesota Press, 2015.

Weil, Simone, and Rachel Bespaloff. *War and the* Iliad. New York: *New York Review of Books,* 2005.

Wexler, Bruce. *Brain and Culture.* Cambridge, MA: MIT Press, 2006.

Wilson, Chris. *The Myth of Santa Fe.* Albuquerque: University of New Mexico Press, 1997.

Wittgenstein, Ludwig. *Tractatus logico-philosophicus.* Translated by G.C.M. Colombo. Rome and Milan: Fratelli Bocca, 1954.

Wu, Timothy. *The Attention Merchants.* New York: Alfred A. Knopf, 2016.

Yaeger, Patricia. "The Death of Nature and the Apotheosis of Trash; or, Rubbish Ecology." *PMLA* 123, no. 2 (2008): 321–39.

Crystal Vortex

Banks, Jamison Chas, and Eliza Naranjo Morse. *Giving Growth* artwork and exhibition presented at the Ralph T. Coe Center for the Arts, Santa Fe, NM, August 18–October 7, 2022.

Brown, Brené. *The Gifts of Imperfection.* Center City, MN: Hazelden Publishing, 2010.

Cameron, Julia. *The Artist's Way.* New York: TarcherPerigee, 1992.

Chödrön, Pema. *How to Meditate.* Louisville, CO: Sounds True audio, 2007.

———. *When Things Fall Apart.* Boston: Shambhala, 1997.

Crary, Jonathan. *24/7: Late Capitalism and the Ends of Sleep.* New York: Verso, 2013.

Desmond, Matthew. "In Order to Understand the Brutality of American Capitalism, You Have to Start on the Plantation." 1619 Project, *The New York Times,* August 14, 2019.

Frankl, Viktor E. *Man's Search for Meaning: An Introduction to Logotherapy,* 3rd ed. Translated by Ilse Lasch. New York: Touchstone, 1984. First published in Austria in 1946 as *Ein Psycholog erlebt das Konzentrationslager.*

Geissler, Heike. *Seasonal Associate.* Los Angeles: Semiotext(e), 2018.

Geuter, Ulfried, Michael C. Heller, and Judyth O. Weaver. "Elsa

Gindler and Her influence on Wilhelm Reich and Body Psychotherapy." *Body, Movement & Dance in Psychotherapy: An International Journal for Theory, Research and Practice* 5.1, 2010.

Gindler, Elsa. "Gymnastik for Busy People." *Gymnastik, the Journal of the Deutscher Gymnastik-Bund (German Gymnastik Association)*, 1926. Reprinted in *International Body Psychotherapy Journal* 3.1, 2004.

Groff, Lauren, and Lucie Shelly. "My Own Boundaries Seem to Be Fading: An Interview with Lauren Groff." *Paris Review*, June 5, 2018.

Hammond, Harmony, and Jenn Shapland. "Studio Visit: Harmony Hammond." *Southwest Contemporary*, March 27, 2019. https://southwestcontemporary.com.

Harris, Malcolm. *Kids These Days*. New York: Little, Brown, 2017.

Heti, Sheila. *Motherhood*. New York: Henry Holt, 2018.

Houston, Pam. "Redefining Success." In *A Little More About Me*. New York: Norton, 1999.

Knaster, Mirka. *Discovering the Body's Wisdom*. New York: Bantam, 2010.

Kodish, Bruce I. "Body Awareness in Theory and Practice." *ETC: A Review of General Semantics* 61, no. 3 (October 2004).

Kraynak, Janet, ed. *Please Pay Attention Please: Bruce Nauman's Words: Writings and Interviews*. Cambridge, MA: MIT Press, 2003.

Lorde, Audre. *A Burst of Light and Other Essays*. Mineola, NY: Ixia Press, 2021.

McClure, Tess. "Dark Crystals: The Brutal Reality Behind a Booming Wellness Craze." *The Guardian*, September 17, 2019.

McGee, Micki. *Self Help, Inc.* Oxford: Oxford University Press, 2005.

Mendelsohn, Meredith. "Harmony Hammond: *Material Witness, Five Decades of Art*." *Brooklyn Rail*. https://brooklynrail.org.

Neff, Kristen. *Self-Compassion*. New York: William Morrow, 2015.

Pollan, Michael. *How to Change Your Mind*. New York: Penguin, 2018.

Riso, Don Richard, with Russ Hudson. *Personality Types: Using the Enneagram for Self-Discovery*. New York: Houghton Mifflin, 1996.

Saltonstall, Ellen. *The Bodymind Ballwork Method*. Berkeley, CA: North Atlantic Books, 2018.

Scarry, Richard. *What Do People Do All Day?* New York: Random House, 1968.

Sher, Barbara. *Wishcraft: How to Get What You* Really *Want.* New York: Ballantine Books, 1979.

Summers, Elaine. *Kinetic Awareness.* Boston: Pub Center Cultural Resources, 1988.

Wooster, Ann-Sargent. "Elaine Summers: Moving to Dance." *Drama Review* 24, no. 4 (1980).

The Meaning of Life

Avison, Margaret, and Adrian Furnham. "Personality and Voluntary Childlessness." *Journal of Population Research* 32, no. 1 (2015).

Batuman, Elif. *Either/Or.* New York: Penguin Press, 2022.

Brandow, Heidi. *Working with Kin.* Exhibition at form & concept gallery. Santa Fe, NM, July 16–October 1, 2022.

Brooks, Christine. "Meaning-Making Among Intentionally Childless Women." *International Journal of Transpersonal Studies* 38, no. 1 (2019).

brown, adrienne maree. *Pleasure Activism: The Politics of Feeling Good.* Chico, CA: AK Press, 2019.

Brown, Jenny. *Without Apology: The Abortion Struggle Now.* New York: Verso Books, 2019.

Buckley, Cara. "Earth Now Has Eight Billion Humans. This Man Wishes There Were None." *The New York Times,* November 23, 2022.

Butler, Octavia. *Bloodchild.* New York: Seven Stories Press, 1996.

Carson, Rachel. *The Sea Around Us.* Oxford: Oxford University Press, 1951.

———. *Silent Spring.* New York: Houghton Mifflin, 1962.

Chee, Alexander. *How to Write an Autobiographical Novel.* New York: Mariner Books, 2018.

Davis, Angela Y. *Women, Race, and Class.* New York: Alfred A. Knopf, 1983.

Edelman, Hope. *Motherless Daughters: The Legacy of Loss.* Philadelphia: Da Capo Press, 2006.

Edelman, Lee. *No Future: Queer Theory and the Death Drive.* Durham, NC: Duke University Press, 2004.

Fausto-Sterling, Anne. *Sexing the Body: Gender Politics and the Construction of Sexuality*. New York: Basic Books, 2000.

Federici, Silvia. *Caliban and the Witch: Women, the Body and Primitive Accumulation*. New York: Autonomedia, 2004.

———. *Revolution at Point Zero: Housework, Reproduction, and Feminist Struggle*. Brooklyn, NY, and Oakland, CA: Common Notions/ PM Press, 2012.

Field, Thalia. "Happy/That you have the body (The Mirror Test)." Nonhuman Rights (blog), August 5, 2019. https://www.non humanrights.org/blog/.

———. *Personhood*. New York: New Directions Publishing, 2021.

Freeman, Martha. *Always, Rachel: The Letters of Rachel Carson and Dorothy Freeman, 1952–1964*. Boston: Beacon Press, 1995.

George, Lynell. *A Handful of Earth, A Handful of Sky: The World of Octavia E. Butler*. Santa Monica, CA: Angel City Press, 2020.

Gillespie, Rosemary. "Childfree and Feminine: Understanding Gender Identity in Voluntarily Childless Women." *Gender and Society* 17, no. 1 (2003).

Heti, Sheila. *Motherhood*. New York: Henry Holt, 2018.

Honig, Bonnie. *Emergency Politics: Paradox, Law, Democracy*. Princeton, NJ: Princeton University Press, 2009.

Jansson, Tove. *Letters from Tove*. Edited by Boel Westin and Helen Svensson. Translated by Sarah Death. Minneapolis: University of Minnesota Press, 2020.

Laurent-Simpson, Andrea. "Considering Alternate Sources of Role Identity: Childless Parents and Their Animal 'Kids.'" *Sociological Forum* 32, no. 3 (2017).

Lear, Linda. *Rachel Carson: Witness for Nature*. New York: Henry Holt, 1997.

Lessin, Tia, and Emma Pildes, dirs. *The Janes*. HBO Documentary Films, 2022.

Lewis, Sophie. *Abolish the Family*. New York: Verso Books, 2022.

———. *Full Surrogacy Now: Feminism Against Family*. New York: Verso, 2019.

Lisicky, Paul. "The New Rhoda." In *Selfish, Shallow, and Self-Absorbed*, edited by Meghan Daum. New York: Picador, 2015.

Manne, Kate. *Entitled: How Male Privilege Hurts Women.* New York: Crown, 2020.

Masson, Jeffrey Moussaieff, and Susan McCarthy. *When Elephants Weep: The Emotional Lives of Animals.* New York: Delta, 1995.

Maxwell, Lida. "Queer/Love/Bird Extinction: Rachel Carson's *Silent Spring* as a Work of Love." *Political Theory* 45, no. 5 (2017).

McClay, B. D. "The New Trend Is Gnomecore." Gawker.com, April 5, 2022.

Museum of International Folk Art. *Yōkai: Ghosts & Demons of Japan.* Santa Fe, NM. December 8, 2019–November 27, 2022.

Myles, Eileen. *For Now (Why I Write).* New Haven, CT: Yale University Press, 2020.

Park, Kristin. "Stigma Management Among the Voluntarily Childless." *Sociological Perspectives* 45, no. 1 (2002).

Rich, Adrienne. *Of Woman Born: Motherhood as Experience and Institution.* New York: Norton, 1976, 1995.

Roberts, Dorothy. "Race, Gender, and Genetic Technologies: A New Reproductive Dystopia?" *Signs: Journal of Women in Culture and Society* 34, no. 4 (2009).

Russo, Nancy Felipe. "The Motherhood Mandate." *Journal of Social Issues* 32, no. 3 (Summer 1976).

Satkunanandan, Shalini. *Extraordinary Responsibility: Politics Beyond the Moral Calculus.* Cambridge: Cambridge University Press, 2015.

Sheldrake, Merlin. *Entangled Life: How Fungi Make Our Worlds, Change Our Minds, and Shape Our Futures.* New York: Random House, 2020.

Slaughter, Anne-Marie. "Why Women Still Can't Have It All." *Atlantic,* July/August 2012.

StopHavingKids.org.

United Nations Population Fund. "Nearly Half of All Pregnancies Are Unintended—A Global Crisis, Says New UNFPA Report." Press release. March 30, 2022. https://www.unfpa.org.

Walter, Brenda Gardenour. "Corrupt Air, Poisonous Places, and the Toxic Breath of Witches in Late Medieval Medicine and Theology." In *Toxic Airs: Body, Place, Planet in Historical Perspective,* edited by James Rodger Fleming and Ann Johnson. Pittsburgh: University of Pittsburgh Press, 2014.

Williams, Joy. "The Case Against Babies." *Ill Nature*. New York: Lyons Press, 2001.

Winant, Carmen. *Notes on Fundamental Joy; seeking the elimination of oppression through the social and political transformation of the patriarchy that otherwise threatens to bury us.* New York: Printed Matter, 2019.

Wynes, Seth, and Kimberly A. Nicholas. "The Climate Mitigation Gap: Education and Government Recommendations Miss the Most Effective Individual Actions." *Environmental Research Letters* 12 (2017).